WAR
AND THE
CHRISTIAN CONSCIENCE:

FROM AUGUSTINE TO MARTIN LUTHER KING, JR.

edited by ALBERT MARRIN

HENRY REGNERY COMPANY
CHICAGO

For Yvette and my parents . . .
the best allies in any campaign

"... the conscience of man is the seat and throne of God in him. ..."

—Robert Barclay

Contents

Introduction

Next to the production of food, which sustains life, the family, which fosters life, and religion, which hallows life and gives it meaning, no sphere of activity has so occupied man's thoughts and usurped his energies as war, which degrades life as it destroys it. Understanding war, its nature, causes, and social role, is almost as complex a problem as exorcising it from the world. To what extent war is an expression of innate and biologically determined impulses leading to aggressiveness is a subject of ongoing discussion among social scientists, as is the role that conflict with others plays in defining the individual's personality and concept of self.[1] This much is certain: in the animal kingdom all the vertebrates, as well as many invertebrates, indulge in fighting. But their fighting is always between individuals or packs that cooperate in bringing down a larger prey. A pack of wolves never fights another pack of wolves, never attacks a whole herd of deer. When individuals of the same species clash, they employ formalized surrender or disengagement gestures to avoid a struggle to the death. A defeated wolf, to give the best-known example, will either run away or bare his throat to his adversary as a sign of submission. The Latin proverb *homo homini lupus* ("Man is a wolf to man") is unfair to the wolf; for it is man, so poorly endowed by nature with aggressive means, in whom the mechanism inhibiting the killing

1. *War: Studies from Psychology, Sociology, Anthropology,* edited by Leon Bramson and George W. Goethals (New York: Basic Books, 1968), is a valuable anthology with an extensive bibliography.

of his own kind is so lamentably defective. Apart from the foraging ants of the tropics, which in any event attack other species exclusively, and rats, which seem to enjoy slaughtering members of other packs, man is the only creature in all of creation that engages in war.

Yet, contrary to the cliché that is a legacy of nineteenth-century Social Darwinism—the doctrine that life is a struggle for survival in which the superior (stronger) overcomes the inferior (weaker)—man is not innately warlike. If he has always been a killer, he has been a warrior for an infinitesimally small portion of his existence. Even today there are peoples—the Arapesh of New Guinea and the Pygmies of the Ituri Forest in the Congo—who know nothing of warfare. Though prehistoric man was far from embodying the idealized view of the good-natured "noble savage," neither was he caught up in the maelstrom of perpetual war. Paradoxically, intergroup conflict on a scale warranting the name "war" became possible only about seven to ten thousand years ago, when certain societies developed enough of a surplus to free the would-be warrior from the day-in and day-out struggle for the necessities of life. In any case, every civilization uncovered thus far has engaged in war, and, as Ruskin observed, has achieved its greatest triumphs culturally while dominant militarily. But civilizations have also seen their aspirations and their accomplishments blasted, their pride and their glory humbled, by war.

In his more lucid moments, man has recognized the incompatibility of war with his better self. This recognition has certainly been true of man as a religious creature. The great religions of East and West have passed a negative judgment on war. Among these, Christianity, like its parent Judaism, is a life-cherishing faith. Christianity regards human life as inherently precious, because man, of all beings the favorite of the Creator, is created in His image. As Erasmus, the prince of Christian humanists, expressed it in *Antipolemus*, man is "a representative of Himself, a kind of terrestrial Deity." Given the Incarnation (the doctrine that the Son of God took human flesh from His human mother), to kill or wound a fellow human being is to assault God as well. Furthermore, within the Gospels themselves there abound exhortations to remain peaceable, to requite hatred with love, to turn the other cheek, and to offer no resistance to evil.

These truths notwithstanding, the question of war, and of Christianity's understanding of it, is more relevant today than at any time in the history of man. Within the past twenty-five years, man's ability to deal death and destruction to his fellows has moved into a new dimension. In purely numerical terms, allowing one ton of TNT to kill ten persons, thirty megatons of nuclear explosive, or the equivalent of 30,000,000 tons of TNT, could dispatch every Russian. The mind cannot fully comprehend statistics of such magnitude, but there is more. The United States now possesses an "overkill" capacity of approximately 67,000 percent! Assuming the Soviet Union has, and China soon will have, an equal force, it may be said that what passes today for war is nothing of the kind. It is suicide, it is genocide, it is the murder of humanity—but it is definitely *not* war. To say this, is not to be paradoxical. For better or worse, the creation of the thermonuclear arsenal has closed a chapter in history, putting an end to war as man in the West has understood it and justified it ever since he first felt the need to do so.

This anthology, originating in discussions with young people concerned about the crisis in which their country presently finds itself, is intended to serve a utilitarian purpose. One hears nowadays the terms "pacifist," "conscientious objector," "unjust war," "crime against humanity," and "war criminal," only to discover on probing further that often the speaker is mouthing partially understood concepts combined with pure misinformation. Slogans such as "Make love not war" (as if the pleasure of the one diminishes automatically the energy available for the other) and posters such as the one announcing "War is not healthy for children and other living things" (as are careless drivers and air pollution) further stimulate the emotions at the expense of the understanding. This anthology is not a tract for or against war in general or a given war in particular; enough of those have been produced throughout the centuries. It aims, rather, at utilizing historical source materials to make intelligible to the modern reader the various ways in which Christians have regarded war. This is hardly an esoteric subject, because these ways, conditioned by historical experience, manifestations of certain sociological types, and the outgrowth of profound religious insights and logic, have contemporary relevance. For a thousand years the Church was the only teacher in the West, thereby assuring for Christianity an influence on thought and action extending far beyond the confines of the Church itself. The foundations of international law, to take an outstanding instance, have rested upon religious bedrock. Of the founders of that science, Francisco de Vitoria was a priest and a professor of theology, while Hugo Grotius was a lawyer and the author of several important theological works. Whatever principle is employed either to defend or to condemn war as an institution, or to regulate what may or may not be done in war, it originated with Christian thinkers who lived long ago, although its full implications may not have been evident at the time it was enunciated. Without some understanding of these ideas and how they were derived, one is left with no standard for assessing issues involving the fate of humanity other than garbled half-truths and personal preference.

The Christian attitude toward war cannot be considered in a vacuum. It must be seen as an aspect of a broader concern, namely, the nature, function, and relationship of the Church (the divine community) to the world (all social institutions outside the Church), and the place of the individual Christian in each. In line with this concern, and before proceeding further, we need to differentiate two socio-religious types. The "church-type" and the "sect-type" of organization, according to Ernst Troeltsch's classic study, *The Social Teaching of the Christian Churches*, differ fundamentally in nature and outlook.

Hierarchical in organization and conservative in social outlook, the church-type organization is a socially inclusive institution that seeks to exert a spiritual influence upon the whole of life through becoming an integral part of existing society. To accomplish its objective without creating intolerable strains between its ideals and reality, it compromises by adapting the absolute law of God to the relativities and exigencies of living in an imperfect world. To put the idea simply, the church-type group affirms the impossibility of living up to the requirements of the Gospel so long as the present dispensation endures. Its watchwords are not "If only men would do such-and-so, then . . ." but "Since men are really this way, therefore. . . ." In the institutionalized asceticism of the monastery it provides a framework for those wishing to approximate the ideal more closely.

In contrast, the sect-type grouping represents a form of perfectionism. Involving select, voluntary associations, frequently grouped around a charismatic leader, it aims at gathering the elect into a community of "saints." Its watchword is "It makes no difference what others believe or do, so long as we. . . ." As members of the sect aspire to personal inward perfection through living in accordance with the absolute law of God, they may resolve their tension with the world in several ways. One way of obeying the law and keeping oneself free from contagion is to withdraw from the world to varying degrees. Whether their attitude toward society at large is indifferent, tolerant, or hostile, their rejection usually involves refusing to go to law, to swear oaths, to serve as magistrates, and to fight. Another, rarer, way of resolving the tension is to overcome the world through violence, making it coterminous with the religious group. Modern totalitarian revolutionaries, though swayed by secular ideologies, share certain of the characteristics of extreme sectarianism. Be they Jacobin, Fascist, Nazi, Bolshevik, or Maoist, they seek, also under the guidance of an inspired leader, to make the world over in their own image.

Historically, Christianity evolved from groups with the characteristics of pacifistic, world-renouncing sects into a church with quasi-imperial qualities. The early apologists—Tertullian, Justin Martyr, Tatian, Origen, Cyprian—insisted not only that their coreligionists abstain from shedding blood, but also that they were a people set apart, a people who must stand aloof from worldly institutions. The strength of their teaching is attested in the innumerable cases in which Christians went to their deaths (often gladly, though under the nastiest circumstances) rather than violate this charge or defend themselves with violence. On the other side of the coin, of course, and still a matter of contention among scholars,[2] are the soldier-martyrs, men like the centurion Marcellus who, though a warrior, suffered because he was unwilling to participate in pagan rites.

Only with the emergence of the Constantinian empire after A.D. 313 did the Church Fathers modify their rigorous principles. They accepted the state, which now recognized and sought to promote Christianity, as a stabilizing and a civilizing influence at a time when barbarians pressed ever harder on the frontiers. In so doing they did not, as they have been accused since the Middle Ages, cynically abandon principle for privilege. There is a vast difference between a select corps of spiritual athletes, bound together by persecution and struggling amid a society in decadence, and the first institution of a universal state. Such an institution must accept responsibilities hitherto shunned. It must accept all who wish to come into the fold, or who are forced into it against their will, hoping all the while to leaven the world with its benign influence. But to change the world it must be prepared to meet the world halfway, to temper its absolute demands to average possibilities. It must become a church.

Having accepted the state, and consequently the violence bound up in the very essence of the state, the Church then faced the question of accommodating this violence within the framework of Christian ethics. Not that the admonition of Jesus to turn the other cheek was ever abandoned; it was transformed instead into a principle exclusively of personal conduct. In an unbroken tradition extending, some would say, from Jesus Him-

2. The following are the most authoritative works on this subject: Adolf von Harnack, *Militia Christi, die christliche Religion und der Soldatenstand in der ersten drei Jahrhunderten* (Tübingen, 1903; Darmstadt, 1963); C.J. Cadoux, *The Early Christian Attitude to War* (London, 1918) and *The Early Church and the World* (Edinburgh, 1925); G.J. Heering, *The Fall of Christianity* (London, 1930); Roland Bainton, *Christian Attitudes toward War and Peace* (Nashville, 1960) and "The Early Church and War," *Harvard Theological Review*, 1946; Edward A. Ryan, "The Rejection of Military Service by the Early Christians," *Theological Studies*, 1952.

self, but certainly from St. Ambrose of Milan through St. Augustine of Hippo to Luther, the Calvinists, and beyond, moralists have maintained the wrongfulness of the good man's defending with violence his own life and property. Said Ambrose in *The Duties of the Clergy* (III, 4, 27): "I do not think a Christian, a just and a wise man, ought to save his own life by the death of another; just as when he meets an armed robber he cannot return his blows, lest in defending his own life he should strain his love toward his neighbor."

The critical word here, and in everything that follows, is *love*. At the root of Christianity, the concept of love stands for infinitely more than the feelings of affection or of sensuality that exist between individuals. It signifies instead a heartfelt desire to sacrifice oneself for another, to will his "true good" as God Himself wills it. Hence love could serve as the touchstone of nonviolence and nonresistance, as well as of the father's chastisement of his errant child, and of the work of the magistrate, the policeman—and the soldier. We have seen that violence was disavowed as a matter of private morality, but the matter was not permitted to rest here. In an insight stemming from the Christian love-ethic, the post-Constantinian Fathers proclaimed that the Christian must function in both a public and a private capacity. The individual cannot live for himself alone. He is his brother's keeper, a trustee for others. Whereas the bachelor may feel obliged to give everything to the poor, he who has wife, children, and perhaps others depending on him cannot; nor, for this same reason (leaving aside the theological case against suicide), is he free to take his own life, as John Stuart Mill recognized in his *Essay on Liberty*.

By the mid-fourth century, Christians must have been asking themselves, relative to a still wider sphere of relationships, a question something like this: "It is desirable for me, through love, to die rather than resist an assailant; but what is my duty toward other life—life that either is incapable of choosing for itself because of tender years, or, having chosen, is incapable of enforcing its choice because of weakness? What would the Good Samaritan have done had he come upon the scene *before* the robbers had completed their work? However well-meant my intention, my 'turning the other cheek' under any and all circumstances means that I have actually turned to the smiter the cheeks of the helpless and the innocent. Consequently, as an act of charity, I am bound to resist evil *for the sake of my brother*; to resist, to be sure, in order to further the true good of my evil-doing brother, who would otherwise be encouraged to endanger his soul further."

Here, then, in the idea of trusteeship for the well-being of others, was found the primary justification for imparting to the state the police power for dealing with criminals and, by analogy, for war. This justification was never meant to imply that war is good in itself. Insofar as it springs from and fosters base passions—hatred, cruelty, pride, revenge, ambition—it is offensive to God. War at best is a necessary purgation, the best choice among many worse choices. It is no more a good than a cancer operation: it is necessary to rid the body of a disease, but it would be better not to have contracted the disease to begin with; nor does the operation guarantee that there will never be a relapse.

Drawing upon Greco-Roman sources, notably Cicero and the Stoics, some of the most profound intellects of Christendom—Ambrose, Augustine, Aquinas, Luther, the authors of the Protestant confessional statements during the Reformation, Vitoria, and, in our own day, Karl Barth, Reinhold Niebuhr, and the popes and priests of Vatican II—developed the theory of the just war, refining it and applying it to new situations as war itself evolved through the centuries.[3] The just war, however, is not the only type of war treated in a Christian context. Although

---

3. The best general accounts of the just war are Bainton, *Christian Attitudes toward War and Peace;* John Eppstein, *The Catholic Tradition of the Law of Nations* (Washington, D.C., 1935); and Charles Plater, S.J., *A Primer of War and Peace* (London, 1915). The Scholastic doctrine is dealt with in four French works: Mgr. Batiffol, et. al., *L'Eglise et la guerre* (Paris, 1913); Alfred Vanderpol, *La doctrine scholastique du droit de guerre* (Paris, 1919) and *La droit de guerre d'après les théologiens et les canonistes du moyen age* (Paris, 1911); Robert Regout, *La doctrine de la guerre juste de saint Augustin à nos jours d'après les théologiens et les juristes canoniques* (Paris, 1935).

the crusade, the apocalyptic war, and the revolution are bound by the rules of the just war, they differ from it in important respects, and are therefore best treated in the proper sections in the main body of the text.

Every aspect of the "just war" theory is deduced from and consistent with the dual principle that justice cannot be left without material resources against evil, and that the use of these resources must be confined within a moral universe, lest they poison the cause they serve. Briefly stated, every war must meet certain criteria, ranging from three to fifteen (depending on the authority), before it can be certified as a just war. It must be waged for a just cause, such as self-defense and the defense of the weak, the honoring of treaties, and the vindication of rights, usually property rights. Yet having a just cause does not automatically put a belligerent in the right. He must have in addition a just intention, a sincere desire to further that which is good and to thwart that which is evil; for example, one acts wrongly in using a provocation as an excuse for aggrandizement. Because war involves suffering and death on a grand scale, it must not be resorted to lightly, but regarded as the *ultima ratio*, the last resort after everything else has been tried and failed; nor should it be commenced without an assurance of success, lest all the sacrifice go for nought. Consistent with this principle, a rule of proportionality must be observed. This rule is binding on police forces on one level and on governments and their armies on another level. As the police cannot shoot into a crowd to get at the criminal hiding in its midst, so a government cannot go to war if the value of the objective sought is vastly outweighed by the probable harm done in gaining it. If victory involves bringing ruination to both sides, or to the human race as a whole, then the party with the just cause must forfeit its rights and suffer the evil in the interests of the common good. Furthermore, as a communal undertaking, war must be declared with due solemnity and conducted under the auspices of the authority representing the community. Just as the private citizen cannot take the law into his own hands, so "private war," condemned in the medieval peace and truce of God, is brigandage. Finally, the settlement concluding the conflict must recognize the right

of each side to exist and must do whatever is necessary to remove the occasion for conflict in the future.

Perhaps the most humanizing feature of the "just war" theory,
which gave rise to the once-familiar term "civilized warfare,"
is its insistence that war be conducted "in the right manner."
Something that is inherently unjust, whether a tactic or a
weapon, by definition cannot be employed as an instrument of
justice. Basic to fighting "in the right manner" is a rule of
discrimination, the setting of limits as to who may be harmed.
Granted, during a siege or an air raid on a military facility near
a populated area, civilians are bound to be hurt. But injuries
arising as a collateral consequence of military operations are
not in the same universe morally as striking intentionally at
noncombatants. As a corollary, once a soldier has surrendered
and has been divested of the means of aggression, he thereby
loses his status as a public functionary and ceases to be a
legitimate target. From the rule of discrimination have been
derived the modern codes of warfare, notably the Geneva
Convention (1864) and the Hague Conventions (1899, 1907),
together with the obligations imposed on the individual conscience and the criteria for determining the "war criminal."

It is at the points of proportionality and discrimination that
the theological justification of war has come up hardest against
the realities of warfare in the twentieth century. From the
flaked-stone arrowhead to the TNT-laden warhead, every
weapon devised before 1945 had one common characteristic:
the man behind it was master and could predict with a fair
degree of accuracy the kind and amount of damage it would
cause. The problem confronting the theologian H.D.A. Major
during World War I and Bishop Bell of Chichester during World
War II was actually the old problem stated in a different way:
Would the use of a certain means (the bomber) against a
specified target (German industrial centers) achieve a limited
objective (crippling Germany's war production and deterring
raids on English population centers)? But to argue on the basis
of the traditional criteria for the justice of thermonuclear war
is to arrive at the *reductio ad absurdum;* indeed, it is open to
question whether a hydrogen bomb should be called a "weapon"

at all, since in common usage a weapon is something that ceases its destructive action the moment its user decides to stop fighting. Yet the very effectiveness of nuclear "devices" (for want of a better word) as deterrents depends on their inherently indiscriminate nature and the fact that, once detonated, they have effectively escaped human control. Phrases such as "megadeaths," "balance of terror," "city busting," and "massive retaliation" capture the quality of injustice that is the essence of this kind of warfare.

In dealing with the various moral aspects of these devices—their controllability, their genetic effects, and the implications of testing and holding them as deterrents—Helmut Gollwitzer, Thomas Merton, the disputants on "The Morality of Nuclear War," and the authors of the Roman Catholic pronouncements concur in the impossibility of squaring them with any recognized moral standard. According to *The Church and the International Order*, the report of the 1948 Amsterdam conference of the World Council of Churches, "the tradition of the just war, requiring a just cause and the use of just means, is now challenged. Law may require the sanction of force, but when war breaks out, force is used on a scale that tends to destroy the basis on which law exists." Two years later, the (then) Federal Council of Churches issued the "Dun Report," which advanced the question to where it stands essentially today. When faced with the necessity of preserving life by employing "measures [that] corrupt the users, and destroy the humanity of the victims," it is incumbent upon the Christian to recognize that "there are certain things which Christians should not do to save self, or family, or nation, or free civilization."

The fear of nuclear holocaust, while averting for the time being a conflict between the superpowers, has lent impetus to insurrectionary and interventionary wars. Since 1945, "people's wars," or "wars of national liberation," have flared from Algeria to Vietnam, from Latin America to the Middle East. Whether, in the case of Vietnam, one concurs with Paul Ramsey's defense of the basic format of the U.S. counterinsurgency strategy or with the assertion of Dr. Martin Luther King and others that the war has been ruinous for all concerned, the fact remains that wars of this type have a high degree of injustice built into them. A guerrilla army, as Chairman Mao reminds us, must be as a fish swimming through the medium of the civilian population. It is the civilian who conceals, provides intelligence, and mans guerrilla armies. Combine this with the tactics and machines designed by technologically advanced societies to wage nuclear or large-scale "conventional" wars, and the toll in innocent lives is bound to be high. What makes this form of warfare even more insidious is that a kind of "irrational rationality" may take hold of both sides. Warfare can escape from emotional control as easily as from technical control when insurgents and counterinsurgents set about, with the best intentions, to destroy a society in order to save it from a fate worse than death: Communist, imperialist, or racist domination.

Long before nuclear and guerrilla war forced their dismal, if inevitable, conclusions, the "just war" theory had come under attack. Some of the most searching criticisms have come not from doctrinaire pacifists, but from those who, accepting the theory as a general principle, rigorously applied its stated criteria to the ways statesmen and nations really behave. To anyone with a rudimentary knowledge of history, it is plain that no nation has ever engaged in a conflict totally consistent with the theory of the just war. If a nation had a just cause, or a right intention, it invariably lacked some other criterion. Erasmus disqualified nearly all wars because they wanted the elements of prudence and proportionality; Charles Sumner saw that the vast armaments kept by powers "justly" intending to discourage aggression actually provoked conflict; William Ellery Channing denounced those who would entrust the authorities with unlimited warmaking powers and then, after these authorities have embroiled the country in war, would abstain from criticizing them for fear of undermining national unity in a time of crisis. When, critics have asked, have leaders *not* proclaimed the justice of their cause? When has protective, self-sacrificing love and the wish to set the enemy right with God been the sole or even the prime consideration in drawing the sword? The truth seems to lie instead in a remark of Reinhold Niebuhr in a 1936 tract, *Europe's Catastrophe and the Christian*

Faith: "No nation defends 'civilization' or 'truth' unless there is some coincidence between these values and its own national self-interest." More often than not, the ideals of the just war have been used merely as a legalistic excuse for one nation's working its will on another, or have been fed into the propaganda mills to grind out high-sounding justifications for the bloody business at hand.

The performance of the churches themselves has tended to discredit the theory further. The very fact that the church-type organization seeks to permeate society has led historically to an overidentification with the host society. From the days when Urban II and St. Bernard of Clairvaux preached the Crusades, to the crusades of our own day, the churches have lent perfervid and undiscriminating support to the wars of their small corner of Christendom. There exist hundreds of sermons like the following, which was preached by the Anglican Bishop of London in 1915:

> . . . to save the freedom of the world, every one who loves freedom and honour, every one who puts principle before ease and life before mere living, is banded in a great crusade— we cannot deny it—to kill Germans, to kill them not for the sake of killing, but to save the world, to kill the good as well as the bad, to kill the young as well as the old, to kill those who have shown kindness to our wounded as well as those friends who crucified the Canadian soldier, who sank the *Lusitania,* and who turned the machine guns on the civilians of Aerschot and Louvain; and to kill them lest the civilization of the world itself be killed.[4]

(Meanwhile the enemy was marching with *Gott mit uns*— "God is with us"—embossed on their belt buckles.) One need only read sermons like this, and recollect ecclesiastical dignitaries acting as recruiting sergeants, baptizing cannon, or blessing tanks, to see that the custodians of the highest ideals of our civilization have not always borne their responsibilities with

4. Arthur Foley Winnington-Ingram, "A Word of Cheer" [*sic*], *Christian World Pulpit,* Dec. 8, 1915.

seemly dignity. Worse still, perhaps, when not preaching war, they have too often been satisfied to sit on the sidelines protesting their neutrality, content to denounce horrendous crimes in the blandest commonplaces. Save for such instances as the actions of the Roman Catholic clergy in French Canada during World War I, and of the spokesmen of the church-led opposition to the Vietnam war, organized religion has seldom stood in the forefront, counselling people on their duty to oppose unjust wars.

The just war is understandably in bad odor nowadays. It has become fashionable to deride it as a legalistic-theological irrelevancy. As the biblical scholar John L. McKenzie, S.J., told an interviewer, "I put the ethics of the just war in the same boat as the ethics of the just adultery or the just murder."[5] This is probably saying too much. Given its view of the sinfulness in human nature, the Church does not look for the immediate abolition of war. From Augustine to the *Pastoral Constitution on the Church in the Modern World* (1965), it has affirmed that there will be no end to the danger of war until the advent of the Messiah. Since there will be contention in the world until that time, and since contention carries with it the possibility of violence, some sort of "just war" theory for conflicts below the nuclear level is essential. For all its shortcomings, the just war embodies values and sanctifies truths essential for man's survival as a moral being. To say that nothing about the just war is true is to topple the last barrier against the claim that everything in war is permissible. Maybe it is the weakening in the contemporary world of the belief that even violence has its bounds, rather than the narcotic effect of the media, that is responsible for the lack of sustained outrage when millions of innocents starve to death in an African civil war or when "freedom fighters" dynamite civilian airliners bound for the Middle Eastern "war zone" or when those in the vanguard of the "proletarian revolution" in Latin America "execute" kidnapped diplomats. All have lost sight of the fundamental differentiation between killing in war and cold-blooded murder.

5. James Finn, *Protest: Pacifism and Politics* (New York: Random House, 1968), p. 53.

The critique of the just war is a position midway between the acceptance of war within bounds, and pacifism—its absolute rejection. The term "pacifism" is as imprecise as the pacifist movement is fragmented. The word itself, unknown before the nineteenth century, did not achieve wide acceptance until World War I. Since then it has been used, frequently as an insult, to define on one level an idealistic antimilitaristic position whose goal is the elimination of war; on another level it has meant the practical expedient of conscientious objection to military service. To complicate matters further, pacifism runs the gamut of responses from "passivism" (total nonresistance), to nonviolent resistance, to the use of certain coercive means. Pacifism may be Christian or, in keeping with a growing contemporary trend, entirely secular in orientation. In the event that it is Christian, it may be based on dualistic, apocalyptic, evangelical, or prudential considerations, among others.

Secular pacifism need not detain us long. Within this category, and occasionally within the same individual, philosophical, prudential, political, sociological, humanitarian, and avowedly hedonistic considerations have all been known to play a part. The movement has been spearheaded by unaffiliated individuals or by small groups with a transient membership, displaying a tendency to split into ideological-personality caucuses or to form brand new entities. The labor movement illustrates this phenomenon well. During World War I, when the majority of the unions sided with their respective governments, socialist groups, including the Independent Labor Party in England and the American Socialist Party under Eugene V. Debs, stood aloof from the "capitalists' war." Yet their opposition to war has always been provisional. Most socialists, certainly those of the Leninist persuasion, would be willing to fight to preserve a "workers' state." By the same token, the pacifism of the intelligentsia has almost invariably been provisional. One would be hard pressed to find more than a handful of leaders in the large pacifist movement that flourished on both sides of the Atlantic who kept the faith between 1939 and 1945. The pacifism of Bertrand Russell, to take a notable example, fluctuated with the political climate. He never disavowed war absolutely, claiming that "a small war for a great cause may do more good than harm." A "pacifist" until the mid-1930s, he supported the struggle against Hitler and, in 1947, advised the Western powers against being too squeamish about employing atomic power to contain Soviet expansionism. With the Cuban missile crisis and the Vietnam war, his pacifism surfaced once again.

With the exception of such peripheral forms as dualism—the belief that the cosmos is the arena of conflict between irreconcilable principles represented as God and spirit and Satan and matter—and such groups as the Christadelphians and the Jehovah's Witnesses—whose opposition to military service is provisional, since they hope to be led in battle by the Lord of Hosts in the last days—Christian pacifism is a more consistent position. It alone states as a categorical imperative that war is inconsistent with a conception of morality deriving its sanction ultimately from God.

As we have seen, the pacifism of the early Christians was relegated after 313 to the monastery and to the realm of personal ethics. From then on, whenever pacifism took a form other than the vocational pacifism of the clergy, it was associated with heretical groups such as the Cathari, Waldensians, and Bohemian Brethren, against whom crusades were launched. Not until the Reformation did pacifism re-emerge as a doctrine of groups hearty enough to survive. The so-called "historic peace churches," consisting in the main of Mennonites, Hutterites, Dunkers (after 1908 The Church of the Brethren), Quakers, and, later, the followers of Adin Ballou and Tolstoy, have been the repositories of the nonviolent, nonresisting tradition. They are truly the spiritual descendants of the martyrs of Roman times; like the martyrs, they are sect-type bodies.

The intensity of the pacifism of the different groups may be regarded as a function of the intensity of their withdrawal from the world. As their ancient forebears, they believed their world corrupted, not by the Roman Empire, but by institutionalized religion, the Roman Catholic and the Protestant state churches, allied with the state. The impulse to withdraw from the world was especially strong among the German and Dutch sects, as may be gathered from the following statement made during a disputation in 1539: "There is a great difference between Christians and the world, the former living by the standards of the Sermon on the Mount, and the other being perverted and governed by Satan." Although admitting that government and the sword were given by the Lord (Romans 13) for the sins of the world, they, Christ's brethren, had to sever every tie with the realm of Satan. They therefore accepted Matthew 5:39 without qualification. No matter what others did, they would suffer, resisting evil neither on their own behalf nor on behalf of others, however innocent. They made no effort to convert evildoers, because evil signified to them a mystery beyond human comprehension, something to be borne with patience. The strongest corrective they employed was the ban. Used only toward their own members, its sole power rested in severing the offender from brotherly association.

Because certain conditions peculiar to seventeenth-century England enabled them to take an active part in every department of civil life except fighting, the Quakers became a kind of bridge between the quietistic pacifism of the Reformation sects and the nonviolent activists of the contemporary world. As with the Reformation sects, the Quakers accepted their sufferings, but with a significant difference: whereas the others suffered without any hope of a transformation of the world within historical time, the Quakers considered their sufferings as a vehicle for change. The followers of the itinerant mystic George Fox were the first Christians to discover that when once a man becomes conscious of the Divine Spirit within himself, he acquires a strength greater than that derived from weapons, possessing in nonviolence a formidable instrument against evil. Though persecuted and faced with seemingly hopeless odds, the early Quakers won toleration, not by cracking the heads, but by changing the hearts of their oppressors. Their attitude is described in the *Apology* of Robert Barclay, an early spokesman and theologian:

> . . . when armed men have come to dissolve [their meetings],
> it was impossible for them to do it, unless they had killed every

one; for they stood so close together, that no force could move anyone to stir, unless violently pulled thence. . . . As this patient but yet courageous way of suffering made their persecutors' work very heavy and wearisome unto them, so the courage and patience of the sufferers, using no resistance, not bringing any weapons to defend themselves, nor seeking any revenge upon such occasions, did secretly smite the hearts of their persecutors, and made their chariot wheels go on heavily.

The Quakers' actions, based on faith in the transforming power of "courageous suffering," initiated a line of development culminating in the great nonviolent movements of the twentieth century. The civil disobedience campaigns mounted by Mahatma Gandhi in India, as well as the sit-in and other devices employed by Martin Luther King and the civil rights movement in the United States, are in large measure derived from the methods and the witness of the Quakers.

Up to a point, the modus operandi and logic of the Quakers and latter-day pacifists closely parallel those of their opposite numbers philosophically.[6] Due to their use of Scripture, the charge was constantly brought against pacifists that they, like the Devil (with whom they are sometimes equated), were adept at wrenching fragments from context (such as the Sixth Commandment and portions of the Sermon on the Mount) and torturing these to fit pacifist preconceptions. Actually, neither pacifist nor bellicist relies on set quotations. Each seeks instead to rest his case on an appreciation of the Christian ethic as presented within and derived from the totality of the New Testament.

In conformity with this ethic, for the pacifist as for the bellicist, love is the indispensable first principle, everything else following from it. But whereas the one conceives love primarily in terms of charity and concern for the victim of wrongdoing, the other focuses on love primarily in its redemptive-rehabilita-

6. A useful general survey of the "new" pacifism is Umphrey Lee's *The Historic Church and Modern Pacifism* (New York, 1943). G.H.C. McGregor's *The New Testament Basis of Pacifism* (Nyack, New York, 1954) is a competent study of the theory of modern pacifism.

tive aspect. The pacifist respects the personality of the wrong-doer and hopes that, through a change of heart, he will be won back from evil to goodness and rescued from the consequences of sin. Concern for the wrongdoer has led to another misconception about the pacifist: that since he supposedly holds to the absolute principle that evil should not be resisted, he will stand by impassively while innocence is assaulted. On the contrary, the pacifist holds that love in its redemptive sense, if it is to be a relevant and a living force in the world, cannot be "passivistic." Evil must be met, restrained, and corrected. "Why then," the pacifist might ask, taking his cue from St. Chrysostom's *Homilies,* "ought we not to resist an evil? Indeed we ought," adding, "but not by retaliation. [For] Christ hath commanded us to give up ourselves to suffering wrong freely, for thus shall we prevail over evil. For fire is not quenched by another fire, but by water."

The pacifist, therefore, claims the validity of his doctrine on two counts: it is consistent with the New Testament teaching of redemptive love, and, as Chrysostom indicates, its method of meeting evil is best suited to human nature. The homeopathic principle is as poor a guide in human relations as it is in medicine. Like calls forth like. The pacifist, more optimistic about human nature than the advocate of violence, holds that goodness is the most efficient way of combating wickedness. If approached with patience and in a spirit of love, even the hardest of hearts will eventually soften; if approached with fear and hatred, it will reciprocate in kind. Accordingly, we can best protect the innocent not by stepping in with weapons at the moment of assault, but before the assault takes place, through anticipating and neutralizing aggressive tendencies.

There is a negative side, however. The pacifist fully recognizes that not everyone may be reached in time, and that the recalcitrant must be compelled to do right and constrained from doing evil. Whether in the relations of individual to individual, of individual to government, or of government to government, the pacifist accepts the necessity of coercion. Yet (and this is the crucial factor) he imposes a qualification, a principle of "discrimination," if we may borrow the bellicist's expression, on the means that may be legitimately employed. In every instance, these means must be consistent with the ends of love. Thus Kirby Page and the exponents of the Social Gospel sanctioned the father's use of force in the home, the magistrate's coercive power over criminals, and, to attain a more just society, pressure on the captains of industry to ameliorate the conditions of their workers. Prayer, fasting, picketing, marching, ultimatum, agitation, confrontation, demonstration, civil disobedience, the sit-in, sit-down, sleep-in, strike, boycott, and propaganda have all been deemed ethical strategies of coercion. Indeed, some followers of Gandhi, himself the exemplar of these techniques, consider it legitimate in the event of occupation by a foreign power to dynamite his railroad trains, provided they are unattended and motionless. Though the methods differ widely, the principle behind them is uniform: restraining the evildoer saves the innocent and sets the stage to reclaim the miscreant for God. Killing, though, is another matter. A judge does not show respect for the criminal's personality or help him repent his sins by having him hung; nor does the state, when it blows its enemies to pieces on the battlefield.

What are the practical implications of pacifism? The most obvious one derives from the insistence that the Christian is prohibited under any circumstances, including protecting the lives of his fellows, from being a party to killings. Some pacifists, notably A. J. Muste, have ventured so far as to link redemptive love with a policy of unilateral disarmament. According to this theory, if a superpower such as the United States or the Soviet Union disarmed unilaterally and unconditionally, the other nations would probably follow suit; if they attacked instead, the superpower would become a "martyr nation" whose self-sacrifice would have a redemptive significance akin to the sacrifice on Calvary.

Although chances for the implementation of such a program remain, and probably always will remain, doubtful, pacifists have struck out in other directions. It is only fitting that they should be in the forefront of the peace movement. From the plans for international peace advanced through the centuries by individuals such as William Penn (*Essay Towards the Pres-*

ent and Future Peace of Europe, 1693) and the Abbé Saint-Pierre (*Projet pour rendre la paix perpetuelle,* 1713) to the proliferation of peace societies in the nineteenth century, pacifists have worked out detailed and, for their own time, practical programs for peace. Thus far they have met with little success. More often than not, they have had to decide upon a course of action to follow in war.

Although there have been exceptions on either extreme, ranging from the young Mennonites who served on the French and Prussian sides in the war of 1870 and the Quakers who fought in World War I to the "absolutists" such as Thomas Lurting, the pacifist when called to the colors has generally declined *only* combatant service. Nor did he thereby become a burden to the nation, allowing others to risk themselves for the common good without reciprocating an iota. Historically, Christian pacifists, other than the members of the peace churches of Germanic origin, have either taken the route of the conscientious objector and remained at home to do socially useful work, or have volunteered for the most hazardous duty—combat stretcher-bearers and sailors on mine sweepers. Arle Brooks, for example, refused to register for the draft, but was fully prepared to risk his life saving others. Well aware that the end result of their choice may be the mending and saving of lives to be put back into the war effort, they have carried on, arguing that the duty of saving a life that is immediately endangered transcends all other considerations. There is, after all, no way of being certain that *this* life, saved at *this* moment, will in the end take the life of another. Even if the certainty existed, allowing this life to perish would be a denial of the basic tenet of Christian pacifism, for it would mean depriving one of the chance of reclamation.

Despite its obvious strengths and the sincerity of its witness, Christian pacifism as outlined above is, like the just war, beset by difficulties. It is undeniably true that the practice of nonresistance has met with success in what have been deemed hopeless situations. For years William Penn's unarmed Quakers lived in peace with the Indians of the Pennsylvania backwoods; nonviolent strikes have been successful in such unlikely places as the Vorkuta slave-labor camp, a hellhole in eastern Russia;

pacifists have been allowed to travel freely in time of war, performing errands of mercy for both sides. Let it also be granted that war is an unutterably horrible, senseless, and dirty business, and that the justifications advanced by its advocates often have about them more the aroma of hogwash than of sweet reason. Yet the strengths of pacifism and the weakness of the opposition mask a blind spot and a lack of decisiveness in coming to grips with the consequences of the doctrine as it applies in certain extreme situations. The pacifist's solicitude for the errant soul, expressed as an imperative against taking life, may actually mean condemning countless innocents to living death. Though determined to resist evil in the world, his resources against it are limited. Reason, goodwill, and example having failed to restrain an aggressor, the pacifist may interpose his own body between the aggressor and his would-be victim. But this will be a futile gesture if an evil man is determined to have his way at all costs; he will step over the pacifist's dead body to get at his victim.

In the final analysis, the refusal to resort to death-dealing force *does* leave the evildoer free to work his will on the innocent. If it be argued that the death of innocents is redemptive, then we have come full circle. For a sacrifice to be redemptive, it is reasonable to assume that the life should be freely given. It is open to question exactly what is redeemed when innocents are murdered because those who might save them shrink from the *ultima ratio*.

There are times in history (fortunately extremely rare) when it is at least arguable that war is morally preferable to submission to evil. If the just war can never be the same after Hiroshima, so pacifism must be viewed against the background of Auschwitz and what it symbolizes: the boundless potentiality for evil locked up in the human personality. When in 1938, Gandhi called upon the Jews to show their superiority to the Nazis by eschewing violence and adopting nonresistance—as if this were a living option for them at the time—the philosopher Martin Buber replied with a question: "Now do you or do you not know, Mahatma, what a concentration camp is like and what goes on there?" In the camps there operated a system, carefully designed and relentlessly applied, calculated to invade the human personality, violating it and robbing it of the last shreds of humanity. The pacifist must ask himself how anyone professing a doctrine of love can prefer evils such as the perversion of education and the emasculation of religion; slavery; enforced prostitution of men, women, and children; obscene medical experiments; planned starvation; and genocide to fighting, even if ending the evils is not the sole objective of the war. In light of such horrors, why is the personality of one evildoer more sacrosanct than that of the hecatombs of his victims? The argument that innocents would not have been placed in jeopardy had war been avoided in the first place, though only partially true in the case before us, becomes quite irrelevant once the evil has materialized. To refuse war then is to make a value judgment in favor of fastening upon innocents a diabolical system, a judgment comparable to that of the fanatic who decides that humanity would be better dead than Red. There is a viciousness in both extremes.

In conclusion, the major Christian responses to war reflect the uneasiness that conscientious men have always felt when confronted by violence. When viewed as closed systems of thought, whose exclusiveness is reinforced by tradition and dogma, the responses are irreconcilable. Yet the fact that they are derived from a common source-principle, Christian love, makes them to a certain extent complementary. For each response has made its own unique contributions to man's pursuit of his supreme goal as a social being: peace on earth based on love, brotherhood, and justice.

The documents that follow have been arranged according to four general categories: early Christianity and war; the "just war" tradition and its variants; pacifism; and Christian thought about the modern modes of warfare. Selections are arranged with the objective of facilitating concentration on a given approach, elucidating its central themes, and seeing how certain elements have been interpreted and developed throughout the ages. As to the documents themselves, in cases other than those where the editions and translations are more than sixty years old and therefore in the public domain, care has been taken to secure permission from the copyright holders to reprint material protected by copyright; any unintentional errors or omissions will be rectified in subsequent editions upon notification of the editor.

I

EARLY CHRISTIANITY AND THE PROBLEM OF WAR

"If the loud trumpet summons soldiers to war, shall not Christ with a strain of peace to the ends of the earth gather up his soldiers of peace? A bloodless army he has assembled by blood and by the word, to give to them the Kingdom of Heaven. The trumpet of Christ is his Gospel. He has sounded, we have heard. Let us then put on the armor of peace."

—Clement of Alexandria, *Protrepticus*, XI.

Tertullian

ca.160–ca.220

A native of Carthage, Quintus Septimius Florens Tertullian received a traditional pagan education, which prepared him to earn his livelihood as a lawyer in Rome. Converted to Christianity late in life, probably in his thirty-fifth year, he became the first Christian theologian to write in Latin. A brilliant stylist, he is best known today for the famous epigram "the blood of martyrs is the seed of the Church."

About six years after becoming a Christian, he joined the rigoristic Montanist sect, eventually founding his own party, the Tertullianists, which survived until the fourth century. *The Chaplet* (ca. 211), named after the soldier's crown of laurel, dates from his Montanist period, and was written on the occasion of the martyrdom of a Christian soldier who refused the gift of money, the *donativium,* bestowed upon the army at the accession of Caracalla and Geta. Valuable as the first work to condemn military service in the name of the Gospel and to argue the absolute imperative of conscientious objection, *The Chaplet* indicates, if only by implication, that, at a time when the rejection of the state and military service by the "official" Church was stronger than it would ever be again, there were many Christians in the army, and that the action of the soldier was so unusual as to cause deep embarrassment among his coreligionists.

The Soldier's Chaplet

Very lately it happened thus: while the bounty of our most excellent emperors was dispensed in the camp, the soldiers, laurel-crowned, were approaching. One of them, more a soldier of God, more steadfast than the rest of this brethren, who had imagined that they could serve two masters, his head alone uncovered, the useless crown in his hand—

From The Soldier's Chaplet, *in* The Writings of Tertullian *in the Ante-Nicene Christian Library.*

27

already even by that peculiarity known to everyone as a Christian—was nobly conspicuous. Accordingly, all began to mark him out, jeering him at a distance, gnashing on him near at hand. The murmur is wafted to the tribune, when the person had just left the ranks. The tribune at once puts the question to him, "Why are you so different in your attire?" He declared that he had no liberty to wear the crown with the rest. Being urgently asked for his reasons, he answered, "I am a Christian." O soldier! boasting thyself in God. Then the case was considered and voted on; the matter was remitted to a higher tribunal; the offender was conducted to the prefects. At once he put away the heavy cloak, his disburdening commenced; he loosed from his foot the military shoe, beginning to stand upon holy ground; he gave up the sword, which was not necessary either for the protection of our Lord; from his hand likewise he dropped the laurel crown; and now, purple-clad with the hope of his own blood, shod with the preparation of the Gospel, girt with the sharper word of God, completely equipped in the apostles' armor, and crowned more worthily with the white crown of martyrdom, he awaits in prison the largesse of Christ. Thereafter adverse judgments began to be passed on his conduct . . . as if he were headstrong and rash, and too eager to die, because, in being taken to task about a mere matter of dress, he brought trouble on the bearers of the Name—he, forsooth, alone brave among so many soldier-brethren, he alone a Christian. . . . Now, as they put forth also the objection—But where are we forbidden to be crowned?—I shall take up this point, as more suitable to be treated of here, being the essence, in fact, of the present contention. . . .

To begin with the real ground of the military crown, I think we must first inquire whether warfare is proper at all for Christians. What sense is there in discussing the merely accidental, when that on which it rests is to be condemned?

Do we believe it lawful for a human oath to be superadded to one divine, for a man to come under promise to another master after Christ, and to abjure father, mother, and all nearest kinsfolk, whom even the law has commanded us to honor and love next to God Himself, to whom the Gospel, too, holding them only of less account than Christ, has in like manner rendered honor? Shall it be held lawful to make an occupation of the sword, when the Lord proclaims that he who uses the sword shall perish by the sword? And shall the son of peace take part in the battle when it does not become him even to sue at law? And shall he apply the chain, and the prison, and the torture, and the punishment, who is not the avenger even of his own wrongs? Shall he, forsooth, either keep watch-service for others more than for Christ, or shall he do it on the Lord's day, when he does not even do it for Christ Himself? And shall he keep guard before the temples which he has renounced? And shall he take a meal where the apostle has forbidden him? And shall he diligently protect by night those whom in the daytime he has put to flight by his exorcisms, leaning and resting on the spear the while with which Christ's side was pierced? Shall he carry a flag, too, hostile to Christ? And shall *he* ask a watchword from the emperor who has already received one from God? Shall *he* be disturbed in death by the trumpet of the trumpeter, who expects to be aroused by the angel's trump? And shall the Christian be burned [cremated] according to camp rule, when he was not permitted to burn incense to an idol, when to him Christ remitted the punishment of fire? When how many other offenses there are involved in the performances of camp offices, which we must hold to involve the transgression of God's law, you may see by a slight survey. The very carrying of the name over from the camp of light to the camp of darkness is a violation of it. Of course, if faith comes later, and finds any preoccupied with military service, their case is different, as in the instance of those whom John used to receive for baptism, and of those most faithful centurions, I mean the centurion whom Christ approves, and the centurion whom Peter instructs; yet, at the same time, when a man has become a believer, and faith has been sealed, there must be either an immediate abandonment of it, which has been the course with many; or all sorts of quibbling will have to be resorted to in order to avoid offending God. . . . A state of faith admits no plea of necessity; they are under no necessity to sin, whose one necessity is, that they do not sin. For if one is pressed to the offering of sacrifice and the sheer denial of Christ by the necessity of torture or of punishment, yet discipline does not connive even at that necessity; because there is a higher necessity to dread denying and to undergo martyrdom, than to escape from suffering, and to render the homage required.

Origen
ca.185–ca.254

Origen towers above the other thinkers of the third century. Born in Egypt of Christian parents, he received a sound religious education at home, later studying under Clement of Alexandria. As a boy of eighteen, he was profoundly shaken by the death of his father in the persecution of 202. Thereafter he led an ascetic life, going so far as to take literally Matthew 19:12—"there be eunuchs, which have made themselves eunuchs for the kingdom of heaven's sake"—as a counsel of perfection. Suffering was certainly his lot. After being deposed from the priesthood and exiled because of the irregularity of his ordination, at the age of sixty-five he was caught in the persecution under Decius. He was imprisoned and tortured, dying soon afterward as a result of the ordeal he had undergone.

A prolific writer, Origen is best known for his doctrinal teaching. The *Contra Celsum* (Against Celsus), written between 246 and 248 at the insistence of a wealthy patron, is a point-by-point vindication of Christianity against a treatise (now lost) by a pagan Platonist. In the excerpt given here, he answers the charge, still leveled against sectarians and pacifists, that though they derive benefits from civil society, they refuse to shoulder any of the responsibility for its maintenance. His reply seems, on the surface at least, to complicate rather than clarify the matter. Simultaneously, he asserts that Christians cannot accept public office or fight, yet he praises their public spirit in praying for the victory of imperial arms in a just cause. The key to Origen's thinking is to be found in the idea of the Christian as one set apart from the rest of humanity for a divine purpose, the service of God. Hence neither fighting nor government service is wrong *per se,* nor does he condemn them for others. They are prohibited only to the Lord's disciples, who are in reality the best citizens; for their prayers speed victory and purify the commonwealth through vanquishing the real foe, sin. Therefore, as was also the case with the pagan priests, Christians must be allowed to approach God free of blood-guiltiness. By extension, this argument looks forward to the claim made in the twentieth century by, among others, the Jehovah's Witnesses and even non-Christian groups such as the Black Muslims, that because every believer is a "minister," he must be exempted from military service.

Against Celsus

. . . Celsus, imagining that the Jews are Egyptians by descent, and had abandoned Egypt, after revolting against the Egyptian state, and despising the customs of that people in matters of worship, says that "they suffered from the adherents of Jesus, who believed in Him as the Christ, the same treatment which they had inflicted upon the Egyptians; and that the cause which led to the new state of

From Origen Against Celsus, *III, 5, 7; VIII, 55, 73, 75, in vol. 4 of the Ante-Nicene Christian Library.*

things in either instance was rebellion against the state."
. . . [Just] as the statement is false "that the Hebrews, being
(originally) Egyptians, dated the commencement (of their
political existence) from the time of their rebellion," so
also is this, "that in the days of Jesus others who were Jews
rebelled against the Jewish state, and became His followers"; for neither Celsus nor they who think with him are
able to point to any act on the part of Christians which
savors of rebellion. And yet, if a revolt had led to the for-
mation of the Christian commonwealth, so that it derived
its existence in this way from that of the Jews, who were
permitted to take up arms in defense of the members of
their families and to slay their enemies, the Christian Law-
giver would not have altogether forbidden the putting of
men to death; and yet He nowhere teaches that it is right
for His own disciples to offer violence to any one, however
wicked. For He did not deem it in keeping with such laws
as His, which were derived from a divine source, to allow
the killing of any individual whatever. Nor would the
Christians, had they owed their origin to a rebellion, have
adopted laws of so exceedingly mild a character as not to
allow them, when it was their fate to be slain as sheep, on
any occasion to resist their persecutors. . . .

Celsus goes on to say: "They must make their choice between two alternatives. If they refuse to render due service
to the gods, and to respect those who are set over this service, let them not come to manhood, or marry wives, or
have children, or indeed take any share in the affairs of
life; but let them depart hence with all speed, and leave no
posterity behind them, that such a race may become extinct
from the face of the earth. Or, on the other hand, if they
will take wives, and bring up children, and taste of the
fruits of the earth, and partake of all the blessings of life,
and bear its appointed sorrows . . . then must they discharge the duties of life until they are released from its

bonds, and render due honor to those beings who control the affairs of this life, if they would not show themselves ungrateful to them. For it would be unjust in them, after receiving the good things which they dispense, to pay them no tribute in return." To this we reply, that there appears to us to be no good reason for our leaving this world, except when piety and virtue require it; as when, for example, those that are set as judges, and think that they have power over our lives, place before us the alternative either to live in violation of the commandments of Jesus, or to die if we continue obedient to them. But God has allowed us to marry, because all are not fit for the higher, that is, the perfectly pure life; and God would have us bring up all our children, and not to destroy any of the offspring given us by His providence. And this does not conflict with our purpose not to obey the demons that are on the earth; for, "being armed with the whole armor of God, we stand" as athletes of piety against the race of demons that plot against us. . . .

In the next place, Celsus urges us "to help the king with all our might, and to labor with him in the maintenance of justice, to fight for him; and if he requires it, to fight under him, or lead an army along with him." To this our answer is, that we do, when occasion requires, give help to kings, and that, so to say, a divine help. . . . And this we do in obedience to the injunction of the apostle, "I exhort, therefore, that first of all, supplications, prayers, intercessions, and giving of thanks to be made for all men; for kings, and for all that are in authority"; and the more any one excels in piety, the more effective help does he render to kings, even more than is given by soldiers, who go forth to fight and slay as many of the enemy as they can.

And to those enemies of our faith who require us to bear arms for the commonwealth, and to slay men, we can reply: "Do not those who are priests at certain shrines, and those who attend on certain gods, as you account them, keep their hands free from blood, that they may with hands unstained and free from human blood offer the appointed sacrifices to your gods; and even when war is upon you, you never enlist the priests in the army. If that, then, is a laudable custom, how much more so, that while others are engaged in battle, these too should engage as the priests and ministers of God, keeping their hands pure, and wrestling in prayers to God on behalf of those who are fighting in a righteous cause, and for the king who reigns righteously, that whatever is opposed to those who act righteously may be destroyed!" And as we by our prayers vanquish all demons who stir up war, and lead to the violation of oaths, and disturb the peace, we in this way are much more helpful to the kings than those who go into the field to fight for them. And we do take our part in public affairs, when along with righteous prayers we join self-denying exercises and meditations, which teach us to despise pleasures, and not to be led away by them. And none fight better for the king than we do. We do not indeed fight under him, although he require it; but we fight on his behalf, forming a special army—an army of piety—by offering our prayers to God.

Celsus also urges us to "take office in the government of the country, if that is required for the maintenance of the laws and the support of religion." But we recognize in each state the existence of another national organization, founded by the Word of God, and we exhort those who are mighty in word and of blameless life to rule over Churches. Those who are ambitious of ruling we reject; but we constrain those who, through excess of modesty, are not easily induced to take a public charge in the Church of God. And those who rule over us well are under the constraining influence of the great King, whom we believe to be the Son of God, God the Word. And if those who govern in the

Church, and are called rulers of the divine nation—that is, the Church—rule well, they rule in accordance with the divine commands, and never suffer themselves to be led astray by worldly policy. [Therefore] it is not for the purpose of escaping public duties that Christians decline public offices, but that they may reserve themselves for a diviner and more necessary service in the Church of God —for the salvation of men.

Lactantius
ca.240–ca.320

Lucius Caelius Firmianus, commonly known as Lactantius, was primarily a teacher and rhetorician. By no means ranking with Tertullian or Origen as a theologian, he is known for two works: *The Deaths of the Persecutors* (ca. 314), a collection of horror stories recounting the fate of the persecutors of the Christians, and *The Divine Institutes* (ca. 304), a treatise demonstrating the falsity of paganism as contrasted with the right worship of God. Written in the purest Ciceronian Latin, and dedicated to Constantine, "greatest of emperors," the *Institutes* are steeped in the traditions of classical humanism. In the Vienna edition of his works (1890), the list of quotations from pagan authors fills twenty pages, whereas quotations from the Bible fill only four. Far from disparaging classical culture, therefore, Lactantius appealed to the educated men of his day by demonstrating the compatibility of their highest philosophical insights with Christianity.

Lactantius's hatred of war derives from two sources, neither belonging to what has been dubbed "Sermon on the Mount pacifism." He shared the Stoic-Christian aversion to violence as an action against the brotherhood of man; the human family being one, killing is fratricide. Moreover, in insisting on the immutability of divine law against the relativity of man-made law, he condemned nationalism as prideful and selfish, no matter how it was couched in sanctimonious phrases, and he deprecated also the doctrine, favored by both nationalists and crusaders, that right makes might, that success in arms is a sign that "God is on our side."

The Divine Institutes

The first head of [the divine] law is, to know God Himself, to obey Him alone, to worship Him alone. For he cannot maintain the character of a man who is ignorant of God, the parent of his soul: which is the greatest impiety. For this ignorance causes him to serve other gods, and no greater crime than this can be committed. Hence there is now so easy a step to wickedness through ignorance of the truth and of the chief good; since God, from the knowledge of whom he shrinks, is Himself the fountain of goodness. Or if he shall wish to follow the justice of God, yet, being ignorant of the divine law, he embraces the laws of his own country as the true justice, though they were clearly devised not by justice, but by utility. For why is it that there are different and various laws amongst all people, but that each nation has enacted for itself that which is deemed useful for its own affairs? But how greatly utility differs from justice the Roman people themselves teach, who, by proclaiming war through the Fetiales [special priestly heralds], and by inflicting injuries according to legal forms, by always desiring and carrying off the property of others, have gained for themselves the possession of the whole world. But these persons consider themselves just if they do nothing against their own laws; which may be even ascribed to fear, if they abstain from crimes through dread of present punishment. But let us grant that they do that naturally . . . of their own accord, which they are compelled to do by the laws. Will they therefore be just,

From Lactantius, The Divine Institutes, *book 6 in the Ante-Nicene Christian Library.*

because they obey the institutions of men, who may themselves have erred, or have been unjust? . . . Civil law is one thing, which varies everywhere according to customs; but justice is another thing, which God has set forth to us as uniform and simple: and he who is ignorant of God must also be ignorant of justice. . . .

. . . However[1], let us suppose that this duty of defending the good belongs only to the good man. Yet to undertake it is easy, to fulfill it is difficult; because when you have committed yourself to a contest and an encounter, the victory is placed at the disposal of God, not in your own power. And for the most part the wicked are more powerful both in number and in combination than the good, so that it is not so much virtue which is necessary to overcome them as good fortune. Is any one ignorant how often the better and the juster side has been overcome? From this cause harsh tyrannies have always broken out against the citizens. . . .

It is not a virtue, therefore, either to be the enemy of the bad or the defender of the good, because virtue cannot be subject to uncertain chances. . . . When the agreement of men is taken away, virtue has no existence at all; for what are the interests of our country, but the inconveniences of another state or nation?—that is, to extend the boundaries which are violently taken from others, to increase the power of the state, to improve the revenues—all which things are not virtues, but the overthrowing of virtues: for, in the first place, the union of human society is taken away, innocence is taken away, the abstaining from the property of others is taken away; lastly, justice itself is taken away, which is unable to bear the tearing asunder of the human race, and wherever arms have glittered, must be banished and exterminated from thence. . . . For how can

1. For stylistic reasons I have changed the order of the chapters here, placing chapter six after chapter nine.—Ed.

a man be just who injures, who hates, who despoils, who puts to death? And they who strive to be serviceable to their country do all these things: for they are ignorant of what being serviceable is, who think nothing useful, nothing advantageous, but that which can be held by the hand; and this alone cannot be held, because it may be snatched away.

Whoever, then, has gained for his country these goods— as they themselves call them—that is, who by the overthrow of cities and the destruction of nations has filled the treasury with money, has taken lands and enriched his countrymen —he is extolled with praises to the heaven: in him there is said to be the greatest and perfect virtue. And this is the error not only of the people and the ignorant, but also of philosophers, who even give precepts for injustice, lest folly and wickedness should be wanting in discipline and authority. Therefore, when they are speaking of the duties relating to warfare, all that discourse is accommodated neither to justice nor to true virtue, but to this life and to civil institutions. . . .

. . . The first office of justice is to be united with God, the second with man. But the former is called religion; the second is named mercy or kindness; which virtue is peculiar to the just, and to the worshippers of God, because this alone comprises the principle of common life. For God, who has not given wisdom to the other animals, has made them more safe from attack in danger by natural defenses. But because He made him naked and defenseless, that He might rather furnish him with wisdom, He gave him, besides other things, this feeling of kindness; so that man should protect, love, and cherish man, and both receive and afford assistance against all dangers. Therefore kindness is the greatest bond of human society; and he who has broken this is to be deemed impious, and a parricide. For if we all derive our origin from one man, whom God created, we are plainly of one blood; and therefore it must be considered the greatest wickedness to hate a man, even though guilty. On which account God has enjoined that enmities are never to be contracted by us, but that they are always to be removed, so that we soothe those who are our enemies, by reminding them of their relationship. Likewise, if we are all inspired and animated by one God, what else are we than brothers? . . . Therefore they are to be accounted as savage beasts who injure man; who, in opposition to every law and right of human nature, plunder, torture, slay, and banish.

On account of this relationship of brotherhood, God teaches us never to do evil, but always good. And He also prescribes in what this doing good consists: in affording aid to those who are oppressed and in difficulty, and in bestowing food on those who are destitute. For God, since He is kind, wished us to be a social animal. Therefore, in the case of other men, we ought to think of ourselves. We do not deserve to be set free in our own dangers, if we do not succor others; we do not deserve assistance, if we refuse to render it. . . .

Therefore humanity is to be preserved, if we wish rightly to be called men. But what else is this preservation of humanity than the loving of a man because he is a man, and the same as ourselves? Therefore discord and dissension are not in accordance with the nature of man; and that expression of Cicero is true, which says that man, while he is obedient to nature cannot injure man. . . . For when God forbids us to kill, He not only prohibits us from open violence, which is not even allowed by the public laws, but He warns us against the commission of those things which are esteemed lawful among men. Thus it will be neither lawful for a just man to engage in warfare, since his warfare is justice itself, nor to accuse anyone of a capital charge, because it makes no difference whether you put a man to death by word, or rather by the sword, since it is

the act of putting to death itself which is prohibited. Therefore, with regard to this precept of God, there ought to be
no exception at all; but that it is always unlawful to put to
death a man, whom God willed to be a sacred animal.

Two Soldier-Martyrs

In Roman times, the Christians' refusal to accept military service or its collateral obligations carried the penalty of death by
the sword. By the third century, the number of Christians in the
legions was increasing steadily. However, there were holdouts.
One of the earliest cases of conscientious objection involved
Maximilianus, martyred at Carthage in 295. Summoned before
Dion, the proconsul of Africa, the young man, who was eligible
for conscription as the son of a veteran, refused on the grounds
that, as a Christian, he could not do wrong. From evidence of
this sort, it would seem that all Christians would have had an
aversion to military service; actually, large numbers of them
were in the armies of the later Roman Empire, and they were
quite prepared to fight. Their martyrdom, as Tertullian indicated, stemmed less from their pacifism than from their
refusal to take part in pagan rites. This was the case with Marcellus, who at the time of his martyrdom in Tangier (298), had
attained the fairly high military rank of centurion. Unfortunately,
while we know why men such as Marcellus suffered, we lack
any accounts in their own words of how they were able to reconcile in their own minds their profession with their faith, if
indeed this was a real problem for them.

Acts of Saint Maximilian the Martyr

During the fourth year of the consulship of Tuscus and
Anulinus, on the fifteenth of March, Fabius Victor and his
son Maximilian were led into the public square of Teviste....

*This selection and the next, the story of the martyrdom of Marcel-
lus, are from P. T. Ruinart, ed., Acta Martyrum (Ratisbon, 1859).
The translations were made by Samuel Kapustin.*

DION THE PROCONSUL: What is your name?

MAXIMILIAN: Why do you want to know my name? I am a Christian, and cannot fight.

DION: Nevertheless you will be measured [under the foot rule]. Officer.

MAXIMILIAN: Have it your own way. But I cannot serve as a soldier; I cannot do evil. I am a Christian.

DION: Let him be measured!

BEADLE [after the measuring]: He is five feet, ten inches tall.

DION: Have him put on the soldier's insignia.

MAXIMILIAN: I do not want it. I cannot serve as a soldier.

DION: Serve lest you perish.

MAXIMILIAN: I will not serve. Cut off my head, if that is your will. But I cannot be a soldier for the world, as I am already a soldier for my God.

DION: Who has persuaded you to behave like this?

MAXIMILIAN: My own mind, and He who called me.

DION [to Victor]: Advise your son.

VICTOR: He knows what he must do; he has his own counsel, which will provide for him.

DION: Accept the insignia and serve.

MAXIMILIAN: I will not accept the insignia. I already have the sign of Christ my God.

DION: Soon I shall send you to your Christ.

MAXIMILIAN: I wish you would only do it. This is my glory.

DION [to the Beadle]: Have him put on the insignia.

MAXIMILIAN: I do not accept the insignia of men; and if you should really mark me, I would tear it up, since it signifies nothing. I am a Christian. I am not permitted to carry a lead ball around my neck [i.e., the leaden insignia with the Emperor's effigy], to salute from beneath it the sign of my Lord, Jesus Christ, the Son of the Living God, whom you do not know, but who God sent for our welfare and who suffered for our sins. All Christians serve Him; we follow Him, the Restorer of life, the Author of our salvation.

DION: Accept the insignia and serve, lest you die miserably.

MAXIMILIAN: I do not die. My name already belongs to my Lord. I cannot serve.

DION: Consider your youth and serve. For military service is fitting for a youth.

MAXIMILIAN: My service is to my Lord. I cannot serve the powers of this world. I have just said that I am a Christian.

DION: There are Christians who serve as soldiers in the august company of our lords Diocletian and Maximian, of Constantius and Maximus; and they fight.

MAXIMILIAN: They know what is best for themselves. I nevertheless am a Christian, and I cannot do evil.

DION: Those who wage war do evil?

MAXIMILIAN: You know what they do.

DION: Serve, lest your refusal be the occasion for a miserable death.

MAXIMILIAN: I shall not die; and if I should depart from this world, my spirit will live with Christ my Lord.

DION: Strike his name from the roster. Because of your rebellious spirit, you have refused to render military service; and you shall be punished according to your deserts, so as to serve as an example for others. [Reading the decree from the tablet.] Maximilian! because you have, with a rebellious spirit, refused to bear arms, you shall die by the sword.

MAXIMILIAN: Thanks be to God!

He was twenty-one years, three months, and eighteen days old. And when he was led to the place of execution, he spoke thus: "My dear brethren, endeavor with all your might, that it may be your portion to see the Lord, and that He may bestow upon you such a crown." And with a cheerful countenance he spoke thus to his father: "Give my new clothes, which you have provided for me for the service, to the executioner; and, when I shall receive thee in the company of the blessed martyrs, we may rejoice together with the Lord." And soon afterwards, he was dispatched. And his mother Pompeina claimed his body from the judge and took it on a litter to Carthage, where she buried it next to the Martyr Cyprian. And after the thirteenth day, she passed away and was also buried there. His father Victor, however, returned home, rejoicing and praising God, that he had sent forth such a gift to the Lord, himself expecting to follow shortly, thanks to God. Amen.

Acts of Saint Marcellus, Centurion and Martyr

In the city of Tangiers, during the administration of Fortunatus, the governor, there was celebrated the birthday of the Emperor. When all were attending festivals and offering sacrifices, a certain Marcellus from among the centurions of the Trajana Legion, thinking about the profane goings-on at those festivals, threw down the military belt in front of the Legion, declaring in a loud voice: "I serve Jesus Christ the everlasting King." He then cast away the centurion's staff and arms, adding: "With this I cease to serve your emperors, and I disdain to worship your wooden and stone gods, who are deaf and dumb idols. If such be the conditions of service that men are compelled to sacrifice to the gods and emperors, then behold, I throw away the staff and belt; I renounce the standards and refuse to serve."

Those nearby hearing him were stunned: they held him and reported to Anastasius Fortunatus, the commander of the Legion, who ordered him to be thrown into prison. When the festivals were over, remaining in the chamber, he ordered that the centurion Marcellus be brought in. When Marcellus had been led in by centurions from the Astasian Legion, Anastasius Fortunatus said to him: "What has come over you that, contrary to military discipline, you have removed your sword-belt and cast away girdle and staff?"

MARCELLUS: Now on the twelfth day of the month, on the Kalends of Augustus [October 12], near the standards of your Legion, when the birthday of the Emperor was being celebrated, I publicly stated in a loud voice that I am a Christian, and that I am unable to adhere to the military oath of allegiance, but rather serve Jesus Christ, the son of the almighty God the Father.

ANASTASIUS FORTUNATUS: I cannot allow your rashness to go unnoticed, and for that reason I am reporting this to the generals and to Caesar. You yourself will be conveyed to my lord Aurelius Agricolanus. . . .

On the third day of the month of November at Tangiers, when Marcellus was led in by the Astasian centurions, the bailiff said: "The governor Fortunatus has transferred to your jurisdiction the centurion Marcellus. I have here a letter concerning him, which, if you please, I shall read."

AGRICOLANUS: Let it be read.
BAILIFF: To you lord Fortunatus, etc. This soldier, having scorned the military belt, has declared himself to be a Christian, and in the presence of all the people he uttered many slanders against the gods and against Caesar. For this reason he has been remanded to you, so that your splendor might deal with him.

AGRICOLANUS: Did you say these things before the court of the governor?

MARCELLUS: I said it.

AGRICOLANUS: Were you serving as a regular centurion?

MARCELLUS: I was serving.

AGRICOLANUS: By what madness were you incited so that you renounced the oaths and spoke such things?

MARCELLUS: There is no madness in those who fear the Lord.

AGRICOLANUS: Did you cast away your arms?

MARCELLUS: I threw them away. For it is not fitting for a Christian man who serves Christ the Lord to serve human powers.

AGRICOLANUS: Thus are the acts of Marcellus, that they ought to be punished with discipline. It is my resolve to punish with death Marcellus, who served as a regular centurion, who abandoned his oath publicly, who desecrated it, and who, moreover, during the proceedings before the governor insanely made other statements.

MARCELLUS [as he was being led away]: May God bless you. . . .

II

THE CHRISTIAN AS WARRIOR

"In war even, if you must needs still be engaged in it, hold to the faith, seek after peace."

—St. Augustine

Marcus Tullius Cicero

106 B.C.–43 B.C.

Cicero was not only famous in his own day as a lawyer, orator, and politician, but his works were for centuries the mainstay in the reading of educated men in the West. It was through his ethical writings, notably *De Officiis* (Of Duties), that Christians acquired the Stoic teaching about the natural law as applied to the affairs of nations. According to this concept, a principle of rationality pervades the cosmos, governing all things, animate and inanimate, in a manner congruous with the nature of each. Thus in man the natural law signifies those eternal and unalterable principles of morality engraved upon the heart and perceived by reason. Simply because he is a rational being, every man is capable of knowing and doing what is right.

By extending this principle beyond the individual to the community and to its relations with other communities, it became possible to deduce a kind of natural society of mankind, which in turn gave rise to mutual rights and responsibilities bearing on the morality of war. Cicero, good Roman that he was, carried this development a step further, fusing the concept of the "just war"—for this is what it has been called since his day—with traditional Roman practices, such as the requirement that war be declared by the priestly Fetiales. The result was not only a theory of universal applicability, but one that squared admirably with the practical needs of empire builders. At best it provided for a humane code of conduct and a generous peace policy, the better to keep the vanquished contented. At worst, when a war could not be presented as defensive, it could at least be claimed that it was being waged in the name of honoring pledges to allies or protecting the innocent. This casuistry led both Lactantius and Augustine, otherwise admirers of Cicero, to remark sardonically that the "just war" had enabled Roman imperialism to claim a lot more than its just share of the things of the world, a comment that retains its sting in the world of the present.

The Roman Version of the Just War

There are certain duties that we owe even to those who have wronged us. For there is a limit to retribution and to punishment; or rather, I am inclined to think, it is sufficient that the aggressor should be brought to repent of his wrong-doing, in order that he may not repeat the offence and that others may be deterred from doing wrong.

Then, too, in the case of a state in its external relations, the rights of war must be strictly observed. For since there are two ways of settling a dispute: first, by discussion; second, by physical force; and since the former is characteristic of man, the latter of the brute, we must resort to force only in case we may not avail ourselves of discussion. The only excuse, therefore, for going to war is that we may live in peace unharmed; and when the victory is won, we should spare those who have not been blood-thirsty and barbarous in their warfare. . . . In my opinion, at least, we should always strive to secure a peace that shall not admit of guile. And if my advice had been heeded on this point, we should still have at least some sort of constitutional government, if not the best in the world, whereas, as it is, we have none at all.

Not only must one show consideration for those whom we have conquered by force of arms but we must also ensure protection to those who lay down their arms and throw themselves upon the mercy of our generals, even though the battering-ram has hammered at their walls. And among our countrymen justice has been observed so conscientiously in this direction, that those who have given promise of protection to states or nations subdued in war become,

Reprinted by permission of the publishers and The Loeb Classical Library from Cicero, De Officiis, trans. Walter Miller (Cambridge, Mass.: Harvard University Press,) bk. I, sec. xi-xii.

after the custom of our forefathers, the patrons of those states.

As for war, humane laws touching it are drawn up in the fetial code of the Roman People under all the guarantees of religion; and from this it may be gathered that no war is just, unless it is entered upon after an official demand for satisfaction has been submitted or warning has been given and a formal declaration made. . . .

This also I observe—that he who would properly have been called "a fighting enemy" (*perduellis*) was called "a guest" (*hostis*), thus relieving the ugliness of the fact by a softened expression; for "enemy" (*hostis*) meant to our ancestors what we now call "stranger" (*peregrinus*). . . . What can exceed such charity, when he with whom one is at war is called by so gentle a name? And yet long lapse of time has given that word a harsher meaning: for it has lost its signification of "stranger" and has taken on the technical connotation of "an enemy under arms."

But when a war is fought out for supremacy and when glory is the object of war, it must still not fail to start from the same motives which I said a moment ago were the only righteous grounds for going to war. But those wars which have glory for their end must be carried on with less bitterness. For we contend, for example, with a fellow-citizen in one way, if he is a personal enemy, in another, if he is a rival: with the rival it is a struggle for office and position, with the enemy for life and honour. So with the Celtiberians and the Cimbrians we fought with as deadly enemies, not to determine which should be supreme, but which should survive; but with the Latins, Sabines, Samnites, Carthaginians, and Pyrrhus we fought for supremacy. . . .

Again, if under the stress of circumstances individuals have made any promise to the enemy, they are bound to keep their word even then. For instance, in the First Punic

War, when Regulus was taken prisoner by the Carthaginians, he was sent to Rome on parole to negotiate an
exchange of prisoners; he came and, in the first place, it
was he that made the motion in the senate that the prisoners
should not be restored; and in the second place, when his
relatives and friends would have kept him back, he chose to
return to a death by torture rather than prove false to his
promise, though given to an enemy. . . .

Our forefathers have given us another striking example
of justice toward an enemy: when a deserter from Pyrrhus
promised the senate to administer poison to the king and
thus work his death, the senate and Gaius Fabricus delivered the deserter up to Pyrrhus. Thus they stamped with
their disapproval the treacherous murder even of an enemy
who was at once powerful, unprovoked, aggressive, and
successful.

Saint Augustine of Hippo
354–430

Of all the giants of the Patristic Age, none led so tempestuous
a life, experienced greater spiritual turmoil, or left so indelible
a mark on Christian thought, indeed upon the entire intellectual
development of the West, as Saint Augustine. Not the least of
his accomplishments was the synthesizing of Ciceronian and
Christian ideas about war. To this day, his synthesis is at the
base of both Roman Catholic teaching and the teaching of the
leading Protestant denominations. Unfortunately, prolific writer
that he was, he left no treatise specifically on the subject, scat-
tering his conclusions throughout his writings. Moreover, certain
ambiguities are introduced as a result of his juxtaposing considerations of private morality with those of society, and then
shifting the terms of discussion from one to the other without
warning. But these difficulties are resolvable in accordance with
a few basic concepts.

We begin with two selections from *The City of God,* written between 413 and 416 to refute charges that Christian "slave morality" and other-worldliness had undermined Roman strength, preparing the way for barbarian invasion. The first of these excerpts is an explication of war as tragic necessity, presented in the form of a warning, strikingly modern in tone, against the evils of imperialism. Whereas Cicero had sought a legalistic rationale for Roman imperialism, Augustine delved more deeply. He asserted that through greed and pride Rome had built an empire whose very size, coupled with its attempt to assimilate vastly differing peoples, provoked its neighbors and spawned civil wars. These wars led in turn to further expansion, more provocations, and more war. But these were, strictly speaking, defensive wars, and therefore "just." In a sense, because good and evil were inextricably intermixed in man, Augustine regarded war as being at once a result *of* sin and a cure *for* sin; hence the closing line about the anguish such cruel necessity must cause the wise man.

Justice and the Relations of States

Justice being taken away . . . what are kingdoms but great robberies? For what are robberies themselves but little kingdoms? The band itself is made up of men; it is ruled by the authority of a prince, it is knit together by the pact of the confederacy; the booty is divided by the law agreed on. If, by the admittance of abandoned men, this evil increases to such a degree that it holds places, fixes abodes, takes possession of cities, and subdues peoples, it assumes the more plainly the name of a kingdom, because the reality is now manifestly conferred on it, not by the removal of covetousness, but by the addition of impunity. Indeed, that was an apt and true reply which was given

From St. Augustine, The City of God, *bk. IV, 4, 15; bk. XIX, 7, in the Nicene and Post-Nicene Christian Library.*

to Alexander the Great by a pirate who had been seized. For when that king had asked the man what he meant by keeping hostile possession of the sea, he answered with bold pride, "What thou meanest by seizing the whole world; but because I do it with a petty ship, I am called a robber, whilst thou who dost it with a great fleet art styled emperor." . . .

Let them ask, then, whether it is quite fitting for good men to rejoice in extended empire. For the iniquity of those with whom just wars are carried on favors the growth of a kingdom, which would certainly have been small if the peace and justice of neighbors had not by any wrong provoked the carrying on of war against them; and human affairs being thus more happy, all kingdoms would have been small, rejoicing in neighborly concord; and thus there would have been very many kingdoms of nations in the world, as there are very many houses of citizens in a city. Therefore, to carry on war and extend a kingdom over wholly subdued nations seems to bad men to be felicity, to good men necessity. But because it would be worse that the injurious should rule over those who are more righteous, therefore even that is not unsuitably called felicity. But beyond doubt it is greater felicity to have a good neighbor at peace, than to conquer a bad one by making war. Your wishes are bad, when you desire that one whom you hate or fear should be in such a condition that you can conquer him. . . .

After the state or city comes the world, the third circle of human society—the first being the house, and the second the city. And the world, as it is larger, so it is fuller of dangers, as the greater sea is the more dangerous. And here, in the first place, man is separated from man by the difference of languages. For if two men, each ignorant of the other's language, meet, and are not compelled to pass, but, on the contrary, to remain in company, dumb animals, though of different species, would more easily hold intercourse than they, human beings though they be. For their common nature is no help to friendliness when they are prevented by diversity of language from conveying their sentiments to one another; so that a man would more readily hold intercourse with his dog than with a foreigner. But the imperial city has endeavoured to impose on subject peoples not only her yoke, but her language, as a bond of peace, so that interpreters, far from being scarce, are numberless. This is true; but how many great wars, how much slaughter and bloodshed, have provided this unity! And though these are past, the end of these miseries has not yet come. For though there have never been wanting, nor are yet wanting, hostile nations beyond the empire, against whom wars have been and are waged, yet, supposing there were no such nations, the very extent of the empire itself has produced wars of a more obnoxious description—social and civil wars—and with these the whole race has been agitated, either by the actual conflict or fear of a renewed outbreak. If I attempted to give an adequate description of these manifold disasters, these stern and lasting necessities, though I am quite unequal to the task, what limit could I set? But, say they, the wise man will wage just wars. As if he would not all the rather lament the necessity of just wars, if he remembers that he is a man; for if they were not just he would not wage them, and would therefore be delivered from all wars. For it is the wrongdoing of the opposing party which compels the wise man to wage just wars; and this wrongdoing, even though it gave rise to no war, would still be matter of grief to man because it is man's wrongdoing. Let every one, then, who thinks with pain on all these great evils, so horrible, so ruthless, acknowledge that this is misery. And if any one either endures or thinks of them without mental pain, this is a more miserable plight still, for he thinks himself happy because he has lost human feeling. . . .

Augustine next takes up the subject of peace, derived from his doctrine of the two cities. There are, he held, two kinds of love in man: prideful, selfish, materialistic love; and heavenly, spiritual love. Upon these two kinds of love are built two communities or "cities": the *civitas terrena,* the earthly community, and the *civitas Dei,* the heavenly community. As different as these cities are, they yet have in common a striving for peace ("the tranquility of order"), an active, all-pervasive principle in the universe. Unfortunately, absolute peace, like perfect justice, is an ideal realizable only at the end of days and in the celestial city. This side of the Second Coming, all attempts at peace on earth are in reality little more than temporary expedients, foredoomed to be short-lived and self-destroying because they contain the element of selfish love. As Augustine says elsewhere in this work (XVII, 13): "Whoever hopes for this so great good [i.e., peace] in this world, in this earth, his wisdom is but folly. . . . For such great security is never given to any people, that it should not dread invasions hostile to its life." Thus man, "aping God," always wages war as a means to securing peace. The tragedy is that peace begins to crumble in his hands the moment it is attained.

The Nature of Peace

. . . For peace is a good so great, that even in this earthly and mortal life there is no word we hear with such pleasure, nothing we desire with such zest, or find to be more thoroughly gratifying. So that if we dwell for a little longer

From The City of God, *bk. XIX, 10-13.*

on this subject, we shall not, in my opinion, be wearisome to our readers. . . .

Whoever gives any moderate attention to human affairs and to our common nature, will recognize that if there is no man who does not wish to be joyful, neither is there any one who does not wish to have peace. For even they who make war desire nothing but victory—desire, that is to say, to attain peace with glory. For what else is victory than the conquest of those who resist us? and when this is done there is peace. It is therefore with the desire for peace that wars are waged, even by those who take pleasure in exercising their warlike nature in command and battle. And hence it is obvious that peace is the end sought for by war. For every man seeks peace by waging war, but no man seeks war by making peace. For even they who intentionally interrupt the peace in which they are living have no hatred of peace, but only wish it changed into a peace that suits them better. They do not, therefore, wish to have no peace, but only one more to their mind. And in the case of sedition, when men have separated themselves from the community, they yet do not effect what they wish, unless they maintain some kind of peace with their fellow-conspirators. And therefore even robbers take care to maintain peace with their comrades, that they may with greater effect and greater safety invade the peace of other men. . . . And thus all men desire to have peace with their own circle whom they wish to govern as suits themselves. For even those whom they make war against they wish to make their own, and impose on them the laws of their own peace. . . . [Even] the most savage animals encompass their own species with a ring of protective peace. . . . For what tigress does not gently purr over her cubs, and lay aside her ferocity to fondle them? What kite, solitary as he is when circling over his prey, does not seek a mate, build a nest, hatch the eggs, bring up the young birds, and maintain with the mother of his family as peaceful a domestic alliance as he can? How much more powerfully do the laws of man's nature move him to hold fellowship and maintain peace with all men so far as in him lies, since even wicked men wage war to maintain the peace of their own circle, and wish that, if possible, all men belonged to them, that all men and things might serve but one head, and might, either through love or fear, yield themselves to peace with him! It is thus that pride in its perversity apes God. It abhors equality with other men under Him; but, instead of His rule, it seeks to impose a rule of its own upon its equals. It abhors, that is to say, the just peace of God, and loves its own unjust peace; but it cannot help loving peace of one kind or other. For there is no vice so clearly contrary to nature that it obliterates even the faintest trace of nature.

In the *Contra Faustus Manichaeum* of 397, a work directed against Faustus of Milevus, a propagandist for the Manichaeans —dualists who believed that Satan is co-eternal with God—under whom he had studied, Augustine presents his fullest statement on war. At the beginning of the discussion he seems merely to be quibbling with a heretic. Actually, he is enunciating a number of complex issues without pausing to clarify them thoroughly: namely, the difference between wars ordained by God in the past and subsequent wars; the proper auspices for a just war, and thus the difference between killing and murder; and, in connection with the evils of war, the question of the rightful intention. At the conclusion he raises the issue of whether the soldier should obey orders regardless of the justice of the cause—an issue that should be considered in light of the Nuremberg trials, the Eichmann case, and the My Lai massacre. In Augustine's view, the soldier is a public functionary who must obey without question those placed over him by God; this view persisted until the sixteenth century, because medieval military law knew nothing of the rights of conscientious objection. The ruler, rather than the individual soldier, bears before God the onus for a wicked command; and this doctrine holds whether the ruler be an infidel such as Julian the Apostate (cf. *Commentaries on the Psalms,* CXXIV, 7) or, pursuing the principle further, a Hitler.

Against Faustus

According to the eternal law, which requires the preservation of the natural order, and forbids the transgression of it, some actions have an indifferent character, so that men are blamed for presumption if they do them without being called upon, while they are deservedly praised for doing them when required. The act, the agent, and the authority for the action are all of great importance in the order of nature. For Abraham the sacrifice of his son of his own accord is shocking madness. His doing so at the command of God proves him faithful and submissive. This is so loudly proclaimed by the very voice of truth, that Faustus, *eagerly* rummaging for some fault, and reduced at last to slanderous charges, has not the boldness to attack this action. It is scarcely possible that he can have forgotten a deed so famous, that it recurs to the mind of itself without any study or reflection, and is in fact repeated by so many tongues, and portrayed in so many places, that no one can pretend to shut his eyes or ears to it. If, therefore, while Abraham's killing his son of his own accord would have been unnatural, his doing it at the command of God shows not only guiltless but praiseworthy compliance, why does Faustus blame Moses for spoiling the Egyptians? Your feeling of disapproval for the mere human action should be restrained by a regard for the divine sanction. Will you

From Reply to Faustus the Manichaean, *bk. XXII, 73-76, in the Nicene and Post-Nicene Christian Library.*

venture to blame God Himself for desiring such actions?
Then "Get thee behind me, Satan, for thou understandest
not the things which be of God, but those which be of
men." . . .

. . . The account of the wars of Moses will not excite
surprise or abhorrence, for in wars carried on by divine
command, he showed not ferocity but obedience; and God,
in giving the command, acted not in cruelty, but in righteous
retribution, giving to all what they deserved, and warning
those who needed warning. What is the evil in war? Is it
the death of some who will soon die in any case, that others
may live in peaceful subjugation? This is mere cowardly
dislike, not any religious feeling. The real evils in war are
love of violence, revengeful cruelty, fierce and implacable
enmity, wild resistance, and the lust of power, and such
like; and it is generally to punish these things, when force
is required to inflict the punishment, that, in obedience to
God or some lawful authority, good men undertake wars,
when they find themselves in such a position as regards the
conduct of human affairs, that right conduct requires them
to act, or to make others act in this way. Otherwise John,
when the soldiers who came to be baptized asked "What
shall we do?" would have replied, "Throw away your arms;
give up the service; never strike, or wound, or disable
any one." But knowing that such actions in battle were not
murderous, but authorized by law, and that the soldiers did
not thus avenge themselves, but defend the public safety,
he replied, "Do violence to no man, accuse no man falsely,
and be content with your wages." But as the Manichaeans
are in the habit of speaking evil of John, let them hear the
Lord Jesus Christ Himself offering this money to be given to
Caesar, which John tells the soldiers to be content with.
"Give," he says, "to Caesar the things that are Caesar's."
For tribute-money is given on purpose to pay the soldiers
for war. Again, in the case of the centurion who said, "I

am a man under authority, and have soldiers under me: and I say to one, Go, and he goeth; and to another, Come, and he cometh; and to my servant, Do this, and he doeth it," Christ gave due praise to his faith; he did not tell him to leave the service. . . .

A great deal depends on the causes for which men undertake wars, and on the authority they have for doing so; for the natural order which seeks the peace of mankind, ordains that the monarch should have the power of undertaking war if he thinks it advisable, and that the soldiers should perform their military duties in behalf of the peace and safety of the community. When war is undertaken in obedience to God, who would rebuke, or humble, or crush the pride of man, it must be allowed to be a righteous war. . . . For there is no power but of God, who either orders or permits. Since, therefore, a righteous man, serving it may be under an ungodly king, may do the duty belonging to his position in the State in fighting by the order of his sovereign —for in some cases it is plainly the will of God that he should fight, and in others, where this is not so plain, it may be an unrighteous command on the part of the king, while the soldier is innocent, because his position makes obedience a duty—how much more must the man be blameless who carries on war on the authority of God, of whom every one who serves Him knows that He can never require what is wrong?

The letter, written in 412 in reply to Count Marcellus's query as to whether one can be simultaneously a good Christian and a good citizen seems out of character, accepting as it does from the outset the texts traditionally advanced by pacifists in support of their cause. The key lies in the fact that a matter of personal morality is juxtaposed with broader social concerns. Augustine praises the good man's refusal to resist evil; it is a psychological

device, almost Gandhian in its appreciation of human nature, to
end wrongdoing by changing the mental state of the wrongdoer.
Suffering in this case is a redemptive act undertaken in the
spirit of charity. Such a choice, however, is never possible for
the state, which is commissioned to step in where the interests
of its citizens as individuals, or its own corporate interests, are
menaced. But whereas it must use violence toward the offender,
domestic or foreign, its *inner disposition* must coincide exactly
with that of the self-sacrificing individual. Even when making
war, the state must be motivated by love, by a determination
to chastise its opponent with the double objective of vindicating
justice and rescuing its adversary from further corruption.

Letter to Marcellus

Let us now observe, in the second place, what follows in
your letter. You have added that they said that the Christian doctrine and preaching were in no way consistent with
the duties and rights of citizens, because among its precepts
we find; "Recompense to no man evil for evil," and, "Whosoever shall smite thee on one cheek, turn to him the other
also; and if any man take away thy coat, let him have thy
cloak also; and whosoever will compel thee to go a mile
with him, go with him twain"—all which are affirmed to
be contrary to the duties and rights of citizens; for who
would submit to have anything taken from him by an
enemy, or forbear him retaliating the evils of war upon an
invader who ravaged a Roman province? . . .

. . . For these things are done only that a wicked man
may be overcome by kindness, or rather that the evil which
is in the wicked man may be overcome by good, and that
the man may be delivered from the evil—not from any evil
that is external and foreign to himself, but from that which

From Letter 138 in Augustine's Letters, *in the Nicene and Post-
Nicene Christian Library.*

is within and is his own, under which he suffers loss more severe and fatal than could be inflicted by the cruelty of any enemy from without. He, therefore, who is overcoming evil by good, submits patiently to the loss of temporal advantages, that he may show how those things, through excessive love of which the other is made wicked, deserve to be despised when compared with faith and righteousness; in order that so the injurious person may learn from him whom he wronged what is the true nature of the things for the sake of which he committed the wrong, and may be won back with sorrow for his sin to that concord, than which nothing is more serviceable to the State, being overcome not by the strength of one passionately resenting, but by the good nature of one patiently bearing wrong. For then it is rightly done when it seems that it will benefit him for whose sake it is done, by producing in him amendment of his ways and concord with others. At all events, it is to be done with this intention, even though the result may be different from what was expected, and the man, with a view to whose correction and conciliation this healing and salutary medicine, so to speak, was employed, refuses to be corrected and reconciled. . . .

In fine, that these precepts pertain rather to the inward disposition of the heart than to the actions which are done in the sight of men . . . is manifest from the fact that our Lord Jesus Himself, our perfect example of patience, when He was smitten on the face, answered: "If I have spoken evil, bear witness of the evil, but if not, why smitest thou me?" . . .

[Therefore], these precepts concerning patience ought to be always retained in the habitual discipline of the heart, and the benevolence which prevents the recompensing of evil for evil must be always fully cherished in the disposition. . . . And on this principle, if the commonwealth observe the precepts of the Christian religion, even its wars them-

selves will not be carried on without the benevolent design
that, after the resisting nations have been conquered, provision may be more easily made for enjoying in peace the
mutual bond of piety and justice. For the person from
whom is taken away the freedom which he abuses in doing
wrong is vanquished with benefit to himself; since nothing
is more truly a misfortune than that good fortune of offenders, by which pernicious impunity is maintained, and
the evil disposition, like an enemy within the man, is
strengthened. But the perverse and froward hearts of men
think human affairs are prosperous when men are concerned
about magnificent mansions, and indifferent to the ruin of
souls; when mighty theaters are built up, and the foundations of virtue are undermined; when the madness of ex-
travagance is highly esteemed, and works of mercy are
scorned; when, out of the wealth and affluence of rich men,
luxurious provision is made for actors, and the poor are
grudged the necessities of life; when that God who, by the
public declarations of His doctrine, protests against public
vice, is blasphemed by impious communities, which demand
gods of such character that even those theatrical representa-
tions which bring disgrace to both body and soul are fitly
performed in honor of them. If God permit these things to
prevail, He is in that permission showing more grievous
displeasure: if He leave these crimes unpunished, such
impunity is a more terrible judgment. When, on the other
hand, he overthrows the props of vice, and reduces to
poverty those lusts which were nursed by plenty, He afflicts
in mercy. And in mercy, also, if such a thing were possible,
even wars might be waged by the good, in order that, by
bringing under the yoke the unbridled lusts of men, those
vices might be abolished which ought, under a just government, to be either extirpated or suppressed.

For if the Christian religion condemned wars of every

kind, the command given in the Gospel to soldiers taking counsel as to salvation would rather be to cast away their arms, and withdraw themselves wholly from military service; whereas the word spoken to such was, "Do violence to no man, neither accuse any falsely, and be content with your wages"—the command to be content with their wages manifestly implying no prohibition to continue in the service. Wherefore, let those who say that the doctrine of Christ is incompatible with the State's well-being, give us an army of soldiers such as the doctrine of Christ requires them to be; let them give us such subjects, such husbands and wives, such parents and children, such kings and judges—in fine, such taxpayers and tax-gatherers, as the Christian religion has taught that men should be, and then let them dare say that it is adverse to the State's well-being; yea, rather, let them no longer hesitate to confess that this docrinc, if it were obeyed, would be the salvation of the commonwealth.

The next letter (419) was written to Boniface, Count of Africa, who was then thinking he might better serve God by abandoning his career for the religious life. It deals with two issues. First, Augustine reaffirms the Christian's duty toward the state. Although he grants that priests occupy a higher place before God than laymen, he nevertheless tries to dissuade Boniface by maintaining that the soldier's task is also blessed. As to this task itself, the second part of the letter is devoted specifically to the question of how the just man is to utilize victory. Of course he who avoids war through negotiation is to be praised above the best of warriors: "It is a greater glory to destroy war with a word than men with a sword, and to secure and maintain peace by means of peace rather than war," he says elsewhere (Letter 229, 2). This failing, there is no alternative but to vindicate justice at the sword's point. But since the end of war is peace, the final settlement must be reached with this end in view. The

victor should be stern without being cruel, haughty, or venge-
ful, because these feelings are the germ of future wars. A counsel
of perfection, perhaps, but nonetheless a principle the statesmen
would always do well to remember. That they cannot is the
tragedy of existence in this aeon.

Letter to Boniface

Do not think that it is impossible for anyone to please
God while engaged in active military service. Among such
persons was the holy David, to whom God gave so great a
testimony; among them also were many righteous men of
that time; among them was also that centurion who said
to the Lord; "I am not worthy that Thou shouldest come
under my roof . . ." and concerning whom the Lord said:
"Verily, I say unto you, I have not found so great faith, no,
not in Israel." . . . Among them were also the soldiers who,
when they had come to be baptized by John—the sacred
forerunner of the Lord, and the friend of the Bridegroom,
of whom the Lord says: "Among them that are born of
women there hath not arisen a greater than John the Baptist,"—and had inquired of him what they should do, received the answer, "Do violence to no man, neither accuse
any falsely; and be content with your wages." Certainly he
did not prohibit them to serve as soldiers when he commanded them to be content with their pay for the service.

They occupy indeed a higher place before God who,
abandoning all these secular employments, serve Him with
the strictest chastity; but "every one," as the apostle says,
"hath his proper gift of God, one after this manner, and
another after that." Some, then, in praying for you, fight
against your invisible enemies; you, in fighting for them,

From Letter 189 in Augustine's Letters, *in the Nicene and Post-
Nicene Christian Library.*

contend against the barbarians, their visible enemies. Would that one faith existed in all, for then there would be less weary struggling, and the devil with his angels would be more easily conquered; but since it is necessary in this life that the citizens of the kingdom should be subjected to temptations among erring and impious men, that they may be exercised, and "tried as gold in the furnace," we ought not before the appointed time to desire to live with those alone who are holy and righteous, so that, by patience, we may deserve to receive this blessedness in its proper time.

Think, then, of this first of all, when you are arming for battle, that even your bodily strength is a gift of God; for, considering this, you will not employ the gift of God against God. For, when faith is pledged, it is to be kept even with the enemy against whom the war is waged, how much more with the friend for whom the battle is fought! Peace should be the object of your desire; war should be waged only as a necessity, and waged only that God may by it deliver men from the necessity and preserve them in peace. For peace is not sought in order to the kindling of war, but war is waged in order that peace may be obtained. Therefore, even in waging war, cherish the spirit of a peace-maker, that, by conquering those whom you attack, you may lead them back to the advantages of peace; for our Lord says: "Blessed are the peacemakers; for they shall be called the children of God." If, however, peace among men be so sweet as procuring temporal safety, how much sweeter is that peace with God which procures for men the eternal felicity of the Angels! Let necessity, therefore, and not your will, slay the enemy who fights against you. As violence is used towards him who rebels and resists, so mercy is due to the vanquished or the captive, especially in the case in which future troubling of the peace is not to be feared.

Saint Thomas Aquinas
ca.1225–1274

The son of Landulf, Count of Aquino, Saint Thomas Aquinas, the "Angelic Doctor," was related to the Holy Roman Emperor and the French royal family. Since, as the youngest son, he was excluded from inheriting the family estates, his parents destined him for the abbacy of the neighboring Monte Cassino, mother-house of Benedictine monasticism, where they sent him to school at the age of five. Continuing his studies at Naples, he defied his parents' wishes, resolving to join the newly founded Dominican order. His furious family held him prisoner for over a year; however, the strong-willed young scholar persisted, finally entering the order in 1244, at the age of nineteen. Sent to complete his education at the University of Paris, then the intellectual center of Europe, he came under the influence of Albertus Magnus, who introduced him to the recently discovered metaphysical writings of Aristotle. In about 1265, he began the *Summa Theologica,* his last work, which he never completed.

In the eight centuries between Augustine and the *Summa Theologica,* probably the highest achievement of scholasticism, little had been added to the theory of the just war. Nor did St. Thomas work out anything really new. Though a creative and systematic thinker when reconciling "the philosopher," Aristotle, with Christian teachings, Aquinas evidently believed that Augustine had said the last word about war. Accordingly, he simply contented himself with incorporating Augustine's statements with little comment or criticism.

Yet Thomas's contribution is important. In an age when priests frequently took part in war, he lent his prestige to the ancient prohibition against bloodshed. Furthermore, he presented a brief, orderly, and reasoned resumé of thought up to his own day, stating the case against absolute pacifism based on Scripture and arguing in a manner that was to become standard in moral treatises until the seventeenth century. Because the code of canon law in force today makes the study of St. Thomas obligatory for all students of theology and philosophy, the selection from the *Summa Theologica* presented here is still considered by the Roman Catholic Church as the normative text for the just war.

Of War

FIRST ARTICLE
Whether it is always sinful to wage war?

We proceed thus to the First Article:
Objection 1. It would seem that it is always sinful to wage war. Because punishment is not inflicted except for sin. Now those who wage war are threatened by Our Lord with punishment, according to Matt. 26:52: *All that take the sword shall perish with the sword.* Therefore all wars are unlawful.

Objection 2. Further, Whatever is contrary to Divine precept is a sin. But war is contrary to Divine precept, for it is written (Matt. 5:39): *But I say to you not to resist evil;* and (Rom. 12:19): *Not revenging yourselves, my dearly beloved, but give place unto wrath.* Therefore war is always sinful. . . .

I answer that, In order for a war to be just, three things are necessary. First, the authority of the sovereign by whose command the war is to be waged. For it is not the business of the private individual to declare war, because he can seek for redress of his rights from the tribunal of his superior. Moreover, it is not the business of a private individual to summon together the people, which has to be done in wartime. And as the care of the common weal is committed to those who are in authority, it is their business to watch over

From St. Thomas Aquinas, Summa Theologica, *trans. English Fathers of the Dominican Order (London: Burns and Oates and New York: Binzinger, Inc.), pt. II, Q.40. Reprinted with special permission.*

the common weal of the city, kingdom or province subject to them. And just as it is lawful for them to have recourse to the sword in defending the common weal against internal disturbances, when they punish evil-doers, according to the words of the Apostle (Rom. 13:4): *He beareth not the sword in vain: for he is God's minister, an avenger to execute wrath upon him that doth evil;* so too, it is their business to have recourse to the sword of war in defending the common weal against external enemies. Hence it is said of those who are in authority (Ps. 81:4): *Rescue the poor: and deliver the needy out of the hand of the sinner;* and for this reason Augustine says (*Contra Faust.*, xxii. 75): *The natural order conducive to peace among mortals demands that the power to declare and counsel war should be in the hands of those who hold the supreme authority.*

Secondly, a just cause is required, namely that those who are attacked, should be attacked because they deserve it on account of some fault. Wherefore Augustine says (*QQ. in Hept.*, qu.x): *A just war is wont to be described as one that avenges wrongs, when a nation or state has to be punished, for refusing to make amends for the wrongs inflicted by its subjects, or to restore what it has seized unjustly.*

Thirdly, it is necessary that the belligerents should have a rightful intention, so that they intend the advancement of good, or the avoidance of evil. . . . For it may happen that the war is declared by the legitimate authority, and for a just cause, and yet rendered unlawful through a wicked intention. Hence Augustine says (*Contra Faust.*, xxii. 74): *The passion for inflicting harm, the cruel thirst·for vengenance, an unpacific and relentless spirit, the fever of revolt, the lust of power, and suchlike things, all these are rightly condemned in war.*

Reply Objection 1. As Augustine says (*Contra Faust.*, xxii. 70): *To take the sword is to arm oneself in order to take the life of anyone, without the command or permission of superior or lawful authority.* On the other hand, to have recourse to the sword (as a private person) by the authority of the sovereign or judge, or (as a public person) through zeal for justice, and by the authority, so to speak, of God, is not to *take the sword,* but to use it as commissioned by another, wherefore it does not deserve punishment. And yet even those who make sinful use of the sword are not always slain with the sword, yet they always perish with their own sword, because, unless they repent, they are punished eternally for their sinful use of the sword.

Reply Objection 2. Suchlike percepts . . . should always be borne in readiness of mind, so that we be ready to obey them, and if necessary, to refrain from resistance or self-defense. Nevertheless it is necessary sometimes for a man to act otherwise for the common good, or the good of those with whom he is fighting. Hence Augustine says (*Letter to Marcellus*): *Those whom we have to punish with a kindly severity, it is necessary to handle in many ways against their will. For when we are stripping a man of the lawlessness of sin, it is good for him to be vanquished, since nothing is more hopeless than the happiness of sinners, whence arises a guilty impunity, and an evil will, like an internal enemy. . . .*

SECOND ARTICLE
Whether it is lawful for clerics and bishops to fight?

We proceed thus to the Second Article:

Objection 1. It would seem lawful for clerics and bishops to fight. For, as stated above (A. 1), wars are lawful and just in so far as they protect the poor and the entire common weal from suffering at the hands of the foe. Now this seems to be above all the duty of prelates, for Gregory says (*Hom. in Ev.* xiv): *The wolf comes upon*

*the sheep, when any unjust and rapacious man oppresses
those who are faithful and humble. But he who was thought
to be the shepherd, and was not, leaveth the sheep and
flieth, for he feareth lest the wolf hurt him, and dares not
stand up against his injustice.* Therefore it is lawful for
prelates and clerics to fight.

Objection 2. Further, Pope Leo IV writes (xxiii., qu.
8, can. *Igitur*): *As untoward tidings had frequently come
from the Saracen side, some said that the Saracens would
come to the port of Rome secretly and covertly; for which
reason we commanded our people to gather together, and
ordered them to go down to the sea-shore.* Therefore it is
lawful for bishops to fight. . . .

I answer that, Several things are requisite for the good of
a human society: and a number of things are done better
and quicker by a number of persons than by one . . . while
certain occupations are so inconsistent with one another, that
they cannot be fittingly exercised at the same time; wherefore those who are deputed to important duties are forbidden to occupy themselves with things of small importance.
Thus according to human laws, soldiers who are deputed to
warlike pursuits are forbidden to engage in commerce.

Now warlike pursuits are altogether imcompatible with
the duties of a bishop and a cleric, for two reasons. The
first reason is a general one, because, to wit, warlike pursuits
are full of unrest, so that they hinder the mind very much
from the contemplation of Divine things, the praise of God,
and prayers for the people, which belong to the duties of a
cleric. Wherefore just as commercial enterprises are forbidden to clerics, because they unsettle the mind too much,
so too are warlike pursuits, according to 2 Tim. 2:4: *No
man being a soldier of God, entangleth himself with secular
business.* The second reason is a special one, because, to wit,
all the clerical Orders are directed to the ministry of the
altar, on which the Passion of Christ is represented sacra-

mentally. . . . Wherefore it is unbecoming for them to slay or shed blood, and it is more fitting that they should be ready to shed their own blood for Christ, so as to imitate in deed what they portray in their ministry. For this reason it has been decreed that those who shed blood, even without sin, become irregular. Now no man who has a certain duty to perform, can lawfully do that which renders him unfit for that duty. Wherefore it is altogether unlawful for clerics to fight, because war is directed to the shedding of blood.

Reply Objection 1. Prelates ought to withstand not only the wolf who brings spiritual death upon the flock, but also the pillager and the oppressor who work bodily harm; not, however, by having recourse themselves to material arms, but by means of spiritual weapons. . . . Such are salutary warnings, devout prayers, and, for those who are obstinate, the sentence of excommunication.

Reply Objection 2. Prelates and clerics may, by the authority of their superiors, take part in wars, not indeed by taking up arms themselves, but by affording spiritual help to those who fight justly, by exhorting and absolving them, and by other like spiritual helps. Thus in the Old Testament (Jos. 6:4) the priests were commanded to sound the sacred trumpets in the battle. It was for this purpose that bishops and clerics were first allowed to go to the front: and it is an abuse of this permission, if any of them take up arms themselves. . . .

The Peace of God, and The Truce of God

With the breakdown of central government in France in the tenth century, the local rulers gained a large measure of independence, settling their disagreements by private war. Worse, these petty feudatories, augmented by all manner of brigands and disreputable characters, burned and plundered the country-side. Neither pilgrims, nor merchants, nor women, nor peasants, nor clergy were immune from their depradations. Like the Vikings and Saracens, they besieged and plundered churches and monasteries. One especially unsavory character, Bernard de Cahuzac, a petty lord of Périgord, is described by the historian Peter de Vaux-de-Cernay as a sadistic lunatic:

> He spends his life in looting and destroying churches, in attacking pilgrims, in oppressing the widow and the poor. It pleases him especially to mutilate the innocent. In a single monastery, that of the black monks of Sarlat, one hundred and fifty men and women were found, whose hands and feet had been cut off, or whose eyes had been put out by him. His wife, as cruel as he, aided his deeds. She took pleasure in torturing these poor women herself. She had their breasts slit, or their nails torn out so that they would not be able to work.

To remedy this deplorable state, the Church at three Councils (Charox, 989; Narbonne, 990; Puy, 990) decreed the *Pax Ecclesiae* or *Pax Dei* ("Peace of the Church" or "Peace of God"). Thereafter, violence against noncombatants and ecclesiastical buildings was banned, under pain of excommunication.

An extension of the Peace of God, the *Treuga Dei* ("Truce of God"), was worked out in the eleventh century in France. Introduced into most continental countries by 1085, The Truce prohibited warfare of any kind on specific weekdays and on special holy days. All told, it allowed for little more than a quarter of the year for fighting: given the frequent interruptions, the time needed to start fighting again, and the fact that the feudal host normally served for no more than forty days, the amount of time remaining for actual combat was cut to the barest minimum. The popes supported the Truce, as they saw in it a powerful tool for forging Christian unity against the growing threat from Islam. Yet despite papal support, and notwithstanding the excommunication of peace-breakers, the results were on the whole disappointing, in that the truces never had more than a local effect. Nevertheless, they were not completely without value or influence for later ages. Their affirmations that there are always certain classes of the population who stand outside of war, and who it is always wrong to attack, are echoed in the modern law of war as formulated by the Hague Conferences and in such theological statements as the recent *Pastoral Constitution on the Church in the Modern World.*

Of the texts reproduced here, "The Peace of God," proclaimed in 990 by Guy of Anjou, Bishop of Puy, though leaving sufficient leeway to the warlike, is among the most strongly worded of these truces. "The Truce of God," which follows, was proclaimed for the diocese of Cologne on April 20, 1083.

The Peace of God

In the name of the divine, supreme, and undivided Trinity, Guy of Anjou, by the grace of God bishop [of Puy], greeting and peace to all who desire the mercy of God. Be it known to all the faithful subjects of God, that because of the wickedness that daily increases among the people, we have called together certain bishops . . . princes, and nobles. And since we know that only the peace-loving shall see the Lord, we urge all men, in the name of the Lord, to be sons of peace.

1. From this hour forth, no man in the bishoprics over which these bishops rule, and in these counties, shall break into a church . . . except that the bishop may enter a church to recover the taxes that are due from it.

2. No man in the counties or bishoprics shall seize a horse, colt, ox, cow, ass, or the burdens which it carries, or a sheep, goat, or pig, or kill any of them, unless he requires it for a lawful expedition. On an expedition a man may take what he needs to eat, but shall carry nothing home with him; and no one shall take material for fortifying or

From O J. Thatcher and E. H. McNeal, eds., Source Book for Medieval History *(New York: Scribners, 1905).*

besieging a castle except from his own lands and subjects.

3.   Clergymen shall not bear arms; no one shall injure monks or any unarmed persons who accompany them; except that the bishop or the archdeacon may use such means as are necessary to compel them to pay the taxes which they owe them.

4.   No one shall seize a peasant, man or woman, for the purpose of making him purchase his freedom, unless the peasant has forfeited his freedom. . . .

5.   From this hour forth no one shall seize ecclesiastical lands, whether those of a bishop, chapter, or monastery. . . .

6.   No one shall seize or rob merchants. . . .

If anyone breaks the peace and refuses to keep it, he shall be excommunicated and anathematized and cut off from the holy mother church, unless he makes satisfaction; if he refuses to make satisfaction, no priest shall say mass or perform divine services for him, no priest shall bury him or permit him to be buried in consecrated ground; no priest shall knowingly give him communion; if any priest knowingly violates this decree he shall be deposed.

The Truce of God for the Diocese of Cologne

Inasmuch as in our own times the church . . . has been extraordinarily afflicted by tribulations and difficulties, so that tranquility and peace were wholly despaired of, we have endeavored by God's help to aid it, suffering so many burdens and perils. And by the advice of our faithful subjects we have at length provided this remedy, so that we might to

From Translations and Reprints from the Original Sources of European History, *series I, vol. I, no. 2 (Philadelphia: University of Pennsylvania Press, 1902).*

some extent re-establish, on certain days at least, the peace which because of our sins we could not make enduring. Accordingly we have enacted and set forth the following. . . .

Namely that from the first day of the Advent of our Lord through Epiphany, and from the beginning of Septuagesima to the eighth day after Pentecost and through the whole day, and throughout the year on every Sunday, Friday and Saturday, and on the fast days of the four seasons, and on the eve of the day of all the apostles, and on all days canonically set apart—or which shall in the future be set apart—for fasts or feasts, this decree of peace shall be observed; so that both those who travel and those who remain at home may enjoy security and the most entire peace, so that no one may commit murder, arson, robbery or assault, no one may injure another with a sword, club, or any kind of weapon. . . . If it shall be necessary for anyone in the time of the decreed peace . . . to go from one bishopric to another in which the peace is not observed, he may bear arms, but on the condition that he shall not injure anyone, except in self-defense if he is attacked; and when he returns into our diocese he shall immediately lay aside his arms. If it shall happen that any castle is besieged during the days which are included within the peace the besiegers shall cease from attack unless they are set upon by the besieged and compelled to beat the latter back.

And in order that this statute of peace should not be violated by anyone rashly or with impunity, a penalty was fixed by the common consent of all: if a free man or noble violates it, i.e., commits homicide or wounds anyone or is at fault in any manner whatever, he shall be expelled from our territory without any indulgence on account of the payment of money or the intercession of friends, and his heirs shall take all his property; if he holds a fief, the lord to whom it belongs shall receive it again. Moreover, if it is learned that his heirs after his expulsion have furnished him any support or aid, and if they are convicted of it, the estate shall be taken from them and given to the king. . . . If a slave kills a man, he shall be beheaded; if he wounds a man, he shall lose a hand; if he does an injury in any other way with his fist or a club, or by striking with a stone, he shall be shorn and flogged. . . .

If anyone attempts to oppose this pious institution and is unwilling to promise peace to God with the others or to observe it, no priest in our diocese shall presume to say a mass for him or shall take any care for his salvation; if he is sick, no Christian shall dare to visit him; on his death-bed he shall not receive the Eucharist unless he repents. The supreme authority of the peace promised to God and commonly extolled by all will be so great that it will be observed not only in our times, but forever among our posterity, because if anyone shall presume to infringe, destroy or violate it, either now or ages hence at the end of the world he is irrevocably excommunicated by us.

Saint Bernard of Clairvaux
1090–1153

Resounding through the Old Testament stories of Deborah, Joshua, Gideon, and the Maccabees are tales of a special type of war—the holy war. Taking on even greater significance in the eleventh century, the holy war has been with us in one form or another ever since. The holy war, or crusade, is not unique to Christianity, although the word "crusade," derived from the Latin verb *cruciare* ("to mark with the Cross"), has a definitely Christian connotation. Judaism has had its struggle against Amalek; and Islam has had its *jihad,* the Koran (5:37) enjoining the faithful to cast out, slay, and crucify unbelievers, and to cut off their hands and feet on alternate sides. Although it affirms all the criteria of the just war, the crusade differs from it in several important respects. At the root of the just war is a legal presumption: waged under the proper authority, its object is peace, achieved through the vindication of justice. The holy war, too, has its proper authority and object, only these are infinitely more exalted. *Deus vult*—"God wills it"—was the cry of the knights assembled at Clermont to hear Pope Urban II preach the First Crusade. Thus the crusade is God's war, willed by Him, proclaimed by His Church, and conducted under its aegis to defend and extend true religion. It goes without saying that victory must be total, as compromise with the enemy of the Lord is unthinkable. As for the soldier, according to the canonist Gratian of Bologna, "whoever dies in battle against the infidels is worthy to enter the heavenly kingdom." Seven centuries later, in 1942, General Douglas MacArthur, professing to read the mind of the Almighty, announced after the fall of Bataan: "To the weeping mothers of [the] dead, I can only say that the halo of Jesus of Nazareth has descended upon their sons and that God will take them to Himself."

A leader of the crusading movement, Saint Bernard of Clairvaux, the founder of the Cistercian order, was a dominant influence on the religious and political life of twelfth-century Europe. Raised in an environment where crusading was, so to speak, "in the air," he brought his enthusiasm and incomparable skill as a preacher to bear in the military sphere. He once told the pope; "You ordered; I obeyed. . . . I opened my mouth; I spoke; and at once the Crusaders have multiplied to infinity."

Not the least of Bernard's accomplishments was his sponsorship of the military orders, brotherhoods of monk-knights founded in the hope of channeling the institutionalized asceticism of monasticism into the holy war against Islam. He was especially interested in the Knights Templars (the Poor Brothers of the Temple of Jerusalem), an order that he helped to found in 1128 as protection for pilgrims to the Holy Land.

The following selection, from a little-known sermon dating from the 1130s, has been included here because it at once portrays the highest ideals of the medieval warrior and captures something more ominous—the fanaticism of which the best of men are capable when a cause is transmuted by religion or ideology.

Sermon on the Knights of the Temple

A new order of knights lately sprung up is heard of on earth, and in that region in which formerly the Light of the World visibly came from on high in fleshy form. A new order of knights, I say, and an order inexperienced in worldly matters—an order which unweariedly engageth in a twofold conflict, warring both against flesh and blood and against spiritual wickedness in high places.

Fearless certainly is the knight, and safe from all surrounding dangers, who, as he clotheth his body with a breastplate of iron, also hath his soul clad with the breastplate of faith. Protected by this twofold armor, he assuredly feareth neither devil nor man. But neither doth he dread death, inasmuch as he desireth to die. For what doth he fear, whether living or dying, to whom to live is Christ and to die is gain? He taketh his stand boldly and gladly for Christ; but more doth he desire to depart and be with Christ; for this is better. Fearlessly then advance, ye knights, and with intrepid souls, drive away the enemies of the cross of Christ, assured that neither death nor life shall be able to separate you from the love of God which is in Christ Jesus, remembering in every danger the words, "Whether we live or die we are the Lord's." How arrayed with glory are they who return from the battle victorious! How blessed are they who die as martyrs in the fight! Rejoice, brave athlete, if thou livest and conquerest in the Lord; and exult and glory more if thou shalt die and be united to the Lord. Life indeed is full of joy, and victory full of glory; but a holy

From St. Bernard, Selections from His Writings, *trans. Horatio Grimley (Cambridge: Cambridge University Press, 1910).*

death transcendeth either. For if blessed are they who die in the Lord, are not they much more blessed who die for the Lord?

And indeed whether we die in bed or in battle, precious will be without doubt in the sight of the Lord the death of His saints. But in battle death is certainly so much more precious as it is the more glorious. O fearless is the life where the conscience is pure! O fearless is the life, I say, in which without dread, death is awaited, yea rather is both desired with delight and welcomed with devotion! O knights truly holy and protected, and free certainly from that two-fold danger, by which such order of men is wont to be threatened when the fighting is certainly not for the sake of Christ! For how often thou who engagest in warfare in a spirit of worldliness, dost thou fear lest thou either kill an adversary in the body, but thyself in the soul, or lest thou perchance be slain by him in body and in soul? According to the disposition of the heart, forsooth, not from the event of the battle, there is meted out either danger or Christian victory. If the cause of the fighting is a good one, the issue of the fight will not be evil. So that the end arrived at will not be judged to be good, if a cause not good and an intention not righteous have preceded. If with the wish to kill another it shall happen that thou thyself art killed, thou wilt die a homicide. But if thou prevailest, and if with the desire of overcoming thine enemy and revenging thyself, thou perchance slayest thine enemy, thou livest a homicide. But it advantageth not, whether dead or living, whether victor or vanquished, to be a manslayer. Unhappy victory, by which thou, overcoming thine enemy, fallest thyself beneath the assault of wrongdoing. And with anger or pride dominating thee thou wilt in vain boast of having conquered thine enemy. He who neither with the desire of avenging himself, nor with the mad resolve of conquering another, slayeth his foe, gaineth a true victory. . . .

The knights of Christ fight safely the battles of their Lord, in no wise bearing either sin from slaying enemies, or the danger of their own destruction. Since indeed death for Christ must be either endured or dealt out to others, it involveth no sin and meriteth abundant glory. Indeed in the one case there is gain for Christ, in the other Christ is gained—Christ, who surely and willingly accepteth an enemy's death as retribution, and more willingly offereth Himself to the knight for consolation. A soldier of Christ, I say, slayeth with more honor to himself, and dieth with more merit. When he dieth, himself is benefited; when he slayeth, he benefiteth Christ. For not without cause he beareth the sword. He is the minister of God for the punishment of those who do ill, but for the praise of those who do good. When he slayeth the doer of evil, he is not a manslayer, but —so I should say—a slayer of evil, and plainly an avenger of Christ against those who do wrong, and so is accounted a defender of Christians. But when he himself is slain, he is deemed not to have perished, but to have achieved triumph. The death therefore which he inflicteth is gain for Christ; the death which he receiveth is his own gain. In the death of a pagan a Christian is exultant, because Christ is glorified. In the death of a Christian the bounty of the King is shown forth when the soldier is led forth to be rewarded. The just will rejoice over the first, seeing in it the punishment of an evildoer. At the death of a Christian, men will say "Verily there is a reward for the righteous; doubtless there is a God who judgeth the earth." But not indeed should pagans be slain, if in any way otherwise they may be restrained from attacking and oppressing the faithful. Now however it is better that they should be slain than that the rod of the sinful should rest upon the lot of the righteous, lest the righteous stretch forth their hands unto iniquity. . . .

Let me tell briefly of the manners and life of the knights,

how they comport themselves whether in warfare or at home; by which it becometh evident how much differ from one another the soldiers of God and the soldiers of the world. . . .

The life of the knights is passed in pleasant association and sober converse with one another, without wives and without children. And lest there should be any lack of evangelic perfection, they without any attention to private rights dwell in one style in one house, anxious to keep the unity of the Spirit in the bond of peace. . . .

Moreover when war threateneth they fortify themselves inwardly with faith, outwardly with steel, not with gold; to the intent that armed and not adorned they may strike fear into the enemy and not provoke avarice. They desire to have horses strong and swift, but not attractive and adorned with trappings; thinking forsooth of fighting and not of display, of victory but not of glory, and striving to arouse fear rather than admiration. Then . . . with every care and forethought, they place themselves in battle array. But when the actual conflict hath commenced, they at last put aside their former deliberateness, as if they should say: "Do not I hate them, O Lord, who hate Thee, and am not I at war with those who are hostile to Thee?" They rush upon their foes, in no wise fearing, if they themselves are very few in number, either wild barbarians or a numerous multitude. They know at least not to count too much on their own strength, but to hope for victory from the strength from the Lord of Sabaoth, with whom, according to the words of Machabaeus, they know it is very easy for many to be shut up in the hands of a few. . . . Such hath God chosen to Himself, and gathered from the ends of the earth as servants from amongst the bravest of Israel, so that they may faithfully guard the resting place of the true Solomon—forsooth the Holy Sepulchre—all with swords in their hands, all prepared for battle.

Francisco de Vitoria

1485–1546

First and last a scholar and a teacher, Vitoria spent his adult life lecturing on Thomistic philosophy at the universities of Paris, Valladolid, and Salamanca, where for his last twenty years he held the Prime Chair in Theology. One aspect of his devotion to Saint Thomas, involving the application of his teaching to contemporary issues, earned for Vitoria the distinction of "Father of International Law." Even the Protestant Hugo Grotius acknowledged his debt to him.

Growing out of a series of *Relectiones,* conferences given between 1527 and 1540, Vitoria's book, *Conferences on the Indies and the Law of War,* remains one of the most thorough and insightful treatises ever composed on the subject of the relation of Christianity to war. In dealing with the chief problem of his day, the moral implications of the conquest of the New World (Cortés had completed the rape of Mexico in 1523, the year Vitoria returned to Spain), he became the first to investigate in detail three questions that were to grow in importance until our own day.

To begin with, in discussing the matter of the just cause, Vitoria drew a distinction that opponents of modern methods of warfare frequently use without being aware of its provenance: the state has a responsibility transcending its own sectional interests. Even if its cause is just by every criterion, it is bound by a principle of proportionality. Justice demands that the state rather forfeit its rights than begin a war destructive of either Christendom or the human family as a whole.

Secondly, Vitoria (and Luther, as will become evident later) loaded a new and a grave burden on the individual's conscience. Whereas Augustine's presumption that the soldier must render unquestioning obedience held throughout the Middle Ages, Vitoria left no room for the pleas made four centuries later, "I was only following orders," and "There was nothing I could do in the face of evil." Naturally the common soldier, lacking all the facts and powerless to influence policy, should defer to higher authority. But if his conscience testifies that a particular war is unjust, he must withdraw regardless of the personal consequences.

Lastly, Vitoria's words on the position of noncombatants are particularly relevant today, now that the hydrogen bomb has "enlarged the target" to make all life in an area liable to extinction. Recognizing that innocent life was bound to be lost as a collateral result of military action, he reiterated that there could never be extenuating circumstances sufficient to justify the intentional slaying of noncombatants; this is always murder and abhorrent to God.

On the Indies and the Law of War

What may be a reason and cause of just war? It is particularly necessary to ask this in connection with the case of the Indian aborigines, which is now before us. Here my first proposition is: Difference of religion is not a cause of just war. This was shown at length in the preceding *Relectio*, when we demolished the . . . alleged title for taking possession of the Indians, namely, their refusal to accept Christianity. And it is the opinion of St. Thomas, and the common opinion of the doctors—indeed, I know of no one of the opposite way of thinking.

Second proposition: Extension of empire is not a just cause of war. This is too well known to need proof, for otherwise each of the two belligerents might have an equally just cause and so both would be innocent. This in its turn would involve the consequence that it would not be lawful to kill them and so imply a contradiction, because it would be a just war.

This selection is from the second Relectio *of* Francisci de Victoria De Indis et de Jure Belli Relectiones, *ed.* Ernest Nys, *Classics of International Law, no. 7 (Washington, D.C.: Carnegie Endowment for International Peace, 1917). Reprinted by special permission.*

Third proposition: Neither the personal glory of the prince nor any advantage to him is a just cause of war. This, too, is notorious. For a prince ought to subordinate both peace and war to the common weal of his State and not spend public revenues in quest of his own glory or gain, much less expose his subjects to danger on that account. . . . Again, this is the difference between freemen and slaves, as Aristotle says, that masters exploit slaves for their own good and not for the good of the slaves, while freemen do not exist in the interest of others, but in their own interest. And so, were a prince to misuse his subjects by compelling them to go soldiering and to contribute money for his campaigns, not for the public good, but for his own private gain, this would be to make slaves of them.

Fourth proposition: There is a single and only just cause for commencing war, namely, a wrong received. The proof of this rests in the first place on the authority of St. Augustine, and it is the conclusion arrived at by St. Thomas and the opinion of all the doctors. Also, an offensive is for the purpose of avenging a wrong and of taking measures against an enemy, as said above. But there can be no vengeance where there is no preceding fault and wrong. . . . Hence it is clear that we may not turn our sword against those who do us no harm, the killing of the innocent being forbidden by natural law. . . .

Fifth proposition: Not every kind and degree of wrong can suffice for commencing a war. The proof of this is that not even upon one's own fellow-countrymen is it lawful for every offense to exact atrocious punishment, such as death or banishment or confiscation of property. As, then, the evils inflicted in war are all of a severe and atrocious character, such as fire and slaughter and devastation, it is not lawful for slight wrongs to pursue the authors of the wrongs with war, seeing that the degree of punishment ought to correspond with the offence. . . .

The [next] question is about the law of war, namely, what kind and degree of stress is lawful in a just war: Here let my first proposition be: In war everything is lawful which the defense of the common weal requires. This is notorious for the end and aim of war is the defense and preservation of the State. Also, a private person may do this in self-defense, as has been proved. Therefore much more may a State and a prince.

Second proposition: It is permissible to recapture everything that has been lost and any part of the same. This is too notorious to need proof. For war is begun or undertaken with this object.

Third proposition: It is lawful to make good out of enemy property the expenses of the war and all damages wrongfully caused by the enemy. This is clear, for the enemy who has done the wrong is bound to give all this redress. Therefore the prince can claim it all and exact it all by war. . . .

Fourth proposition: Not only are the things just named allowable, but a prince may go even further in a just war and do whatever is necessary in order to obtain peace and security from the enemy; for example, destroy the enemy's fortress and even build one on enemy soil, if this be necessary in order to avert a dangerous attack of the enemy. This is proved by the fact that, as said above, the end and aim of war is peace and security. Therefore a belligerent may do everything requisite to obtain peace and security. . . .

Fifth proposition: Not only is all this permissible, but even after victory has been won and redress obtained and peace and security been secured, it is lawful to avenge a wrong received from the enemy and to take measures against him and exact punishment from him for the wrongs he has done. . . . Confirmation hereof is furnished by the fact that in reality peace and tranquility, which are the end and aim of war, cannot be had unless evils and damages be visited on the enemy in order to deter him from the like conduct in the future. . . . Moreover, shame and disgrace are not wiped away from a State merely by the rout of its enemies, but also by its visiting severe punishment and castigation on them. Now, among the things which a prince is bound to defend and preserve for his State are its honor and authority.

Many doubts are suggested by what has just been said. In the first place, there is a doubtful point in connection with the justice of a war, whether it be enough for a just war that the prince believes himself to have a just cause. On this point let my first proposition be: This belief is not always enough. And for proof I rely, first, on the fact that in some matters of less moment it is not enough either for a prince or for private persons to believe that they are acting justly. This is notorious, for their error may be vincible and deliberate, and the opinion of the individual is not enough to render the act good, but it must come up to the standard of a wise man's judgment. . . . Also the result would otherwise be that very many wars would be just on both sides, for although it is not a common occurrence for princes to wage war in bad faith, they nearly always think theirs is a just cause. In this way all belligerents would be innocent and it would not be lawful to kill them. Also, were it otherwise, even Turks and Saracens might wage just wars against Christians, for they think they are thus rendering God service.

Second proposition: It is essential for a just war that an exceedingly careful examination be made of the justice and causes of the war and that the reasons given on grounds of equity be listened to. . . . For truth and justice in moral questions are hard of attainment and so any careless treatment of them easily leads to error, an error which will be inexcusable, especially in a concern of great moment, involving danger and calamity to many, and they our neighbors, too, whom we are bound to love as ourselves.

Second doubt: Whether subjects are bound to examine the cause of a war or whether they may serve in the war without any careful scrutiny thereof, just as the lictors [of ancient Rome] had to enforce the praetor's decree without questioning. On this doubt let my first proposition be: If a subject is convinced of the injustice of a war, he ought not to serve in it, even on the command of the prince. . . . Again, a prince sins when he commences a war in such a case. But "not only are they who commit such things worthy of death, but they, too, who consent to the doing thereof" (Rom. 1). Therefore soldiers also are not excused when they fight in bad faith. Again, it is not lawful to kill innocent citizens at the prince's command. Therefore not aliens either.

Hence flows the corollary that subjects whose conscience is against the justice of a war may not engage in it whether they be right or wrong. This is clear, for "whatever is not of faith is sin" (Rom. 14).

Second proposition: Senators and petty rulers and in general all who are admitted on summons or voluntarily to the public council or the prince's council ought, and are bound, to examine into the cause of an unjust war. This is clear; for whoever can save his neighbor from danger and harm is bound to do so, especially when the danger is that of death and greater ills, as is the case in war. But the persons referred to can avert war, supposing it to be unjust, if they lend their wisdom and weight into an examination of its causes. Therefore they are bound so to do. Again, if by their neglect an unjust war be entered on, they are consenting parties thereto, for that which a man could and ought to prevent is imputed to him, if he does not prevent it. Again, a king is not by himself capable of examining into the causes of a war and the possibility of a mistake on his part is not unlikely and such a mistake would bring great evil and ruin to multitudes. Therefore war ought not to be made on the sole judgment of the king, nor, indeed, on the judgment of a few, but on that of the many, and they wise and upright men.

Third proposition: Other lesser folk who have no place or audience in the prince's council or in the public council are under no obligation to examine the causes of a war, but may serve in it in reliance on their betters. This is proved, first, by the fact that it is impossible and inexpedient to give reasons for all acts of state to every member of the commonality. Also by the fact that men of the lower orders, even if they perceived the injustice of a war, could not stop it, and their voice would not be heeded. Therefore, any examination by them of the causes of a war would be futile. Also by the fact that for men of this sort it is enough proof of the justice of the war (unless the contrary is quite certain) that it is being waged after public counsel and by public authority. Therefore no further examination on their part is needed.

Fourth proposition: Nevertheless the proofs and tokens of the injustice of the war may be such that ignorance would be no excuse even to subjects of this sort who serve in it. . . .

. . . Now, much attention must be paid to the admitted fact that a war may be just and lawful in itself and yet owing to some collateral circumstance may be unlawful. For it is admitted that one may be entitled to recapture a city or a province and yet that, because of some scandal, this may become quite unlawful. For inasmuch as wars ought to be waged for the common good, if some one city cannot be recaptured without greater evils befalling the State, such as the devastation of many cities, great slaughter of human beings, provocation of princes, occasions for new wars to the destruction of the Church (in that an opportunity is given to pagans to invade and seize the lands of Christians), it is indubitable that the prince is bound rather to give up his own rights and abstain from war. For it is clear that if the King of France, for example, had a right to take Milan, but by the war both the Kingdom of France and the Duchy of Milan would suffer intolerable ills and heavy woes, it would not be right for him to retake it. This is because that war ought to take place either for the good of France or for the good of Milan. Therefore, when, on the contrary, great ills would befall each side by the war, it would not be a just war. . . .

With regard to another question, namely, what degree of stress is lawful in a just war, there are also many doubts. The first is: Whether it is lawful in war to kill the innocent. It seems that it is; because, in the first place, the Sons of Israel slew children at Jericho and afterwards Saul slew children in Amalek, and in both these cases it was by the authority and the bidding of God. . . . Therefore, if a war of the present day be just, it will be lawful to kill the innocent.

With regard to this doubt, let my first proposition be: The deliberate slaughter of the innocent is never lawful in itself. . . . The basis of a just war is a wrong done. But wrong is not done by an innocent person. Therefore war may not be employed against him. . . . All this is confirmed by Deuteronomy 20, where the Sons of Israel were ordered to take a certain city by force and to slay every one except women and little ones.

Hence it follows that even in war with the Turks it is not allowable to kill children. This is clear, because they are innocent. Aye, and the same holds with regard to the women of unbelievers. This is clear, because, so far as war is concerned, they are presumed innocent; but this does not hold in the case of any individual woman who is certainly guilty. Aye, and this same pronouncement must be made among Christians with regard to harmless agricultural folk, and also with regard to the rest of the peaceable civilian population, for all these are presumed innocent until the contrary is shown. . . . The same principle applies to clerics and members of a religious order, for they in war are presumed innocent unless the contrary be shown, as when they engage in actual fighting.

Second proposition: Sometimes it is right, in virtue of collateral circumstances, to slay the innocent even knowingly, as when a fortress or city is stormed in a just war, although it is known that there are a number of innocent people in it and although cannon and other engines of war can not be discharged or fire applied to buildings without destroying innocent together with guilty. The proof is that war could not be otherwise waged against even the guilty and the justice of the belligerents would be balked. In the same way, conversely, if a town be wrongfully besieged and rightfully defended, it is lawful to fire cannon-shot and other missiles on the besiegers and into the hostile camp, even though we assume that there are some children and innocent people there.

Great attention, however, must be paid to the point already taken, namely, the obligation to see that greater evils do not arise out of the war than the war would avert. For if little effect upon the ultimate issue of the war is to be expected from the storming of a fortress or fortified town wherein are many innocent folk, it would not be right, for the purpose of assailing a few guilty, to slay the many innocent by use of fire or engines of war or other means likely to overwhelm indifferently both innocent and guilty. In sum, it is never right to slay the guiltless, even as an indirect and unintended result, except where there is no other means of carrying on the operations of a just war. . . .

All this can be summarized in a few canons or rules of

warfare. First canon: Assuming that a prince has authority to make war, he should first of all not go seeking occasions and causes of war, but should, if possible, live in peace with all men, as St. Paul cnjoins us (Rom. 12). Moreover, he should reflect that others are his neighbors, whom we are bound to love as ourselves, and that we all have one common Lord, before whose tribunal we shall have to render our account. For it is the extreme of savagery to seek for and rejoice in grounds for killing and destroying men whom God has created and for whom Christ died. But only under compulsion and reluctantly should we come to the necessity of war.

Second canon: When war for a just cause has broken out, it must not be waged so as to ruin the people against whom it is directed,[1] but only so as to obtain one's rights and the defense of one's country and in order that from that war peace and security may in time result.

Third canon: When victory has been won and the war is over, the victory should be utilized with moderation and Christian humility, and the victor ought to deem that he is sitting as judge between two States, the one which has been wronged and the one which has done the wrong, so that it will be as judge and not as accuser that he will deliver the judgment whereby the injured state can obtain satisfaction, and this, so far as possible should involve the offending state in the least degree of calamity and misfortune, the offending individuals being chastised within lawful limits; and an especial reason for this is that in general among Christians all the fault is to be laid at the door of their princes, for subjects when fighting for their princes act in good faith and it is thoroughly unjust, in the words of the poet, that—

1. This would preclude the idea of unconditional surrender and the idea of taking measures so harsh as to prevent an enemy from ever "rising" again.—Ed.

Quidquid delirant reges, plectantur Achivi.

("For every folly their Kings commit the punishment should
fall upon the Greeks.")

Protestant Confessional Statements

During the Protestant Reformation, formal statements of belief
were vital instruments of education as well as of propaganda.
Not only did they publish to the world precisely what a group
believed, thereby functioning as a unifying force, they also
served to parry accusations and to avoid misinterpretations. The
following brief excerpts, taken from the most famous confessional statements, place the reformed churches squarely in the
center of the Catholic tradition as regards war; they are taken
from Philip Schaff's edition of *The Evangelical Protestant Creeds,*
New York, 1877.

THE AUGSBURG CONFESSION
(LUTHERAN) 1530

Article XVI, Of Civil Affairs:

Concerning civil affairs, [the churches] teach that such
civil ordinances as are lawful are good works of God; that
Christians may lawfully bear civil office, sit in judgments,
determine matters by the imperial laws, and other laws in
present force, appoint just punishments, engage in just war,
act as soldiers, make legal bargains and contracts, hold
property, take an oath when the magistrates require it,
marry a wife, or be given in marriage. They condemn the
Anabaptists who forbid Christians these civil offices.

THE THIRTY-NINE ARTICLES OF
THE CHURCH OF ENGLAND 1571

Article XXXVII:
It is lawful for Christian men, at the commaundement of the Magistrate, to weare weapons, and serve in the warres.

THE ARTICLES OF RELIGION OF
THE IRISH EPISCOPAL CHURCH 1615

Article 62:
It is lawful for Christian men, at the commandment of the magistrate, to bear arms and serve in just wars.

THE WESTMINSTER CONFESSION OF FAITH
(PRESBYTERIAN) 1647

Article XXII, Of the Civil Magistrate:
It is lawful for Christians to accept and execute the office of a magistrate when called thereunto; in the managing thereof, as they ought especially to maintain piety, justice, and peace, according to the wholesome laws of each commonwealth, so, for that end, they may lawfully, now under the New Testament, wage war upon just and necessary occasion.

Thomas Müntzer
ca.1490–1525

Thomas Müntzer was one of the most remarkable characters of the Reformation era; and, as is usual with remarkable characters, friends and foes have painted him larger than life. For Luther, denouncing him in his tirade *Against the Robbing and Murdering Hordes of Peasants* (1525), Müntzer was "that arch-devil who . . . does nothing except stir up robbery, murder, and bloodshed." For Friedrich Engels, glorifying him in *The Peasant War in Germany* (1850), he was "the plebeian revolutionary" against a moribund social order. Actually, he was a parish priest at Zwickau and Allstedt in Saxony. Claiming direct inspiration from the Holy Ghost, he became a rebel against all authority, demanding radical reforms in religion and society.

The sermon reprinted here, preached to the Saxon princes in July of 1524, deals with that classic passage of apocalyptic imagery, Daniel's dream of the multi-metallic statue destroyed by a stone that grows into a mountain (Dan. 2). The Scriptures speak of two kinds of war: those waged in the past by the chosen people at God's behest, and that to come in the last days, the denouement of history, when Good will triumph over Evil at the battle of Armageddon. Jewish apocalypticism, the expression of the yearnings of a persecuted people for divine intervention in its affairs, was taken over by the Church during its own time of tribulations. The theme of messianic warfare permeates the book of Revelation, where it is prophesied that the Messiah, a sword issuing from His mouth, will return to conquer the Beast, inaugurate the millennial reign, and overthrow Gog and Magog, and that finally the New Jerusalem shall descend from heaven.

These ideas, basically harmless as long as they are interpreted allegorically or in terms of a supernatural agent acting in the indeterminately remote future, became dangerous in the hands of fanatics who demanded the Second Coming "now." But the Second Coming, they held, would be delayed until such time as the enemies of God were exterminated; hence Müntzer's call for the saints to prepare His way by bathing the world in the blood of the reprobate. Müntzer himself was killed while leading the great peasant rebellion of 1525.

These beliefs, because they expressed yearnings within the human heart, did not die with Müntzer. Instead, through that strange chemistry of the intellect known as "secularization," they have come to form part of the intellectual baggage of twentieth-century man. Men today no longer fight for the messianic kingdom, but wage wars and revolutions to end all war or to usher in the dictatorship of the proletariat or to bring about other versions of the Kingdom of God on earth. In each case, the premise is the same: the existing order is unspeakably evil, and will be ended suddenly, by a bolt from the blue. Those to be exterminated are no longer the enemies of true religion but, among others, communists, imperialists, in fact, all those tainted ideologically. The final battle is no longer called Armageddon, but "the showdown," "the final clash," "the battle of destiny." Finally, the prophetic leader, who embodies in himself the divine spirit and who kindles the divine wrath in the people, is no longer a Daniel, but a Führer, a Duce, a Chairman.

The Call to Apocalyptic War

It is true, and [I] know it to be true, that the Spirit of God is revealing to many elect, pious persons a decisive, inevitable, imminent reformation [accompanied] by great anguish, and it must be carried out to completion. Defend oneself against it as one may, the prophecy of Daniel remains unweakened, even if no one believes it. . . . This passage of Daniel is thus as clear as the sun, and the process of ending the fifth monarchy of the world is in full swing.

The first [kingdom] is set forth by the golden knop.[1] That was the kingdom of Babylon. The second [was represented] by the silver breast and arms. This was the kingdom of the Medes and Persians. The third was the kingdom of the Greeks, which, resounding with its science, was symbolized by the [sounding] brass. The fourth [was] the Roman Empire, which was won by the sword and a kingdom of coer-

From Spiritual and Anabaptist Writers, *edited by George H. Williams and Angel M. Mergal. Volume XXV,* The Library of Christian Classics. *Published simultaneously in Great Britain and the United States of America by the S.C.M. Press, Ltd., London, and The Westminister Press, Philadelphia. First published in 1957. Used by permission.*

cion. But the fifth [symbolized by the iron and clay feet] is this which we have before our eyes, which is also of iron and would like to coerce. But it is matted together with mud,² as we see before our discerning eyes— vain, pretentious schemes of hypocrisy which writhe and wriggle over the whole earth. . . . O beloved lords, how handsomely the Lord will go smashing among the old pots with his rod of iron. Therefore, you much beloved and esteemed princes, learn your judgments directly from the mouth of God and do not let yourselves be misled by your hypocritical parsons nor be restrained by false consideration and indulgence. . . .

Seek only straightway the righteousness of God and take up courageously the cause of the gospel! For God stands so close to you that you wouldn't believe it! . . . If you could only as clearly recognize the harm being [done] to Christendom and rightly consider it, you would acquire just the same zeal as Jehu the king; and the same as that which the whole book of Revelation proclaims. And I know for a certainty that you would thereupon hold yourselves back only with great effort from [letting] the sword exert its power. For the pitiable corruption of holy Christendom has become so great that at the present time no tongue can tell it all. Therefore a new Daniel must arise and interpret for you your vision and this [prophet], as Moses teaches, must go in front of the army. He must reconcile the anger of the princes and the enraged people. For if you will rightly experience the corruption of Christendom and the deception of the false clerics and the vicious reprobates, you will become so enraged at them that no one can think it through. Without doubt it would vex you and go right to your heart that you have been so kindly after they, with the very sweetest words, misled you into the most shameful conceptions against all established truth. For they have made fools of you so that everyone swears by the saints that the princes are in respect to their office a pagan people. They are said to be able to maintain nothing other than a civil unity. O beloved, yea, the great Stone there is about to fall and strike these schemes of [mere] reason and dash them to the ground, for he says: I am not come to send peace but a sword. What should be done, however, with the same? Nothing different from [what is done with] the wicked who hinder the gospel: Get them out of the way and eliminate them, unless you want to be ministers of the devil rather than of God. . . . You need not doubt it. God will strike to pieces all your adversaries who undertake to persecute you, for his hand is by no means shortened, as Isaiah says. Therefore he can still help you and wishes to, as he supported the elect King Josiah and others who defended the name of God. Thus you are angels, when you wish to do justly, as Peter says. Christ commanded in deep gravity, saying: Take mine enemies and strangle them before mine eyes. Why? Ah! because they ruin Christ's government for him and in addition want to defend their rascality under the guise of Christian faith and ruin the whole world with their insidious subterfuge. . . . Now if you want to be true governors, you must begin government at the roots, and, as Christ commanded, drive his enemies from the elect. For you are the means to this end. Beloved, don't give us any old jokes about how the power of God should do it without your application of the sword. Otherwise may it rust away for you in its scabbard! . . . Therefore let not the evildoers live longer who make us turn away from God. For the godless person has no right to live when he is in the way of the pious. . . . God is your protection and will teach you to fight against his foes. He will make your hands skilled in fighting and will also sustain you. . . . For he himself commanded through Moses where he says: Ye are a holy people. Ye ought not to have pity on account of the superstitious. Break down their altars, smash up their images and burn them up, that I be not angry with you. These words Christ has not abrogated, but rather he wishes to fulfill them for us. . . . Therefore no justification is given us in the inadequacy and the negligence of the saints to let the godless have their way. . . . That our learned divines, however, should come along and, in their godless prevaricating manner, say in reference to Daniel (2:34) that the Antichrist ought to be destroyed without [human] hands is as much as to say he [Antichrist] is already inwardly collapsed. . . . The sword is necessary to wipe out the godless. That this might now take place, however, in an orderly and proper fashion, our cherished fathers, the princes, should do it, who with us confess Christ. If, however, they do not do it, the sword shall be taken from them. For they confess him all right with words and deny him with the deed. They [the princes], accordingly, should proffer peace to the enemies. If the latter wish to be spiritual [in the outmoded sense] and do not give testimony of the knowledge of God, they should be gotten out of the way. But I pray for them with the devout David where they are not against God's revelation. Where, however, they pursue the opposition, may they be slain without any mercy as Hezekiah, Josiah, Cyrus, Daniel, Elijah destroyed the priests of Baal, otherwise the Christian church cannot come back again to its origin. The weeds must be plucked out of the vineyard of God in the time of harvest. Then the beautiful red wheat will acquire substantial rootage and come up properly. The angels, however, who sharpen their sickles for this purpose are the serious servants of God who execute the wrath of the divine wisdom. . . .

1. A disparaging reference to the head.
2. In German, a secondary meaning for "mud" is "ordure."—Ed.

Martin Luther
1485–1546

For Luther, the former Augustinian monk and the author of a tract discussing *Whether Soldiers, too, Can Be Saved* (1526), there was no question that the citizen could, indeed must, take arms at the command of the magistrate. But for Luther, "at the command of the magistrate" was the critical phrase. In the eyes of the man who touched off one of the profoundest spiritual, and ultimately political, upheavals in the history of Christendom, another type of war—revolution—was still automatically unjust. The warrants against revolution, originating both with the assertion in Romans 13 that the powers that be are ordained of God and with Augustine's doctrine of the two cities, had always been strong. The rebel, so the theory went, was an agent of Satan, one who would overthrow the order of the universe as established by God. When oppressed, the Christian had no alternative but to pray and hope for better times. If they came, fine; if not, God's will be done. The Christian's motto, Luther affirmed, must be *Leiden, leiden, Kreuz, kreuz, ist der Christen Recht: das und kein anderes!* ("Suffering, suffering, Cross, cross; there is nothing else in the Christian law").

The rebellion that brought Müntzer to the headsman's block also damaged irreparably the chances of Lutheranism becoming a mass movement. Luther's *Admonition to Peace* (1525) having failed to restore calm among the peasants, whose grievances he supported but whose methods he deplored, in his next work, *Against the Robbing and Murdering Hordes of Peasants,* he urged the princes to "smite, slay, and stab, secretly and openly" the "mad-dog" peasants. They did. The revolt crushed, thousands killed, and Luther himself criticized for brutality, he penned the following tract in self-vindication. Despite its harsh, earthy language, it is a remarkable work, being at once a statement of his views on revolution and, of more enduring value, a reaffirmation of the individual's responsibility in the face of overwhelming evil. One cannot help seeing in it the outline of what was to become the Nuremberg Principle: nobody can be "ordered" or "forced" to sin.

An Open Letter on the Harsh Book Against the Peasants

. . . I must warn those who criticize my book to hold their tongues and to be careful not to make a mistake and lose their own heads; for they are certainly rebels at heart, and . . . those who are fellow-travelers with rebels sympathize with them, feel sorry for them, justify them, and show mercy to those on whom God has no mercy, but whom he wishes to have punished and destroyed. For a man who thus sympathizes with the rebels makes it perfectly clear that he has decided in his heart that he will also cause disaster if he has the opportunity. The rulers, therefore, ought to shake these people up until they keep their mouths shut and realize that the rulers are serious.

If [my critics] think this answer is too harsh, and that this is talking violence, and only shutting men's mouths, I reply, "That is right." A rebel is not worth rational arguments, for he does not accept them. You have to answer people like that with a fist, until the sweat [i.e., blood] drips off their noses. The peasants would not listen; they would not let anyone tell them anything, so their ears must now be unbuttoned with musket balls till their heads jump off their shoulders. Such pupils need such a rod. He who will not hear God's word when it is spoken with kindness, must listen to the headsman, when he comes with his axe. If anyone says that I am being uncharitable and unmerciful about this, my reply is: This is not a question of mercy; we are talking of God's word. It is God's will that the king be

From "An Open Letter on the Harsh Book Against the Peasants" in The Works of Martin Luther (Philadelphia: Fortress Press, 1967), vol. 47. Reprinted by special permission.

honored and the rebels destroyed; and he is as merciful as we are.

Here I do not want to hear or know about mercy, but to be concerned only about what God's word requires. . . . My good friends, you praise mercy so highly because the peasants are beaten; why did you not praise it when the peasants were raging, smiting, robbing, burning, and plundering, in ways that are terrible to see or even to hear about? Why were they not merciful to the princes and lords, whom they wanted to exterminate completely? No one spoke of mercy then. Everything was "rights"; nothing was said of mercy, it was nothing. "Rights, rights, rights!" They were everything. Now that the peasants are beaten, and the stone that they threw at heaven is falling back on their own heads, no one is to say anything of rights, but to speak only of mercy.

And yet they are stupid enough to think that no one notices the rascal behind it! Ah, no! We see you, you black, ugly devil! You praise mercy not because you are seriously concerned about mercy, or you would have praised it to the peasants; on the contrary, you are afraid for your own skin, and are trying to use the appearance and reputation of mercy to escape God's rod, and punishment. That will not work, dear fellow! You must take your turn, and die without mercy. . . . Suppose I were to break into a man's house, rape his wife and daughters, break open his strong box, take his money, put a sword to his chest, and say, "If you will not put up with this, I shall run you through, for you are a godless wretch"; then if a crowd gathered and were about to kill me, or if the judge ordered my head off, suppose I were to cry out, "Hey, Christ teaches you to be merciful and not to kill me," what would people say? . . .

The Scripture passages which speak of mercy apply to the kingdom of God and to Christians, not to the kingdom of the world, for it is a Christian's duty not only to be merciful, but also to endure every kind of suffering—robbery, arson,

murder, devil, and hell. It goes without saying that he is
not to strike, kill, or take revenge on anyone. But the kingdom of the world, which is nothing else than the servant of
God's wrath upon the wicked and is a real precursor of hell
and everlasting death, should not be merciful, but strict,
severe, and wrathful in fulfilling its work and duty. Its tool
is not a wreath of roses or a flower of love, but a naked
sword; and a sword is a symbol of wrath, severity, and punishment. It is turned only against the wicked, to hold them
in check and keep them at peace, and to protect and save
the righteous. Therefore God decrees, in the law of Moses
and in Exodus 22 where he institutes the sword, "You shall
take the murderer from my altar, and not have mercy on
him." And the Epistle to the Hebrews acknowledges that he
who violates the law must die without mercy. This shows
that in the exercise of their office, worldly rulers cannot
and ought not be merciful—though out of grace, they may
take a day off from their office. . . .

The Scriptures, therefore, have good, clear eyes and see
the temporal sword aright. They see that out of great mercy,
it must be unmerciful, and from utter kindness, it must exercise wrath and severity. As Peter and Paul say, it is God's
servant for vengeance, wrath, and punishment upon the
wicked, but for the protection, praise, and honor of the
righteous. It looks upon the righteous with mercy, and so
that they may not suffer, it guards, bites, stabs, cuts, hews,
and slays, as God has commanded; and it knows that it
serves God in doing even this. The merciless punishment
of the wicked is not being carried out just to punish the
wicked and make them atone for the evil desires that are in
their blood, but to protect the righteous and to maintain
peace and safety. And beyond all doubt, these are precious
works of mercy, love, and kindness, since there is nothing
on earth worse than disturbance, insecurity, oppression,
violence, and injustice. Who could or would stay alive if

such things were the rule? Therefore the wrath and severity of the sword is just as necessary to a people as eating and drinking, even as life itself. . . .

One of their more important distortions of the situation is this: They claim that many righteous people participated in the revolt innocently—because they were forced to do so. To execute them would be unjust in God's sight. I answer: They are talking like people who never heard a single word of God, and therefore I must reply here as I would to heathen or to little children; for so little has been accomplished among these people by all the books and sermons!

I say, in the first place, that no injustice is done to those whom the peasants forced to participate. No Christian stayed among them, and these men did not get involved innocently, as they pretend. . . . Who ever heard of anyone being compelled to do good or evil? Who can compel a man's will? This argument does not hold water. Nor does it make sense for a man to say, "I have to do wrong: I am forced to do it." To deny Christ and the word of God is a great sin and wrong, and many are forced to do it, but do you think that that excuses them? Likewise, to start an insurrection, to become disobedient and faithless to rulers, to perjure oneself, to rob and burn—that is a great wrong, and some of the peasants were forced to do it; but how does that help them? Why do they let themselves be forced?

"No," they say, "but they threatened to take my life and my property." Come now, friend, are you willing to break God's commandments, to kill me, and to abuse my wife and children to keep your life and property? But how did God and I get involved in that? Would you be willing to suffer the same things at my hands? If the peasants had forced you to go along with them by tying you hand and foot, and carried you along by force, and you had defended yourself with your mouth, and rebuked them for doing it, and your heart had thus confessed and borne witness that it was unwilling and refused to consent, then your honor would have been preserved; you would have been compelled in body, but not in will. But as it is, you kept silent and did not rebuke them; you went along with the crowd and did not make your unwillingness known, and thus nothing helps you. . . . It is our duty to call upon God for help and to resist sin and wrong. If you die or suffer for it, good for you! Your soul is blessed before God and honored by the world! But if you yield and obey, you must die anyhow, and your death is shameful before God and the world because you have allowed yourself to be forced to do wrong. Thus it would be better to die with honor and blessedness, in praise of God, than to have to die with shame, in punishment and pain. . . .

Finally it may be said, "You yourself teach rebellion, for you say that everyone who can, should hew and stab among the rebels, and that, in this case, everyone is both supreme judge and executioner." I reply: My little book was not written against ordinary evildoers, but against rebels. You must make a very, very great distinction between a rebel and a thief, or a murderer, or any other kind of evildoer. A murderer or evildoer lets the head of the government alone and attacks only the members or their property; indeed, he fears the ruler. So long as the head remains, no one ought to attack such a murderer, because the head can punish. Everyone ought to await the judgment and command of the head, to whom God has committed the sword and the office of punishment. But a rebel attacks the head himself and interferes with the exercise of his sword and his office, and therefore his crime is not to be compared with that of a murderer. . . . Rebellion is no joke, and there is no evil deed on earth that compares with it. Other wicked deeds are single acts; rebellion is a flood of all wickedness.

I am called a clergyman and am a minister of the word, but even if I served a Turk and saw my lord in danger, I would forget my spiritual office and stab and hew as long as my heart beat. If I were slain in so doing, I should go straight to heaven. For rebellion is a crime that deserves neither a court trial nor mercy, whether it be among heathen, Jews, Turks, Christians, or any other people; the rebel has already been tried, judged, condemned, and sentenced to death and everyone is authorized to execute him. Nothing more needs to be done than to give him his due and to execute him. No murderer does so much evil, and none deserves so much evil. For a murderer commits a punishable offense, and lets the penalty stand; but a rebel tries to make wickedness free and unpunishable, and attacks the punishment itself. . . .

John Knox
ca.1513–1572

Whereas Luther and the early followers of John Calvin, the Genevan reformer, condemned revolutionary wars on scriptural grounds, circumstances in the mid-sixteenth century dictated a radical departure from their teaching. In terms of a human response to intolerable persecution, this departure is thoroughly understandable; for the Protestants faced at this time assaults upon their lives and their faith by a resurgent Catholicism.

The following debate in the Scottish Assembly in June, 1565, between John Knox, the moving spirit in the Reformation in Scotland, and William Maitland of Lethington, the Secretary of Mary Queen of Scots, marks a turning point in the abandonment of nonresistance. Knox, vain and tactless, had for four years tried to bully the young Queen into accepting his "true" religion. She, equally vain and tactless, but Catholic to her fingertips, resisted his exhortations and prayers to free her from "the venom of idolatry" and "the thraldom of Satan." Such wrongheadedness could not long be endured; and although Knox rejected revolution for worldly ends, he regarded it as a necessity where God's interests were concerned. It was he, more than anyone else, who was responsible for fomenting the rebellion that drove Mary from the throne into exile in England, where she was eventually executed for high treason.

As testimony to the fact that ideas from the religious sphere have always tended to influence thought in other areas, one need only glance at subsequent developments. In later centuries the arguments justifying revolution in God's name were to furnish, when stripped of their religious qualifications and applied in a new social-political context, the rationale for revolution for the sake of man. It is partly because Knox and his followers insisted that ungodly and idolatrous rulers, no less than their humblest subjects, must be punished here, on earth and by their fellow men, that later generations could hold their governments accountable for more mundane infractions.

The Right of Revolution in Scotland

"Well, Mr. Knox" (said he [Secretary Lethington]), "yesterday we heard your judgment upon the 13th [chapter of the Epistle] to the Romans; we heard the mind of the Apostle well opened; we heard the causes why God has established Powers upon the earth; we heard the necessity that mankind has of the same; and we heard the duty of Magistrates sufficiently declared. But in two things I was offended, and I think some more of my Lords that then were present. The one thing was, ye made difference betwixt the ordinance of God and the persons that were placed in authority; and ye affirmed that men might refuse the persons and not yet offend against God's ordinance. This is the one; the other ye had no time to explain; but this, methought, ye meant, that subjects were not bound to obey their princes if they commanded unlawful things; but that

From William Croft Dickinson, ed., John Knox's History of the Reformation in Scotland (New York: The Philosophical Library, 1950), II. Reprinted with special permission.

they might resist their princes, and were not ever bound to suffer."

"In very deed," said the other [Knox], "ye have rightly both marked my words, and understood my mind; for of that same judgment I have long been, and so yet I remain."

"How will ye prove your division and difference," said Lethington, "and that the person placed in authority may be resisted, and God's ordinance not transgressed, seeing that the Apostle says, 'He that resists [the power], resisteth the ordinance of God.' "

"My Lord," said he [Knox], "the plain words of the Apostle make the difference; and the facts of many approved by God prove my affirmative. First, the Apostle affirms, that the powers are ordained of God, for the preservation of quiet and peaceable men, and for the punishment of malefactors; whereof it is plain, That the ordinance of God, and the power given unto man, is one thing, and the person clad with the power or with the authority, is another; for God's ordinance is the conservation of mankind, the punishment of vice, the maintaining of virtue, which is in itself holy, just, constant, stable, and perpetual. But men clad with the authority, are commonly profane and unjust; yea, they are mutable and transitory, and subject to corruption, as God threateneth them by his Prophet David, saying, 'I have said, Ye are gods, and every one of you the sons of the Most Highest; but ye shall die as men, and the Princes shall fall like others.' Here I am assured, that persons, the soul and body of wicked princes, are threatened with death. . . . And now, my Lord, that the Prince may be resisted, and yet the ordinance of God not violated, it is evident; for the people resisted Saul, when he had sworn by the living God that Jonathan would die. The people (I say), swore in the contrary, and delivered Jonathan, so that one hair on his head fell not. Now, Saul was the annointed King, and they were his subjects, and yet they so resisted him that they made him no better than mansworn. . . .

"And now, my Lord, to answer to the place of the Apostle who affirms, 'That such as resists the power, resists the ordinance of God'; I say that the power in that place is not to be understood of the unjust commandment of men, but of the just power wherewith God has armed his Magistrates and Lieutenants to punish sin and maintain virtue. As if any man should enterprise to take from the hands of a lawful judge a murderer, an adulterer, or any other malefactor that by God's law deserved death, this same man resisted God's ordinance, and procured to himself vengeance and damnation, because that he stayed God's sword to strike. But so it is not, if that men in the fear of God oppose themselves to the fury and blind rage of princes; for so they resist not God, but the Devil, who abuses the sword and authority of God." . . .

"Then will ye," said Lethington, "make subjects to control their princes and rulers?"

"And what harm," said the other, "should the commonwealth receive, that if the corrupt affections of ignorant rulers were moderated, and so bridled by the wisdom and discretion of godly subjects, that they should do wrong nor violence to no man?"

"All this reasoning," said Lethington, "is not of the purpose; for we reason as if the Queen should become such an enemy of our religion, that she should persecute it, and put innocent men to death; which I am assured she never thought, nor never will do. For if I should see her begin at that end, yea, if I should suspect any such thing in her, I should be as far forward in that argument as ye or any other within this Realm. But there is not such a thing. Our question is, Whether that we may and ought to suppress the Queen's Mass? Or whether her idolatry shall be laid to our charge?"

"What ye may [do]," said the other, "by force, I dispute not; but what ye may and ought to do by God's express commandment, that I can tell. Idolatry ought not only to be suppressed, but the idolater ought to die the death, unless that we will accuse God."

"I know," said Lethington, "the idolater is commanded to die the death; but by whom?"

"By the people of God," said the other; "for . . . a commandment was given, That if it be heard that idolatry is committed in any one city, inquisition shall be taken; and if it be found true, that then the whole body of the people shall arise and destroy that city, sparing in it neither man, woman, nor child."

"But there is no commandment given to the people," said the Secretary, "to punish their King if he be an idolater."

"I find no more privilege granted unto kings," said the other, "by God, more than unto the people, to offend God's majesty."

"I grant," said Lethington; "but yet the people may not be judges unto their King to punish him, albeit he be an idolater."

"God," said the other, "is the Universal Judge, as well unto the King as to the people; so that what his word commands to be punished in the one, is not to be absolved in the other."

"We agree in that," said Lethington; "but the people may not execute God's judgment, but must leave it unto Himself, who will either punish it by death, by war, by imprisonment, or by some other plagues." . . .

"Ye know, my Lord [said Knox], that Elisha sent one of the children of the Prophets to anoint Jehu, who gave him in commandment to destroy the house of his master Ahab for the idolatry committed by him, and for the innocent blood that Jezebel his wicked wife had shed. Which he obeyed, and put in full execution; for which God promised unto him the stability of the kingdom to the fourth generation. Now," said he, "here is the fact of one Prophet, that proves that subjects were commanded to execute judgments upon their King and Prince. . . . [And since] God of his nature is constant, immutable, so can he not damn in the ages subsequent that which he has approved in his servants before us. But in his servants before us, He by his own commandment has approved that subjects have not only destroyed their kings for idolatry, but also have rooted out their whole posterity, so that none of that race was left after to empire over the people of God."

"Whatever they did," said Lethington, "was done at God's commandment."

"That fortifies my argument," said the other; "for by God's commandment He approved that subjects punish their princes for idolatry and wickedness by them committed."

"We have not the like commandment," said Lethington.

"That I deny," said the other, "for the commandment, 'the idolater shall die the death,' is perpetual, as [ye] yourself have granted. You doubted only who should be executors against the King; and I said the people of God, and have sufficiently proved, as I think, that God has raised up the people, and by his Prophet has anointed a King to take vengeance upon the King, and upon his posterity. Which fact, God . . . has never retreated; and therefore, to me it remains for a constant and clear commandment to all the people professing God, and having the power to punish vice, what they ought to do in the like case. If the people had enterprised anything without God's commandment, we might have doubted whether they had done well or evil; but seeing that God did bring the execution of his law again in practice, after that it was come to oblivion and contempt, what reasonable man can doubt now of God's will, unless he will doubt of all things which God renews not unto us by miracles, as it were from age to age? . . . For my assertion is, that kings have no privilege more than the people to offend God's majesty; and if that so they do, they are no more exempted from the punishment of the law than is any other subject; yea, and that subjects may not only lawfully oppose themselves to their kings, whensoever they do anything that expressly repugns to God's commandment, but also that they may execute judgment upon them according to God's law; so that if the king be a murderer, adulterer, or idolater, he should suffer according to God's law, not as a king, but as an offender; and that the people may put God's laws in execution, this history clearly proves. . . . And now, my Lords" (said he), "I will reason no longer, for I have spoken more than I intended."

J. B. Mozley
1813–1878

John Bowling Mozley was Regius Professor of Divinity at Oxford University, where for many years he championed the cause of conservatism and the rights of the Church of England against a liberalizing, secularistic state. A prodigious writer and lecturer in theology, he was also deeply interested in the political problems of his day. In 1871, the year the Franco-Prussian War was raging, he preached before the university his sermon on war, regarded by the Church of England until World War I as a normative statement on the subject.

Mozley's views, the product of the nationalism that came to dominate Christendom after its unity had been shattered by the tumults of the Reformation, are like nothing we have encountered thus far. Whereas older thinkers—Lactantius and Augustine immediately come to mind—had condemned nationalism as sinful because it was selfish and predatory, Mozley and his contemporaries placed the nation-state at the center of their thought, deriving from it a doctrine of the inevitability of war. Because God created nations, with their differing natures, irreconcilable interests and conflicting appraisals of their "rights," these writers treated war with almost an Augustinian sense of predestination. As the only means of resolving serious differences, war is as predictable as the change of the seasons. To be sure, the drive toward nation-building is manifested even in peoples historically disunited and oppressed; in this Mozley anticipates much of the history of the "Third World" in the twentieth century. Worse still, all cosmopolitan ideologies, all schemes for world government, and all international organizations for keeping the peace (including, he would probably have said, the United Nations) were doomed. They would either degenerate into universal despotisms or founder on nationalism. The function of the Christian Church, then, was to unite spiritually the worst of enemies, recognizing all the while the inevitability of war and condemning the evil motives that may lead to that *ultima ratio.*

Christianity, War, and Nationalism

The Christian recognition of the right of war was contained in Christianity's original recognition of *nations,* as constituting at the same time the division and the structure of the human world. Gathering up the whole world into one communion spiritually, the new universal society yet announced its coalescence with mankind's divisions politically; it was one body of one kind, in many bodies of another kind. It did not interfere with the established fabric of human society; its ancient inclosures, those formations of nature or events which collected mankind into separate

From J. B. Mozley, "War," in Sermons Preached before the University of Oxford (London: Longmans, 1900).

masses, those great civil corporations into which mankind was distributed; in a word with *nations;* it gathered up into itself not only the unions but the chasms of the human race, all that separated as well as all that united; all that divided, and by dividing created variety and individuality in our human world. The nation was one of those wholes to which the individual man belonged, and of which he was part and member; it existed prior to Christianity, and was admitted into it with other natural elements in us; Christians were from the outset members of States; and the Church could no more ignore the State than it could the family. And as one of those wholes to which the individual belonged, a sentiment and affection attached to it; Christianity admitted this sentiment; it gave room for national feeling, for patriotism, for that common bond which a common history creates, for loyalty, for pride in the grandeur of the nation's traditions, for joy in its success. . . .

The Christian Church, then, recognized and adopted nations, with their inherent rights; took them into her inclosure. But war is one of these rights, because under the division of mankind into distinct nations it becomes a necessity. Each of these is a center to itself, without any amenableness to a common center. Questions of right and justice must arise between these independent centers; these cannot be decided except by mutual agreement or force, and when one fails the other only remains—not that it necessarily settles questions rightly indeed, because it is force and not right which decides; but the right side makes the trial. In the act, then, of recognizing and including within herself, nations, collecting within one spiritual area so many independent political sources, the Christian Church necessarily admitted also war within her pale. . . .

Christianity does not admit, indeed, but utterly denounces and condemns the motives which lead to war— selfish ambition, rapacity, tyranny, and vanity; but the condemnation of one side is the justification of the other; these very motives give the right of resistance to one side. And, inasmuch as the Church has no authority to decide which is the right side—is not judge of national questions or of national motives, not having been made by her Divine Founder a "judge or a divider" in this sphere, the Church cannot, in her ignorance, exclude the other side either. The Church therefore stands neutral, and takes in both sides; that is to say, both sides fight within the bond of Christian unity. She only contemplates war forensically, as a mode of settling national questions, which is justified by the want of any other mode. . . .

It must be observed that individuals are enabled to settle their disputes peaceably by the fact of being under a government. It is not that individuals are less pugnacious than nations, but they are differently circumstanced. Being under a government, they are obliged, if they do not voluntarily come to terms, to accept the arbitration of a court. Nobody supposes that the suitors for justice in our courts agree with the judge when he decides against them. They think him in error, but they submit because they are obliged. Every judgment of a court is backed by the whole force of the nation, as against the force of the individual who dissents. Individuals then are able to settle their disputes peaceably because they are governed by the nation; but nations themselves are not governed by a power above them. . . . [Thus] the aim of the nation in going to war is exactly the same as that of the individual in entering a court; it wants its rights, or what it alleges to be its rights; but it is not in the situation in which the individual is of being compelled by force to accept the decision of a judge upon them. For indeed a court of justice possesses, only in reserve, exactly the same identical force as that which exerts and demonstrates itself in war. It is one and the same force in principle; only in the court it is confessedly superior to all opposition, and therefore has not to make any demonstration of itself, *i.e.,* it acts peaceably. In war it has to make a demonstration, to come out, *i.e.,* its action is warlike. It acts as a contending force; because it is only as a superior force that it is effective; and its superiority can only be proved by contention. It exists in its compressed form in the court, like the genius shut up in the chest in the eastern legend; in war it rises to a colossal height, like the same genius let out. In civil government the force of final resort is a stationary force at the nation's center; in war it is a moving and nomad force, going about the world, and showing itself by the proof of the event in battle, in whatever place the occasion may arise; but it is the same force in different circumstances. . . .

. . . When we go further, we find that there is a spring in the very setting and framework of the world; whence movements are ever pushing up to the surface—movements for recasting more or less the national distribution of the world; for establishing fresh centers and forming States into new groups and combinations. Much of this is doubtless owing to the mere spirit of selfish conquest; for conquest as such is change and reconstruction; but conquest does not account for the whole of it. There is doubtless an instinctive reaching in nations and masses of people after alteration and readjustment, which has justice in it, and which arises from real needs. The arrangement does not suit as it stands; there is want of adaptation; there is confinement and pressure—people kept away from each other that are made to be together; and parts separated that were made to join. Thus there is uneasiness in States, and an impulse rises up toward some new coalition; it is long an undergrowth of feeling, but at last it comes to the top, and takes steps for putting itself in force. Strong States then, it is true, are ready enough to assume the office of reconstructors, and yet we must admit there is sometimes a natural justice in these movements, and that they are instances of a real self-correcting process which is part of the constitution of the world, and which is coeval in root with the political structure which it remedies. . . . But such just needs when they arise must produce war; because a *status quo* is blind to new necessities, and does not think such an alteration to be for the better, but much for the worse. . . . And as Christianity at its commencement took up the national divisions of mankind, with war as a consequence contained in them, so it assumes this root of change and reconstruction with the same consequence—this fundamental tendency to re-settlement, this inherent corrective process in political nature. . . .

The natural remedy for war would then appear to be a government of nations; but this would be nothing short of universal empire, and can this be accomplished by any progress? It is indeed a physical improbability. The Church, indeed, in the Middle Ages put forth pretensions to this power; the Roman Empire was in its day an approach to it; and so are all large conquests in their degree, keeping the nations under them distinct, but only partially self-governing, and depending on the center. Nor is the dream of a universal government or empire confined entirely to such shapes, or to such sources. Great popular causes, powerful tides of opinion, as they spread and advance over the world, tend to level the barriers of nations, to reduce patriotic sentiment, and to throw open the whole of human society into one vast area, in which the interests of collective humanity alone reign. The first French revolution was such a movement; it bound together the disciples of revolutionary philosophy all over the world; and tended to erect one immense brotherhood, whose common ground was stronger and more connecting than their differencing one; the union of ideas more forcible than the separation of country. At the present time that vast common fellowship, co-extensive with the world—the great uniting bond of labor, man's universal yoke, has produced a move in a like direction. . . . But whatever approach may occasionally take place toward a relaxation of the national tie, the alternative is still an inexorable one between independent nations and a universal empire; and as a universal empire is impossible the division of nations only remains. The waves of universalism can only dash themselves against that rock; they cannot possibly shake the seat of distributed power and government; and by a fortunate necessity nations must ever form the barriers and breakwaters in that boundless ocean of humanity, which would otherwise drive with irresistible and wild force in the direction of particular great movements and ideas; they are the groins which divide the beach, whose immeasurable expanse of sands would otherwise crowd up into over-whelming piles and masses.

Thus we fall back again upon independent States, which must decide their own rights, otherwise they are not full and integral States. . . . But such States meet equal rights in other States, for the conflict of which no solution is provided but war.

James Martineau
1805–1900

The excerpt presented here, from a sermon delivered in 1855 at the height of the Crimean War, is the work of the foremost English Unitarian theologian of the nineteenth century. Intended as a refutation of pacifism, it is perhaps the best modern example of the "police analogy" as a justification of war. Basing his theory on a view of human nature and history, Martineau held that God had implanted in man two faculties—resentment of injustice and fellow-feeling—that in normal human beings often express themselves violently. The first enables the individual to mobilize his energies and strike out against injustice on his own behalf; by extension, the second, fellow-feeling, which Martineau saw manifested throughout history as a movement toward justice in ever-widening circles of human association, enables the individual to combine with others to achieve this end. As the individual is his brother's keeper, so the state has a corresponding responsibility in the international sphere. Unlike his contemporary, J. B. Mozley, he saw the inevitable culmination of this movement in a system of universally recognized law, enforced (it would have to be) by a universal peace-keeping body. Finally, since the state occupies the same position morally as the individual, it is bound to use the police to keep the domestic peace and the army, its analogue, only on a vastly expanded scale, to vindicate justice abroad. Selfishness in states, Martineau held, pushing the analogy further, is as reprehensible as selfishness in individuals. The state must intervene anywhere in the world to prevent evil having a free hand; in fact, he would have considered a "lost generation," the decimation of a nation's young manhood as in 1914–1918, an acceptable price to pay for the vindication of righteousness.

The "Police Analogy"

The Christian rule of "forgiveness" . . . does not enable us to pardon *moral guilt,* but only *personal affront.* It does not release us from the obligations of justice, which constrain us to deal with men according to their character, to hinder the wrong and help the right. It exempts no one of the resources at our disposal—persuasion, discipline, power—from free use in this service; and if, by letting any of them lie idle, we permit an injustice we might prevent, we are in the sight of heaven accomplices in its perpetration. Bodily strength, and the skill which arms it with mechanical increase, are as much entrusted to us for this end as any faculty of thought and affection; and to main-

From James Martineau, "Right of War," in National Duties and other Sermons and Addresses *(London: Longmans, 1903).*

tain that we may employ it in the service of our own convenience and luxury, but not in the defense of innocence and the repulse of guilt, is an incomprehensible and untenable paradox. Indeed everyone who puts his money in an iron safe, or a chain upon his house door, relinquishes his reliance on the appeal of reason and conscience, and accepts the aid of material power. And if, further, he has ever restrained the arm, or chastened the disobedience of a passionate child; if he has availed himself of the services of the police to arrest and the courts to try the offender against his person or goods; if, in short, he consents to have a place in civil society at all; he has engaged himself, by active coercion, in resistance to evil, and in his private capacity *gone to war* with the delinquencies he meets.

Nay, in the earlier stages of every historical community, the ends of justice, now so quietly obtained, were literally accomplished no otherwise than by *going to war*. Natural resentment, individual moral indignation, rising against the evildoer and hurling him out, is the first protection which heaven provides against unjust aggression. The sympathy of observers prevents the strife remaining single, and soon supplies a law which one combatant is glad to accept, and the other forced to obey. The neighborhood however long continues small through which the same authority is acknowledged, and the weapons of personal defense laid down on its behalf. In the next village, or the next barony, another tribunal is obeyed; and a dispute between the two circles is settled by trial of local arms, adjoining districts often taking sides. A succession of such struggles disengages at last, and fixes in distinct form, the moral judgment of a wider circle, and erects a court of larger jurisdiction to interpret and enforce it. But while private feuds are thus banished between barony and barony, they still break out between county and county, till by similar experience a common feeling is found which covers a broader area, and insists on its verdict of right. With widening intercourse and more settled relations the range of public law extends; till at last province has no longer border-wars with province, but settles its cause by Imperial appeal. Throughout this process, what is the moving spring, the real natural force, which conducts the march of security and order?—what but the human indignation at wrong, at first isolated and momentary; but gradually feeling its way to concurrence in expanding circles, till it organizes itself into national law? Had that primitive anger never struck a blow, no rudiment of social rights would have appeared. It is the arms of yesterday that have won the field of justice for today; and the fairest growths of peace have roots not unwatered by blood. And after all, Law in the last resort can but *economize* force, and does not *dispense with it*. It transfers the weapon from the private to the public hand, and stops the lavish violence of individual passion. But what would be the value of a judiciary without an executive visible behind it? What else is the whole penal administration of a country but its perennial civil war against its own incorrigible criminals?

Far be it for me to say that the process of pacification which replaces the warrior by the judge must necessarily stop with the limits of each country. As the barriers disappear which hinder the sympathy of land with land, the sense of common justice and an eventual common interest cannot fail to spread; and already its beginnings are traced in the faint and uncertain outlines of International Law. But at present the group of European nations are in corresponding relative position to baronies of the same country, ere yet there was any dominant power to summon them to its tribunal; and as the struggle of castle with castle, and of alliances of chief with chief, were the means of ascertaining the common feeling, and working out the balance of common right; so, if States are ever to be brought into a court of general jurisdiction, they have yet to win by a like experience of conflict both the code which is to be there administered, and the cosmopolitan executive which shall enforce its decrees. Meanwhile, we are neighbors, each with his own trust, his own conscience, and his own force; bound to keep what is committed to us, and not to stand by while wanton wrong is done. For these ends we have no guiding law but the sympathies of justice which bring States into generous alliance; and no administrative power but those armed battalions which are the only police of nations. A people without an army is chargeable with more than folly. It refuses its fair contribution to the police of the world; and if, while the power is there, it selfishly looks on, though murder it might prevent is passing before its eyes, its standard blazons forth a lie, and becomes the symbol, not of order, but of anarchy. As the feuds of individuals and clans have been the parents of municipal law, so the hostile collisions of nations are the necessary conditions under which, if at all, an authoritative code can clear itself for the States of the civilized world. The path to the court of justice lies, alas! through the camp of war. . . .

No doubt, this openness, on adequate occasion, to mingle in moral struggles of the world involves a readiness for war; and must be regulated by the clear sense of how dreadful is the scourge of war. On its miseries and horrors I will not dwell; they are such as to render a selfish, a rash, an ill-ordered war the greatest of crimes; but they are *not* such as to justify us in preferring, when we can prevent, the triumph of wrong. Those who in this argument draw in detail the picture of the battlefield, the siege, the hospital, the mourning homes, the crippled bodies, the wasted treasures, involved in the conflict of great nations, practice deception on themselves and contribute little to the solution of the moral problem . . . . [For] even to decimate one of its generations, what would this be as the price of that self-respect and faithfulness without which the very terms of existence are ignoble, and the most comfortable of populations is nothing but a blot upon the world? Where God embodies great principles in historic forms, and makes mighty nations the organs and medium of moral conflict, it cannot be expected that the arbitrament should take place without a piercing shriek of the hour, wailing and dying down the winds of time. There is no chloroform for earthquakes; the giant mountain heaves and cracks with its throes; but when the equilibrium returns, the villages rise again, the plough cleaves again through the resting soil, the vine-trellice reappears upon the slope, and the Spring field smiles beneath the sun once more. . . .

. . . The terrible right—or rather the stern trust—of Arms, I do not hesitate to claim for every righteous State. With that last arbitrament, however, all questions cease. It is the confession of something irresolvable by Reason, irresolvable by Right; it is a solemn appeal to the collective forces, spiritual no less than material, which God has shut up in our humanity. Here, therefore, the Christian moralist comes to the end of his theme; owns that his principles avail to settle nothing more; that all beyond is indeterminate except in the counsels of eternal Providence. . . .

H. D. A. Major
1872–1961

The following selection, the work of a leading theologian of the Modernist school, represents the reopening of an issue thought resolved at least since the days of Vitoria in the sixteenth century. The military technology brought into play for the first time on a large scale during World War I altered radically the position of the civilian population. War became "total." Because the combat effectiveness of the armies facing each other on the Western Front was linked ultimately to the productive capacity of technologically sophisticated societies, the workers behind the lines became as important for victory as the forces in the field. The result was a blurring of the traditional distinction between soldier and civilian. To defeat the armies of an opponent—so the logic went—one would not only have to destroy the industrial plant supplying them, but also break the morale of those on the "home front."

Although civilians have always suffered in war, atrocities usually have been ordered on the initiative of individual commanders or have been carried out by soldiers gone berserk. Rarely in the history of the West before 1914 had *governments* pursued a policy aimed directly at civilians or their places of habitation. The industrialization and democratization of warfare imposed new "necessities." In 1917, the Germans, anticipating the raids that were to obliterate their own cities in a later war, attacked "military" targets in London, killing and wounding in one raid alone (June 13) hundreds of civilians, including schoolchildren and babies.

Immediately, amid the cries for revenge that swept the nation, agonizing questions were raised for men of goodwill, especially those schooled in the canons of the just war. How, if at all, does reprisal differ from revenge? Can attacks against the civilian population of the enemy, undertaken to discourage his forces from attacking other innocent populations, be squared with the ideal of justice and the law of love? Who is more of a humanitarian, he who prolongs a war through refusing to employ his strength fully, or he who would "get it over with" quickly, in one grand paroxysm of violence? Dr. Major's articles, written shortly after the German raid, are an attempt to justify a policy of reprisals against the strictures of the "sentimentalists," those who would rather see their country perish than survive tainted with the blood of innocents. Although his opinions represent a minority position among ethicists, the issues he raises are still very much alive. Guerrilla warfare and low-level wars of attrition may raise such questions on a less massive scale, but governments such as that of Israel, engaged in what they deem a life and death struggle for survival, must grapple daily with the moral implications of reprisals against civilians.

Revenge, Reprisals, and the Innocent

Reprisals seem essentially un-Christian. The thought of them shocks the Christian consciousness. Shall we fall to the level of the German barbarians? Shall we outrage all the rules of civilized warfare and kill women and children? We declare that the Psalmist offends against Christian feeling when he sings:

> Blessed shall be he that serveth thee as thou hast served us. Yea, blessed shall he be that taketh thy little ones and dasheth them against the stones. . . .

"An eye for an eye and a tooth for a tooth" is condemned by Christ as a motive for action. To wish to knock out another man's eye because he has knocked out one's own eye, however natural, is highly un-Christian, but to blind a man to prevent him from blinding others is not un-Christian at all. Is it not doing what is best for the man himself as well as what is best for his neighbours? Justice and love ought to be our motives in our conduct towards our fellows. We need both motives as our guide: Justice, giving every man what is due to him; Love, giving every man what is best for him. Each has to be kept in line if our course is to be straight, otherwise it will wobble between hardness and sentimentality. The two ideals must not be separated, for they are really one. To give a man what is due him is to give him what is best for him, and *vice versa*. According to our character, God in the experience of our life comes to us either in the form of justice or of love. . . .

The Christian sentimentalist is one who will not face the

From H. D. A. Major, "Reprisals" and "Sentimentalists and Casuists," The Modern Churchman (1917), pp. 154-155, 207-213. Reprinted with special permission.

facts of life. He will not see things as they are. The world for him is not the world as it is, but the world of his dreams. The world as he would like it to be. The Christian Religion is for him the religion of this world of dreams. It is the sweet Galilaean vision, which as soon as it shines on human life makes it good, beautiful, and joyous. Now, while we admit that imagination and idealism serve great purposes in life, we ought to observe that what is really useful is scientific imagination and rational idealism, not the sentimental varieties. . . .

. . . The sentimentalists are in the ranks of the pacifists.[1] Yet at this stage the sentimentalists have largely departed from the pacifist ideal. They recognise with sorrow, as every humane being must, that in this world, human nature being what it is, there are occasions when war is a dire necessity— occasions when armed force which sheds human blood must be called into use. In this view they are true to the best and sanest of Christian teaching. . . .

. . . The question . . . which is now vexing the soul of the sentimentalist is whether the Christian Church should sanction reprisals for German atrocities? It seems clear to him she ought not. He does not, as many do, protest on the ground that reprisals are ineffective (that is not a sentimental but a practical ground for protest), but on the ground that they are inhuman and therefore un-Christian. On the other hand, those who advocate the lawfulness of reprisals declare that their motive in advocating them is a humanitarian one. As to whether reprisals are protective, they leave the military and naval experts to decide; they, the Christian teachers, inheritors of the authority of the Keys, faced with the duty of deciding what is and what is not in accordance with Christian principles, declare that if reprisals are the best means of protecting noncombatants, they are morally permissible. In speaking thus, they incur a most serious responsibility, but, at least, they do not shirk it by remaining silent. While forbidding reprisals on the ground of revenge they permit them on the ground of humanitarianism, i.e., with the object of putting an end to such treacherous outrages as the Germans have committed. The Germans have deliberately adopted these methods, because they hope to win the war by them. They hold that one instrument of success which such outrages gives them is "frightfulness," or the power to terrorize their enemies. The Germans, and all who would follow their example, need to learn that frightfulness is a weapon which not only does not avail, but may be used with terrible effect against themselves. To show a criminal that he can be hoist with his own petard is the best way to prevent criminals from making use of petards. With other sorts of men direct appeals to their moral feelings not to use petards are more effective.

Our sentimentalists need to study human nature more closely than they do . . . [for they] often seem to err in three directions.

First, they have *compassion as an emotion*, and so they cry out against such terrible acts as those of which the Germans have been guilty, but they do not seem to have *compassion as a motive,* or they would support the most effective steps (which experts advise) to put a stop to such horrid crimes.

Secondly, they seem to be weak in their power of moral resentment, that "generous movement of the mind" as [Bishop] Butler calls it. They do not seem to realise how needful it is from the point of view of morality and the higher good of humanity—that horrid crimes should be severely punished. They do not seem to recognise that softness and readiness to forgive (not personal injuries but evil conduct) may be a vice and do most deadly injury to human character, and cause most pernicious results in human society. . . .

Thirdly, they do not see human nature as the experience of life exhibits it to us both at its best and at its worst. While regarding it as sacred on the one hand, as reflecting the image of God, they do not seem to realise that human nature can act divinely. They do not seem to realise that it is possible to punish with a powerful feeling of good-will towards the criminal, and to be ever-ready to forgive him on seeing signs of penitence. Such action seems to them to savour of hypocrisy. . . . On the other hand they do not seem to realise that some human beings can become so callous or perverted morally that direct moral appeals are made in vain. They must be appealed to through suffering. . . .

The strongest moral argument against reprisals is that some are punished by them who are not actually guilty. Insofar as unarmed Germans approve of the atrocious methods of their government they are guilty of its crimes, as guilty as though they had themselves actually bombed London or torpedoed the *Lusitania*. In the cases of others, particularly children, they are not guilty, and those who undertake reprisals would spare them if they could separate them from their guilty countrymen. This they are hardly able to do. In this their situation is, if we may say it with reverence, that of the Divine Being Himself. Bishop Butler points out in his *Analogy* that God governs the world by general laws, laws framed for men as a race of related beings, not as an aggregate of separate individuals. The advantage of government by these general laws is much greater than the disadvantage. One advantage is that men benefit greatly by the virtues of others, and the general progress of mankind. But the disadvantage of government by general laws is that we suffer for the sins of others—children for the sins of their parents, and parents for the sins of their children. However, even the fact that others suffer for our sins has certain compensating results. For instance, the knowledge that our evil conduct will involve others, even those nearest and dearest to us, is one of the greatest deterrents to evil doing. The knowledge by the Germans that in killing English babes they are also killing their own may well prove a greater deterrent than the loss of their own lives. But the question is this: If the innocent cannot be separated from the guilty, ought the guilty therefore to be spared and allowed to continue unpunished their evil ways? It is not for the good of humanity that the guilty should be spared even though the innocent should suffer with them. When Germans advanced behind Belgian women to invade Belgium, Belgian patriots fired on the Germans though they slew their own women in doing so.

It is terrible to have to face such questions, and it may seem utterly repulsive to have to decide in this way. It would give to many (including the writer of this article) an immense sense of emotional relief to say: Though all the babes in England are to be blown to pieces by German airmen, and though you might protect them all by blowing to pieces a single German babe, it is better for you as a nation, and for humanity as a whole in regard to its future moral progress, that your nation should perish but leave this memorial behind it that you would not do this deed, and defile your hands with innocent blood. But if the writer decided thus, his reason and conscience would tell him ere the applause had died away that he had lapsed into sentimentalism. If the only way to protect adequately an English babe is to kill a German babe, then it is the duty of our authorities, however repugnant, to do it. More particularly is this so, when we reflect that that innocent German babe will in all probability grow up to be a killer of babes himself, or at least an enthusiastic advocate of that horrible policy of frightfulness of which the killing of babes is one of the features. Whereas the English babe whose life is saved by this means will, we may reasonably anticipate, grow up to be a protector of babes, and a detestor of those who would slay them.

1. That is, pacifists merely in the sense of wanting to abolish war, not absolutely nonresistant Christians.—Ed.

Reinhold Niebuhr

1892–

For thirty-two years professor of Christian ethics at Union Theological Seminary (New York), and the author of innumerable books and articles, Reinhold Niebuhr has exerted a profound influence upon religious thought in America. In ethics, his most significant work was done in the years before World War II. In the afterglow of the "war to end war" and the hopes for peace embodied in the League of Nations, there flourished in the West a naïve pacifism, a syrupy, optimistic faith in human goodness and rationality and (as Niebuhr would say) in the possibility of realizing the ideal of love in history. Pacifist feeling permeated the intellectual community; and students, who would, after all, be the cannon fodder in a future war, responded with resolutions of the sort passed by the Oxford Union in February, 1933:"This House will in no circumstance fight for its King and Country."

Niebuhr rebelled against the ideology of liberal optimism and its political manifestation, appeasement. Originally a pacifist and an early sponsor of the Fellowship of Reconciliation, he began his pilgrimage from pacifism with the publication in 1932 of *Moral Man and Immoral Society. An Interpretation of Christian Ethics,* the Rauschenbush Lectures for 1934, carried him further away. *Why the Christian Church is Not Pacifist,* published shortly after the German invasion of Poland, placed him squarely in the opposing camp. Significantly, he resigned from the Fellowship of Reconciliation in 1933, the year of both the Oxford Union resolution and of Hitler's accession to power.

As the foremost spokesman of what has come to be called

"neo-orthodoxy" in theology, Niebuhr's criticism of pacifism rests on a doctrine of man that rests in turn on the rehabilitation of the doctrine of sin. As the Barthians harkened back to Calvin's view of human depravity, so Niebuhr owes a debt to Luther's pamphlet of 1523, *On Secular Authority*. But instead of following exactly Luther's distinction between real and nominal Christians, who need the law, Niebuhr shifted the reference point, distinguishing rather between individuals and collectivities. Taken individually, he asserted, men are capable of a degree of altruism and of considering interests other than their own. Taken in groups, however, their innate sinfulness tends to be magnified. Justice, therefore, can be established only through a creative tension, tragically disturbed from time to time, between the various forces, dynamisms, and interests in society and between societies. Maintaining this tension, and restoring it when it lapses into tyranny, is a necessary function of force, even armed force, as in war. Pacifists, who on grounds of human rationality and Christian love denounced all war, he accused of preaching a perfectionism incompatible with historical experience; to be sure, he charged them with showing a preference for slavery and despotism. Niebuhr was instrumental in mobilizing American Protestantism for the inevitable struggle with fascism; recently, however, he has modified some of his views in the light of the nuclear threat and the Vietnamese war.

Love, Justice, Sin, and Force

There may be an advantage in stating the thesis with which we enter this debate immediately. The thesis is, that the failure of the Church to espouse pacifism is not apostasy, but is derived from an understanding of the Christian Gospel which refuses simply to equate the Gospel with the "law of love." Christianity is not simply a new law, namely, the law of love. . . . Christianity is a religion which measures the total dimension of human existence not only in terms of the final norm of human conduct, which is expressed in the law of love, but also in terms of the fact of sin. . . .

The good news of the Gospel is not the law that we ought to love one another. The good news of the Gospel is that there is a resource of divine mercy which is able to overcome a contradiction within our own souls, which we cannot ourselves overcome. This contradiction is that, though we know we ought to love our neighbor as ourself, there is a "law in our members which wars against the law that is in our mind," so that, in fact, we love ourselves more than our neighbor. . . .

. . . In this doctrine of forgiveness and justification, Christianity measures the full seriousness of sin as a permanent force in human history. Naturally, the doctrine has no meaning for modern secular civilization, nor for the secularized and moralistic versions of Christianity. They cannot understand the doctrine precisely because they believe there is some fairly simple way out of the sinfulness of human history. . . .

Nevertheless, it is not possible to regard pacifism simply as a heresy. In one of its aspects modern Christian pacifism is simply a version of Christian perfectionism. It expresses a genuine impulse in the heart of Christianity, the impulse to take the law of Christ seriously and not to allow the political strategies, which the sinful character of man makes necessary, to become final norms. In its profounder forms this Christian perfectionism did not proceed from a simple faith that the "law of love" could be regarded as an alternative to the political strategies by which the world achieves a precarious justice. These strategies invariably involve the balancing of power with power; and they never completely escape the peril of tyranny on the one hand, and the peril of anarchy and warfare on the other.

In medieval ascetic perfectionism and in Protestant sectarian perfectionism (of the type of Menno Simons, for instance) the effort to achieve a standard of perfect love in individual life was not presented as a political alternative. On the contrary, the political problem and task were specifically disavowed. This perfectionism did not give itself to the illusion that it had discovered a method for eliminating the element of conflict from political strategies. On the contrary, it regarded the mystery of evil as beyond its power of solution. It was content to set up the most perfect and unselfish individual life as a symbol of the Kingdom of God. It knew that this could only be done by disavowing the political task and by freeing the individual from all responsibility for social justice. . . .

There is thus a Christian pacifism which is not a heresy. Yet most modern forms of Christian pacifism are heretical. Presumably inspired by the Christian gospel, they have really absorbed the Renaissance faith in the goodness of man, have rejected the Christian doctrine of original sin as an outmoded bit of pessimism, have re-interpreted the Cross so that it is made to stand for the absurd idea that perfect love is guaranteed a simple victory over the world, and have rejected all other profound elements of the Christian gospel as "Pauline" accretions which must be stripped from the "simple gospel of Jesus." This form of pacifism is not only heretical when judged by the standards of the total gospel. It is equally heretical when judged by the facts of human existence. There are no historical realities which remotely conform to it. It is important to recognize this lack of conformity to the facts of experience as a criterion of heresy. . . .

The pacifists do not know human nature well enough to be concerned about the contradictions between the law of love and the sin of man, until sin has conceived and brought forth death. They do not see that sin introduces an element of conflict into the world and that even the most loving relations are not free of it. They are, consequently, unable to appreciate the complexity of the problem of justice. They merely assert that if only men loved one another, all the complex, and sometimes horrible, realities of the political order could be dispensed with. They do not see that their "if" begs the most basic problem of human history. It is because men are sinners that justice can be achieved only by a certain degree of coercion on the one hand, and by resistance to coercion and tyranny on the other hand. The political life of man must constantly steer between the Scylla of anarchy and the Charybdis of tyranny. . . .

To look at human communities from the perspective of the Kingdom of God is to know that there is a sinful element in all the expedients which the political order uses to establish justice. That is why even the seemingly most stable justice degenerates periodically into either tyranny or anarchy. But it must also be recognized that it is not possible to eliminate the sinful element in the political expedients. They are, in the words of St. Augustine, both the consequence of, and the remedy for, sin. If they are the remedy for sin, the ideal of love is not merely a principle of indiscriminate criticism upon all approximations of justice. It is also a principle of discriminate criticism between forms of justice.

As a principle of indiscriminate criticism upon all forms of justice, the law of love reminds us that the injustice and tyranny against which we contend in the foe is partially the consequence of our own injustice, that the pathology of modern Germans is partially a consequence of the vindictiveness of the peace of Versailles, and that the ambition of a tyrannical imperialism is different only in degree and not in kind from the imperial impulse which characterizes all of human life.

The Christian faith ought to persuade us that political

controversies are always conflicts between sinners and not between righteous men and sinners. It ought to mitigate the self-righteousness which is an inevitable concomitant of all human conflict. The spirit of contrition is an important ingredient in the sense of justice. If it is powerful enough it may be able to restrain the impulse of vengeance sufficiently to allow a decent justice to emerge. This is an important issue facing Europe in anticipation of the conclusion of the present war. It cannot be denied that the Christian conscience failed terribly in restraining vengeance after the last war. It is also quite obvious that the natural inclination to self-righteousness was the primary force of this vengeance (expressed particularly in the war guilt clause of the peace treaty). The pacifists draw the conclusion from the fact that justice is never free from vindictiveness, that we ought not for this reason ever to contend against a foe. This argument leaves out of account that capitulation to the foe might well subject us to a worse vindictiveness. It is as foolish to imagine that the foe is free of the sin which we deplore in ourselves as it is to regard ourselves as free of the sin which we deplore in the foe.

The fact that our own sin is always partly the cause of the sins against which we must contend is regarded by simple moral purists as proof that we have no right to contend against the foe. They regard the injunction "Let him who is without sin cast the first stone" as a simple alternative to the schemes of justice which society has devised and whereby it prevents the worst forms of antisocial conduct. This injunction of Christ ought to remind every judge and every judicial tribunal that the crime of the criminal is partly the consequence of the sins of society. But if pacifists are to be consistent they ought to advocate the abolition of the whole judicial process in society. It is perfectly true that national societies have more impartial instruments of justice than international society possesses to date. Nevertheless, no impartial court is as impartial as it pretends to be, and there is no judicial process which is completely free of vindictiveness. Yet we cannot dispense with it; and we will have to continue to put criminals into jail. There is a point where the final cause of the criminal's antisocial conduct becomes a fairly irrelevant issue in comparison with the task of preventing his conduct from injuring innocent fellows. . . .

The recognition of the law of love as an indiscriminate principle of criticism over all attempts at social and international justice is actually a resource of justice, for it prevents the pride, self-righteousness and vindictiveness of men from corrupting their efforts at justice. But it must be recognized that love is also a principle of discriminate criticism between various forms of community and various attemps at justice. The closest approximation to a love in which life supports life in voluntary community is a justice in which life is prevented from destroying life and the interests of the one are guarded against unjust claims by the other. Such justice is achieved when impartial tribunals of society prevent men "from being judges in their own cases," in the words of John Locke. But the tribunals of justice merely codify certain equilibria of power. Justice is basically dependent upon a balance of power. Whenever an individual or a group or a nation possesses undue power, and whenever this power is not checked by the possibility of criticizing and resisting it, it grows inordinate. . . .

Naturally the tension of such a balance may become overt; and overt tensions may degenerate into conflict. The center of power, which has the function of preventing this anarchy of conflict, may also degenerate into tyranny. There is no perfectly adequate method of preventing either anarchy or tyranny. But obviously the justice established in the so-called democratic nations represents a high degree of achievement; and the achievement becomes the more impressive when it is compared with the tyranny into which alternative forms of society have fallen. . . .

If we do not make discriminate judgments between social systems we weaken the resolution to defend and extend civilization. Pacifism either tempts us to make no judgments at all, or to give an undue preference to tyranny in comparison with the momentary anarchy which is necessary to overcome tyranny. It must be admitted that the anarchy of war which results from resistance to tyranny is not always creative; that, at given periods of history, civilization may lack the resource to fashion a new and higher form of unity out of momentary anarchy. The defeat of Germany and the frustration of the Nazi effort to unify Europe in tyrannical terms is a negative task. It does not guarantee the emergence of a new Europe with a higher level of international cohesion and new organs of international justice. But it is a negative task which cannot be avoided. All schemes for avoiding this negative task rest upon illusions about human nature. Specifically, these illusions express themselves in the failure to understand the stubbornness and persistence of the tyrannical will, once it is fully conceived. It would not require great argumentative skill to prove that Nazi tyranny could never have reached such proportions as to be able to place the whole of Europe under its ban, if sentimental illusions about the character of the evil which Europe was facing had not been combined with less noble motives for tolerating Nazi aggression.

A simple Christian moralism is senseless and confusing. It is senseless when, as in the World War, it seeks uncritically to identify the cause of Christ with the cause of democracy without a religious reservation. It is just as senseless when it seeks to purge itself of this error by an uncritical refusal to make any distinctions between relative values in history. The fact is that we might as well dispense with the Christian faith entirely if it is our conviction that we can act in history only if we are guiltless. This means that we must either prove our guiltlessness in order to be able to act; or to refuse to act because we cannot achieve guiltlessness. Self-righteousness or inaction are the alternatives of secular moralism. If they are also the only alternatives of Christian moralism, one rightly suspects that Christian faith has become diluted with secular perspectives.

In its profoundest insights the Christian faith sees the whole of human history as involved in guilt, and finds no release from guilt except in the grace of God. The Christian is freed by that grace to act in history; to give his devotion to the highest values he knows; to defend those citadels of civilization of which necessity and historic destiny have made him the defender; and he is persuaded by that grace to remember the ambiguity of even his best actions. If the providence of God does not enter the affairs of men to bring good out of evil, the evil in our good may easily destroy our best efforts and frustrate our highest hopes. . . .

Karl Barth
1886–1968

Karl Barth, the founder of the school of "dialectical theology," was a moving force in twentieth-century Protestant thought. A student of Adolf von Harnack, the dean of liberal theologians, Barth found that his faith in a system presenting God as a kind of big brother, religion as human wish fulfillment, had been shattered by World War I. He returned instead to the prophetic teaching of the Bible, reaffirming the omnipotence of God and reviving the Calvinistic picture of human depravity.

There was sufficient confirmation of the latter view in the

world of the 1930s. Totalitarianism was on the march and Barth, as a leader in the Confessing Church, a group of Evangelical Christians formed to resist the Nazi-sponsored German-Christian Movement, became the guiding spirit in the Barmen Declaration (1934) denouncing the profanation of the Gospel by the state.

Conceding the "almost infinite" arguments supporting the "inflexible negative" of pacifism, and condemning nearly all wars as unjust, Barth nonetheless went on to revivify and purify the classic teaching about the just war, bringing it into line with modern developments. With restrained eloquence he affirmed that modern machine warfare is total war; and that because every citizen has become at once combatant and target, he can no longer shunt the moral responsibility for war's consequences on to his rulers. As never before, war also demanded that the Church be something more than the chaplain of the state. If it is to have relevance to modern life, it must act as the conscience of the nation, speaking out fearlessly against almost every war without regard to the consequences to itself.

Yet Barth regarded certain wars as justified, indeed, as positively commanded by God. There is, he affirmed in a letter to a French pastor (*Theology,* March 1940) and in a slim volume on *The Church and the War* (1940), a world of difference between the state and the anti-state, the state of Romans 13, and that of Revelation 13. The one, always imperfect and subject to corruption, still cleaves to its purpose as the instrument of justice and the trustee of certain divinely imparted values; the other is the "beast out of the abyss" which performs the "miracles of Antichrist." At this point Barth abandoned a basic criterion for the just war, the moral certainty of success. For when confronted with a state such as Nazi Germany, the incarnation of evil, the just state offends God by surrendering; rather it must fight on regardless of its losses.

The following selection from *Church Dogmatics,* his masterwork, expresses Barth's most mature thinking about war.

Church Dogmatics

. . . We shall begin by trying to stab our consciences awake in relation to certain illusions which may have been feasible once but cannot be entertained any longer.

1. There was a time when it was possible not only for monks and ecclesiastics but also for very wide circles of secular society to throw the problem of military action wholly on the so-called military classes. The very word "soldier," with its suggestion of a being apart, has its origin in this period. War was a matter for princes and rulers and their relatively small armies. It did not concern others unless they were accidentally involved. . . .

Those days have gone. Today everyone is a military person, either directly or indirectly. That is to say, everyone participates in the suffering and action which war demands. All nations as such, and all their members, have long since become responsible military subjects. It would be ridiculous today to throw the responsibility on the collective body, i.e., the fatherland which calls, the people which rallies, and the state which orders. Each individual is himself the fatherland, the people, the state; each individual is himself a belligerent. Hence each individual must act when war is waged, and each has to ask whether the war is just or unjust. This is the first thing which today makes the problem of war so serious from the ethical standpoint. It is an illusion to think that there can be an uncommitted spectator.

2. It has always been realized that war is concerned with the acquisition and protection of material interests, more specifically the possession of land and property. In times past, however, it was easier to lose sight of the ma-

From Church Dogmatics *(Edinburgh: T. & T. Clark, 1961), III/4, pp. 450-457, 461-463. Reprinted with special permission.*

terial aspect in all kinds of notions about the honour, justice, freedom and greatness of the nation as represented in its princely houses and rulers, or about the supreme human values at stake, so that something of the character of a crusade, of a religious or cultural war, could be conferred upon the conflict, when in reality the decisive if not the exclusive point was simply the deployment of power for the acquisition of power in the elemental sense. Political mysticism, of course, is still to be found; but it is now much more difficult to believe in it sincerely. Certain fog patches have lifted. . . .

Today . . . the increasing scientific objectivity of military killing, the development, appalling effectiveness and dreadful nature of the methods, instruments and machines employed, and the extension of the conflict to the civilian population, have made it quite clear that war does in fact mean no more and no less than killing, with neither glory, dignity nor chivalry, with neither restraint nor consideration in any respect. The glory of the so-called military profession, which has incidentally become the profession of everybody either directly or indirectly, can now feed only on the relics of ancient illusions long since stripped of their substance. Much is already gained if only we do at last soberly admit that, whatever may be the purpose or possible justice of a war, it now means that, without disguise or shame, not only individuals or even armies, but whole nations as such, are out to destroy one another by every possible means. It only needed the atom and hydrogen bomb to complete the self-disclosure of war in this regard. . . . How unequivocally ugly war now is! . . .

A first essential [to a right understanding of the question] is that war should not on any account be recognized as a normal, fixed and in some sense necessary part of what in the Christian view constitutes the just state, or the political order demanded by God. Certainly the state as such possesses power and must be able to exercise it. But it does this in any case, and it is no primary concern of Christian ethics to say that it should do so, or to maintain that the exercise of power constitutes the essence of the state, i.e., its *opus proprium* [primary function], or even a part of it. What Christian ethics must insist is that it is an *opus alienum* [deviation from its primary function] for the state to have to exercise power. It cannot assure the state that in the exercise of power either the state or its organs may do gaily and confidently whatever they think is right. In such cases it must always confront them with the question whether there is really any necessity for this exercise. Especially the state must not be given *carte blanche* to grasp the *ultima ratio* of organising mass slaughter in its dealings with other states. Christian ethics cannot insist too loudly that such mass slaughter might well be mass murder, and therefore that this final possibility should not be seized like any other, but only at the very last hour in the darkest of days. The Church and theology have first and supremely to make this detached and delaying movement. If they do not first and for a long time make this the burden of their message, if they do not throw in their weight decisively on this side of the scales, they have become savourless salt, and must not be surprised if they are freely trampled underfoot on every side. It is also to be noted that, if the Church and theology think otherwise, if they do not say this first, if they do not throw in their weight on this side, if they speak tediously and tritely of war as a political *opus proprium,* then at the striking of the last hour in the darkest of days they will be in no position to say authentically and authoritatively what they may say at such a time. That is to say, they will be in no position authentically and authoritatively to issue a call to arms, to the political *opus alienum*. For they can do this only if they have previously held aloof, calling for peace right up to the very last moment. . . .

Perhaps a state desires to expand politically, geographically or economically, and therefore to extend its frontiers and dominion. Perhaps it thinks it necessary to rectify its internal conditions, e.g., to bring about political unity, by external adventure. Perhaps it considers that its honour and prestige are violated by the attiude of another state. Perhaps it feels that it is threatened by a shift in the balance of power among other states. Perhaps it thinks it sees in the internal conditions of another state, whether revolutionary or reactionary, a reason for displeasure or anxiety. Perhaps it believes it can and should ascribe to itself a historical mission, e.g., a call to lead and rule other nations. All this may well be so. Yet it certainly does not constitute a valid reason for setting one's own great or little war machine in motion, for sending out one's troops to the battlefield to kill and be killed. Such aims may be well worth striving for. But they are too paltry to be worth the terrible price involved in their realisation by war. War for such reasons could always have been avoided. War for such reasons is an act of murder. . . . The Christian Church has to testify unambiguously that wars waged for such reasons are not just, and therefore ought not to be undertaken.

Even the existence or non-existence of a state does not always constitute a valid reason for war. It can sometimes happen that the time of a state in its present form of existence has expired, that its independent life has no more meaning nor basis, and that it is thus better advised to yield and surrender, continuing its life within a greater nexus of states. There are times when this kind of question has to be raised and answered. As is well-known, Jeremiah did not repeat the message of Isaiah in an earlier situation, but summoned the people to submit rather than resist. We may well imagine a case in which the witness of the Christian Church ought to have a similar material content.

Indeed, it is only in answer to this particular question that there is a legitimate reason for war, namely, when a people or state has serious grounds for not being able to assume responsibility for the surrender of its independence, or, to put it even more sharply, when it has to defend within its borders the independence which it has serious grounds for not surrendering. The sixth commandment is too urgent to permit of the justification of war by Christian ethics on any other grounds.

Why do we have to allow the possibility that in the light of the divine commandment this is a justifiable reason for war, so that a war waged for this reason must be described as a just war in spite of all the horrors which it will certainly entail? The obvious answer is that there may well be bound up with the independent life of a nation responsibility for the whole physical, intellectual and spiritual life of the people comprising it, and therefore their relationship to God. It may well be that in and with the independence of a nation there is entrusted to its people something which, without any claim or pretension, they are commissioned to attest to others, and which they may not therefore surrender. It may well be that with the independence of the state, and perhaps in the form of the legally constituted society guaranteed by it, they would also have to yield something which must not be betrayed, which is necessarily more important to them than the preservation of life itself, and which is thus more important than the preservation of the lives of those who unfortunately are trying to take it from them. It may well be that they are thus forbidden by God to renounce the independent status of their nation, and that they must therefore defend it without considering either their own lives or the lives of those who threaten it. Christian ethics cannot possibly deny that this case may sometimes occur. The divine command itself posits and presents it as a case of extreme urgency. . . .

But a similar situation may arise in a different form, e.g., when a state which is not itself directly threatened or attacked considers itself summoned by the obligation of a treaty or in some other way to come to the aid of a weaker neighbour which does actually find itself in this situation. In solidarity with the state which it tries to help, it will then find itself in a position of true emergency. At such a time Christian ethics can no longer be absolutely pacifist. It cannot, therefore, oppose all military action, nor resist all military armament. If it has said all there is to be said about true peace and the practical avoidability of war; if it has honestly and resolutely opposed a radical militarism, it may then add that, should the command of God require a nation to defend itself in such emergency, or in solidarity with another nation in such an emergency, then it not only may but must do so. It may also add that if this is basically the only reason for war on the basis of its constitution and history and in the minds of all its responsible citizens, then it may and must prepare for it even in peacetime. For even though this preparation has in view the terrible venture of killing and being killed, with all that this entails, the venture itself is inescapably demanded.

A distinctively Christian note in the acceptance of this demand is that it is quite unconditional. That is to say, it is independent of the success or failure of the enterprise, and therefore of the strength of one's own forces in comparison with those of the enemy.

George Bell and Viscount Cranborne

At the beginning of World War II, Englishmen, their sentiments voiced by Winston Churchill, had condemned air raids on population centers as unworthy of a civilized people. Yet the animosity created by the Blitz, with its senseless destruction of English towns, coupled with the increased capability of English bombers to strike at the heartland of the Reich, heightened the outcry for retaliation. Once again Churchill spoke for the nation, declaring in the House of Commons in September, 1943: "There are no sacrifices we will not make, no lengths of violence to which we will not go" to achieve victory. He was as good as his word. The Allied air offensive against Germany reached a crescendo of ferocity during the next two years. "Area," "obliteration," or "saturation" raids were launched against German cities. Whole sections, sometimes practically entire cities, were wiped out as though they were blemishes on the face of the earth. Hamburg was hit so severely by a mixture of high explosive and incendiary bombs that firestorms, created by air heated to over a thousand degrees, swept the city; casualties numbered about 43,000 dead, among them 5,000 children. Dresden, raided by over 3,000 bombers in three waves of attack, lost 135,000 people in thirty-six hours.

Not all public men, however, supported such tactics. The dilemma of decent men confronted by a welter of evil choices was expressed nowhere more poignantly than in the following debate. The questions involved lay at the very center of Christian thinking about war. Having chosen the *end,* have we not also to a certain extent chosen the *means* of attaining it? To what extent may evil be done in the hope of good growing out of it?

Each side marshalled its arguments, all logical, high-minded, and humanitarian in intent, yet mutually contradictory. The Bishop of Chichester, George Bell, represented the antireprisalists. An outspoken man, Bell had a knack for discovering and making his own those causes that others would not touch, such as German refugees and relief for the hunger caused by the British economic blockade. Bell was also deeply committed to the war as a struggle for Christian civilization; but it had to be carried on in the right way. Viscount Cranborne, Secretary of State for Dominion Affairs, answered for the government (in the long run more persuasively, judging by events), arguing that the long-range interests of humanity would be served rather than hindered by continuing the attacks. Similar arguments were heard the following year, when the U.S. dropped atomic bombs on Hiroshima and Nagasaki.

The Debate on Obliteration Bombing in the House of Lords (February 9, 1944)

THE RIGHT REVEREND PRELATE [George Bell, Bishop of Chichester] said: My Lords, the question which I have to ask is beset with difficuties. It deals with an issue which must have its own anxieties for the Government, and certainly causes great searchings of heart amongst large numbers of people who are as resolute champions of the Allied cause as any member of your Lordships' House. If long-sustained and public opposition to Hitler and the Nazis since 1933 is any credential, I would humbly claim to be one of the most convinced and consistent anti-Nazis in Great Britain. But I desire to challenge the Government on the policy which directs the bombing of enemy towns on the present scale, especially with reference to civilians, non-combatants, and non-military and non-industrial objectives. I also desire to make it plain that, in anything I say on this issue of policy, no criticism is intended of the pilots, the gunners, and the air crews who, in circumstances of tre-

From Parliamentary Debates (Lords), *1944, columns 737-755.*

mendous danger, with supreme courage and skill, carry out the simple duty of obeying their superiors' orders.

Few will deny that there is a distinction in principle between attacks on military and industrial objectives and attacks on objectives which do not possess that character. At the outbreak of the war, in response to an appeal by President Roosevelt, the Governments of the United Kingdom and France issued a joint declaration of their intention to conduct hostilities with a firm desire to spare the civilian population and to preserve in every way possible those monuments of human achievement which are treasured by all civilized countries. At the same time explicit instructions were issued to the Commanders of the Armed Forces prohibiting the bombardment, whether from the air or from the sea or by artillery on land, of any except strictly military objectives in the narrowest sense of the word. Both sides accepted this agreement. . . .

I turn to the situation in February, 1944, and the terrific devastation by Bomber Command of German towns. I do not forget the *Luftwaffe,* or its tremendous bombing of Belgrade, Warsaw, Rotterdam, London, Portsmouth, Coventry, Canterbury and many other places of military, industrial and cultural importance. Hitler is a barbarian. There is no decent person on the Allied side who is likely to suggest that we should make him our pattern or attempt to be competitors in that market. It is clear enough that large-scale bombing of enemy towns was begun by the Nazis. I am not arguing that point at all. The question with which I am concerned is this: Does the Government understand the full force of what area bombardment is doing and is destroying now? Are they alive not only to the vastness of the material damage, much of which is irreparable, but also to the harvest they are laying up for the future relationships of the peoples of Europe as well as its moral implications? . . . I recognize the legitimacy of concentrated attack on industrial and military objectives, on airfields and air bases, in view especially of the coming of the Second Front. I fully realize that in attacks on centers of war industry and transport the killing of civilians when it is the result of bonafide military activity is inevitable. But there must be a fair balance between the means employed and the purpose achieved. To obliterate a whole town because certain portions contain military and industrial establishments is to reject the balance. . . .

Berlin, the capital of the Reich, is four times the size of Hamburg. The offices of the Government, the military, industrial, war-making establishments in Berlin are a fair target. Injuries to civilians are inevitable. But up to date half Berlin has been destroyed, area by area, the residential and the industrial portions alike. Through the dropping of thousands of tons of bombs, including fire-phosphorus bombs, of extraordinary power, men and women have been lost, overwhelmed in the colossal tornado of smoke, blast, and flame. It is said that 74,000 persons have been killed and that 3,000,000 are already homeless. The policy is obliteration, openly acknowledged. This is not a justifiable act of war. Again, Berlin is one of the great centers of art collections in the world. . . . Those works of art and those libraries will be wanted for the reeducation of the Germans after the war. I wonder whether your Lordships realize the loss involved in [their destruction]. . . .

How is it, then, that this wholesale destruction has come about? The answer is that it is the method used, the method of area bombing. . . . It is no longer definite military and industrial objectives which are the aim of the bombers, but the whole town, area by area, is plotted carefully out. This area is singled out and plastered on one night; that area is singled out and plastered on another night; a third, a fourth, a fifth area is similarly singled out and plastered

night after night, till, to use the language of the Chief of
Bomber Command with regard to Berlin, the heart of Nazi
Germany ceases to beat. How can there be discrimination
in such matters when civilians, monuments, military objectives and industrial objectives all together form the target?
How can the bombers aim at anything more than a great
space when they see nothing and the bombing is blind? . . .

I wish to offer a few concluding remarks on the policy
as a whole. It will be said that this area bombing . . . is
definitely designed to diminish the sacrifice of British lives
and to shorten the war. We all wish with all our hearts that
these two objects could be achieved, but to justify methods
inhumane in themselves by arguments of expediency smacks
of the Nazi philosophy that Might is Right. In any case the
idea that it will reduce the sacrifice is speculation. . . . If
there is one thing absolutely sure, it is that a combination
of the policy of obliteration with a policy of complete nega-
tion as to the future of a Germany which has got free from
Hitler is bound to prolong the war and make the period
after the war more miserable. . . .

Why is there this blindness on the psychological side?
Why is there this inability to reckon with the moral and
spiritual facts? Why is there this forgetfulness of the ideals
by which our cause is inspired? How can the War Cabinet
fail to see that this progressive devastation of cities is
threatening the roots of civilization? How can they be blind
to the harvest of even fiercer warring and desolation, even
in this country, to which the present destruction will inevitably lead when the members of the War Cabinet have
long passed to their rest? How can they fail to realize that
this is not the way to curb military aggression and end
war? This is an extraordinarily solemn moment. What we
do in war—which, after all, lasts a comparatively short
time—affects the whole character of peace, which covers a
much longer period. . . . The Allies stand for something

greater than power. The chief name inscribed on our banner is "Law." It is of supreme importance that we who, with our Allies, are the liberators of Europe should so use power that it is always under the control of law. It is because the bombing of enemy towns—this area bombing—raises the issue of power unlimited and exclusive that such immense importance is bound to attach to the policy and action of His Majesty's Government. . . .

THE SECRETARY OF STATE FOR DOMINION AFFAIRS [Viscount Cranborne] said: My Lords, the right reverend Prelate, the Bishop of Chichester, in his very eloquent, moving, and sincere speech this afternoon, raised the question of our bombing policy towards enemy countries. If he asked for some assurance from His Majesty's Government that the purpose of these intensive attacks upon German cities is to hamper and, if possible, to bring to a standstill enemy war production, and not merely to sprinkle bombs broadcast with the object of damaging ancient monuments and spreading terror among the civilian population, I am very ready to give him that assurance. Indeed I am very happy to have the opportunity of doing so. . . .

. . . The hard, inescapable fact is that war is a horrible thing, and that it cannot be carried on without suffering, often caused to those who are not immediately responsible for causing the conflict. In the situation with which we are faced today we cannot expect to find means of conducting hostilities which do not involve suffering. What we have to do, to the best of our ability, is to weigh against each other how much suffering is going to be caused or saved by any action which we may feel obliged to take. . . .

The targets which have been attacked are the administrative centers, the great industrial towns, the ports and the centers of communication. These targets have been chosen with the definite object of making it more difficult for Germany and her Allies to carry on war. That is why the Royal Air Force attacked Essen, why it attacked Mannheim, Cologne, Hamburg, Magdeburg, Berlin and many other towns. Your Lordships will remember that we have never concentrated upon sleepy country towns and villages. That would not only have been unnecessarily brutal; it would have been entirely futile from our point of view. But I would emphasize this to the right reverend Prelate: the great centers of administration, of production and of communication are themselves military targets in a total war. You cannot escape that fact. . . .

Therefore, when considering what I fully agree is a most difficult question, I do ask the right reverend Prelate and other Lords not only to think of the Germans who are suffering from these raids, but to think also of the Russians and the Poles and the Czechs, the Dutch, the Belgians, the Norwegians, the Yugoslavs, the Greeks, the French and the Danes who are at present enduring terrible anguish at the hands of the Armies of the Axis. Every day, appalling stories flown in from the occupied countries of men, women and children who are being starved, subjected to fiendish tortures, mental and physical, at the hands of the German Secret Police, who are being slaughtered in droves. We must remember that. We must also remember our own soldiers and airmen who at present are engaged in mortal combat in Italy, and those others who are soon to engage in yet greater attacks in other parts of Europe. We must remember our men who are languishing at present in intolerable conditions in Japanese prison camps, and the soldiers and sailors of our Allies. Their lives are our responsibility.

I sometimes wondered as I listened to the right reverend Prelate—I appreciate his sincerity—whether he really wants to help these people, because if he does want to get them out of their misery he must accept the implications of that policy. The only way to end this horror is to beat our enemies rapidly and completely and restore enduring peace. That is the only way. From that aim we must not avert our eyes, however kind our hearts, however deep our sentiments. While, therefore, I deeply respect the high motives which have inspired the right reverend Prelate . . . I cannot hold out hope that we shall abate our bombing policy. On the contrary, we shall continue it against proper and suitable targets with increasing power and more crushing effects until that final victory is achieved. So alone, in my view, shall we be able to fulfil our obligations to our people, to our Allies, and to the world. . . .

III

THE PACIFIST TRADITION

"Hear me, my warriors; my heart is sick and sad.
Our chiefs are killed;
The old men are all dead;
It is cold, and we have no blankets;
The little children are freezing to death.
Hear me, my warriors; my heart is sick and sad.
From where the sun now stands, I will fight no more
forever."

—Chief Joseph

Desiderius Erasmus

ca.1466–1536

The greatest humanist of the Renaissance, the associate of the best minds of his age, the intimate of popes and princes, Erasmus of Rotterdam was also an articulate critic of society, particularly of its wars. His condemnations of war, as passionate as they are voluminous—his major statements being the *Querela Pacis* ("Complaint of Peace"), *Antipolemus,* and *Dulce Bellum Inexpertis* ("War is sweet to those who know it not")—are masterpieces of their kind.

Erasmus has usually been placed squarely in the center of the pacifist tradition; correctly so, but with an important qualification. He never rejected war absolutely, maintaining rather that wars to repel aggression, while admittedly rare, were unquestionably justified.

His denunciation of war was based on a combination of classical, evangelical, and prudential arguments. In a sense he invalidated much of the "just war" theory by "overloading" it, by taking certain of its criteria and demonstrating how they could not usually stand up to the test of reason when applied to concrete situations. Like his infamous contemporary, Machiavelli, whose *Prince* was attracting attention at the same time as Erasmus's own works, he insisted that governments be judged according to what they *did,* not by what they were *supposed* to do or say. It seemed to him pure cant to insist on combatants' having a righteous motive and on their fighting in a spirit of love; real men kill in hatred, not love. To require governments to put aside selfish motives is as realistic as sheep passing resolutions supporting vegetarianism in their dealing with wolves. Most important of all, war, to use an expression from nuclear "Newspeak," is counterproductive; the price it exacts from the innocent is invariably disproportionate to the hoped-for objective.

Erasmus expressed his abhorrence of war nowhere more emphatically than in the following selection from *The Education of a Christian Prince,* composed in 1516 for the instruction of the future Emperor Charles V. It is a resounding plea for rulers to

157

do something that, judging from the actions of Charles V and subsequent history, they have usually found distasteful: to think rationally and humanely and Christianly before plunging their peoples into war.

The Education of a Christian Prince:
"On Beginning War"

Although a prince ought nowhere to be precipitate in his plans, there is no place for him to be more deliberate and circumspect than in the matter of going to war. Some evils come from one source and others from another, but from war comes the shipwreck of all that is good and from it the sea of all calamities pours out. Then, too, no other misfortune clings so steadfastly. War is sown from war; from the smallest comes the greatest; from one comes two; from a jesting one comes a fierce and bloody one, and the plague arising in one place, spreads to the nearest peoples and is even carried into the most distant places.

A good prince should never go to war at all unless, after trying every other means, he cannot possibly avoid it. If he were of this mind, there would hardly be a war. Finally, if so ruinous an occurrence cannot be avoided, then the prince's main care should be to wage the war with as little calamity to his own people and as little shedding of Chrisian blood as may be, and to conclude the struggle as soon as possible. The really Christian prince will first weigh the great difference between man, who is an animal born for peace and good will, and beasts and monsters, who are born to predatory war; [he will weigh also] the difference between men and Christian men. Then let him think over how earnestly peace is to be sought and how honorable

From Erasmus, The Education of a Christian Prince, *trans. Lester K. Born (New York: Columbia University Press, 1936), Chapter XI. Reprinted by special permission.*

and wholesome it is; on the other hand [let him consider] how disastrous and criminal an affair war is and what a host of all evils it carries in its wake even if it is the most justifiable war—if there really is any war which can be called "just." Lastly, when the prince has put away all personal feelings, let him take a rational estimate long enough to reckon what the war will cost and whether the final end to be gained is worth that much—and if victory is certain, victory which does not always happen to favor the best causes. . . .

The wisdom of princes will be too costly for the world if they persist in learning from experience how dreadful war is, so that when they are old men, they may say: "I did not believe that war was so utterly destructive!" But— and I call God to witness—with what countless afflictions on the whole world have you learned that idea! The prince will understand some day that it was useless to extend the territory of the kingdom and that what in the beginning seemed a gain was [in reality] tremendous loss, but in the meantime a great many thousands of men have been killed or impoverished. These things should better be learned from books, from the stories of old men, from the tribulations of neighbors. . . .

Some princes deceive themselves that any war is certainly a just one and that they have a just cause for going to war. We will not attempt to discuss whether war is ever just; but who does not think his own cause just? Among such great and changing vicissitudes of human events, among so many treaties and agreements which are now entered into, now rescinded, who can lack a pretext—if there is any real excuse—for going to war? But the pontifical laws do not disapprove of war. Augustine approves of it in some instances, and St. Bernard praises some soldiers. But Christ himself and Peter and Paul everywhere teach the opposite. Why is their authority less with us than that

of Augustine and Bernard? Augustine in one or two places
does not disapprove of war, but the whole philosophy of
Christ teaches against it. There is no place in which the
apostles do not condemn it; and in how many places do
those very holy fathers, by whom, to the satisfaction of
some, war has been approved in one or two places, condemn and abhor it? Why do we slur over all these matters
and fasten upon that which helps our sins? Finally, if any
one will investigate the matter more carefully, he will find
that no one has approved the kind of wars in which we
are now commonly involved.

Certain arts are not countenanced by the laws on the
ground that they are too closely allied to imposture and
are too frequently practiced by deceit; for example, astrol-
ogy and the so-called "alchemy," even if someone happens
to be employing them for an honorable purpose. This restriction will be made with far more justice in the case of
wars, for even if there are some which might be called
"just," yet as human affairs are now, I know not whether
there could be found any of this sort—that is, the motive
for which was not ambition, wrath, ferocity, lust, or greed.
It too often happens that nobles, who are more lavish than
their private means allow, when the opportunity is presented stir up war in order to replenish their resources at
home even by the plunder of their peoples. It happens
sometimes that princes enter into mutual agreements and
carry on a war on trumped-up grounds so as to reduce still
more the power of the people and secure their own positions through disaster to their subjects. Wherefore the good
Christian prince should hold under suspicion every war, no
matter how just.

People may lay down the doctrine that your rights must
not be forsaken. In the first place those rights are connected to a large extent with the private affairs of the prince
if he has acquired them through alliances. How unfair it

would be to maintain them at the expense of such great suffering to the people; and while you are seeking some addition or other to your power, to plunder the whole kingdom and to plunge it into deadliest turmoil. If one prince offends another on some trivial matter (probably a personal one such as a marriage alliance or other like affair) what concern is this to the people as a whole? A good prince measures everything by the advantage of his people, otherwise he is not even a prince. He does not have the same right over men as over animals. A large part of the ruling authority is the consent of the people, which is the factor that first created kings. If a disagreement arises between princes, why not go to arbiters? There are plenty of bishops, abbots, and learned men, or reliable magistrates, by whose judgment the matter could better be settled than by such slaughter, despoliation, and calamity to the world.

The Christian prince must first question his own right, and then if it is established without a doubt, he should carefully consider whether it should be maintained by means of catastrophes to the whole world. Those who are wise sometimes prefer to lose a thing rather than to gain it, because they realize that it will be less costly. . . . But what will be safe, they say, if no one maintains his rights? Let the prince insist by all means, if there is any advantage to the state, only do not let the right of the prince bear too hard on his subjects. But what is safe anywhere while everyone is maintaining his rights to the last ditch? We see wars arise from wars, wars following wars, and no end or limit to the upheaval! It is certainly obvious that nothing is accomplished by these means. Therefore other remedies should be given a trial. Not even between the best of friends will relations remain perfectly harmonious unless sometimes one gives in to the other. A husband often makes some concession to his wife so as not to break their harmony. What does war cause but war? Courtesy, on the other hand, calls forth courtesy, and fairness, fairness. . . .

After the prince has reckoned and added up the total of all the catastrophies [which would come] to the world (if that could ever be done), then he should think over in his own mind: "Shall I, one person, be the cause of so many calamities? Shall I alone be charged with such an outpouring of human blood; with causing so many widows; with filling so many homes with lamentation and mourning; with robbing so many old men of their sons; with impoverishing so many who do not deserve such a fate; and with such utter destruction of morals, laws, and practical religion? Must I account for all these things before Christ?" The prince cannot punish his enemy unless he first brings hostile activities upon his own subjects. He must fleece his people, and he must receive [into his realm] the soldier, who has been called ruthless (and not without justification) by Vergil. He must cut off his subjects from those districts which they formerly enjoyed for their own advantage; [or else the reverse], he must shut up his subjects in order to hem in the enemy. And it frequently happens that we inflict worse sufferings upon our own people than upon the enemy. It is more difficult, as well as more desirable, to build a fine city than to destroy it. But we see flourishing cities which were established by inexperienced and common people, demolished by the wrath of princes. Very often we destroy a town with greater labor and expense than that with which we could build a new one, and we carry on war with such great expense, such zeal, such pains, that peace could be maintained at one-tenth of these costs. . . .

We have written elsewhere more extensively on the evils of war and should not repeat here. I will only urge princes of Christian faith to put aside all feigned excuses and all false pretexts and with wholehearted seriousness to work for the ending of that madness of war which has persisted so long and disgracefully among Christians, that among those whom so many ties unite there may arise a peace and concord. Let them develop their genius to this end, and for this let them show their strength, combine their plans, and strain every nerve. Whoever desires to appear great, let him prove himself great in this way. If any one accomplishes this, he will have done a deed far more magnificent than if he had subdued the whole of Africa by arms.

Jonathan Dymond
1796–1828

The death of Jonathan Dymond at the age of thirty-two cut short a promising career as a philosopher and moralist. Yet his influence persisted in peace circles until the twentieth century, for besides helping to found peace organizations in his native England, his writings were a source of inspiration to the American peace movement. Originally published in 1828, after his death, as part of a larger and unfinished work *(Essays on the Principles of Morality and on the Private and Political Rights and Obligations of Mankind), Dymond on War* (as it is called for short) became a standard work for the Society of Friends. In slightly over a hundred pages, every argument for and against war is presented and analyzed in a Christian perspective. There is little, if anything, in it that is not applicable to the contemporary debate.

The following excerpt, on the incompatibility of self-defense with Christianity, is especially significant because it strikes at the "natural law" argument legitimatizing violence under certain conditions, an argument accepted even by Erasmus. According to Dymond, the fact that all creatures have certain natural propensities does not mean that *men* should always be led by them; indeed these propensities were subsumed for men under the higher law of the Gospel. Violent self-defense and war, its logical outgrowth, were therefore forbidden to Christians. On another level, Dymond recognized that, when once commenced, violence follows an inexorable logic leading to its expansion in ever-widening circles. There always reaches a point where "protective reactions" and "defensive wars" pass over into aggression. Finally, human nature being what it is, Dymond affirmed that preparations for self-defense must set in motion a self-fulfilling prophecy, inasmuch as others will regard these preparations as aimed *at* them, and they will react accordingly.

Self-Defense Incompatible with Christianity

The lawfulness of defensive war is commonly simplified to *The Right of Self-Defense*. This is one of the strongholds of the defender of war, the almost final fastness to which he retires. *The instinct of self-preservation, it is said, is an instinct of nature; and since this instinct is implanted by God, whatever is necessary to self-preservation is accordant with his will.* This is specious, but like many other specious arguments, it is sound in its premises, but, as I think, fallacious in its conclusions. That the instinct of self-preservation is an instinct of nature is clear—that, because it is an instinct of nature, we have a right to kill other men, is *not* clear.

The fallacy of the whole argument appears to consist in this, that it assumes that an instinct of nature is a law of *paramount* authority. God has implanted in the human system various propensities or instincts, of which the purposes are wise. These propensities tend in their own nature to *abuse;* and when gratified or followed to excess, they become subversive of the purposes of the wisdom which implanted them, and destructive of the welfare of mankind. He has therefore instituted a *superior* law, sanctioned by his immediate authority: by this law, we are required to regulate these propensities. The question therefore is, not

From Jonathan Dymond, An Enquiry into the Accordancy of War with the Principles of Christianity *(Philadelphia, 1828).*

whether the instinct of self-preservation is implanted by nature, but whether Christianity has restricted its operation. . . .

The establishment of this position is, indeed, the great object of the present inquiry. What are the dispositions and actions to which the instinct of self-preservation prompts, but actions and dispositions which Christianity forbids? They are non-forbearance, resistance, retaliation of injuries. The truth is, that it is to *defense* that the peaceable precepts of Christianity are directed. *Offence* appears not to have even suggested itself. It is "Resist not *evil*"; it is "Overcome *evil* with good"; it is "Do good to them that *hate* you"; it is "Love your *enemies*"; it is "Render not evil for *evil*"; it is "Whoso *smiteth thee on one cheek.*" All this supposes previous offence, or injury, or violence; and it is *then* that forebearance is enjoined. . . .

. . . The case of an assassin will doubtless be brought against me. I shall be asked—Suppose a ruffian breaks into your house, and rushes into your room with his arm lifted to murder you, do you not believe that Christianity allows you to kill him? This is the last refuge of the cause; my answer to it is explicit—*I do not believe it.* . . .

The mode of proving, or of stating, the right to kill an assassin, is this: "There is one case in which all extremities are justifiable; namely, when our life is assaulted, and it becomes necessary for our preservation to kill the assailant. This is evident in a state of nature; unless it can be shown that we are bound to prefer the aggressor's life to our own; that is to say, to love our enemy *better* than ourselves, which can never be a debt of justice nor anywhere appears to be a duty of charity."[1] If I were disposed to hold argumentation like this, I would say, that although we may not be required to love our enemies *better* than ourselves, we are re-

1. A quotation from William Paley (1743-1805), author of the influential *Principles of Moral and Political Philosophy* (1785).—Ed.

quired to love them *as* ourselves; and that in the supposed case, it still would be a question equally balanced, which life ought to be sacrificed; for it is quite clear, that if we kill the assailant, we love him *less* than ourselves, which may, perhaps, militate a little against "a duty of charity." But the truth is, that the question is not whether we should love our enemy better than ourselves, but whether we should sacrifice the laws of Christianity in order to preserve our lives—whether we should prefer the interests of religion to our own—whether we should be willing to "lose our life, for Christ's sake and the gospel's."

This system of *counter-crime* is of very loose tendency. The assailant violates his duties by attemping to kill me, and I, therefore, am to violate mine by actually killing him. Is his meditated crime, then, a justification of my perpetrated crime? In the case of a condemned Christian martyr who was about to be led to the stake, it is supposable, that in having contrived a mine, he may preserve his life by suddenly firing it and blowing his persecutors into the air. Would Christianity justify the act? Or what should we say of him if he committed it? We should say that whatever his *faith* might be, his *practice* was very unsound; that he might *believe* the gospel, but that he certainly did not fulfil its duties. Now I contend that for all the purposes of the argument, the cases of the martyr and the assaulted person are precisely similar. He who was about to be led to the stake, and he who was about to lose his life by the assassin, are both required to regulate their conduct by the same laws, and are both to be prepared to offer up their lives in testimony of their allegiance to Christianity: the one in allegiance to her, in opposition to the violation of her moral principles and her moral spirit; and the other, in opposition to errors in belief or to ecclesiastical corruptions. It is therefore in vain to tell me that the victim of persecution would have suffered for religion's sake, for so also would the victim of the ruffian. There is nothing in the sanctions of Christianity which implies that obedience to her moral law is of less consequence than of adherence to her faith; nor, as it respects the welfare of the world, does the consequence appear to be less; for he who, by his fidelity to Christianity, promotes the diffusion of Christian dispositions and of peace, contributes, perhaps, as much to the happiness of mankind, as he who by the same fidelity recommends the acceptance of an accurate creed.

A great deal hangs upon this question, and it is therefore necessary to pursue it farther. We say, then, first—that Christianity has not declared that we are ever at liberty to kill other men: secondly—that she virtually prohibits it, because her principles and the practice of our Saviour are not compatible with it: and, thirdly—that if Christianity allowed it, she would in effect and in practice allow *war*, without restriction to defense of life.

The first of these positions will probably not be disputed: and upon the second, that Christianity virtually prohibits the destruction of human life . . . I would . . . only observe, that the conduct of the Founder of Christianity, when his *enemies approached him "with swords and staves,"* appears to apply strictly to self-defense. These armed men came with the final purpose of murdering him; and although he knew this purpose, he would not suffer the assailants to be killed or even to be wounded. Christ, therefore, would not preserve his own life by sacrificing another's.

But we say, thirdly, that if Christianity allows us to kill one another in self-defense, she allows *war,* without restriction to self-defense. Let us try what would have been the result if the Christian Scriptures had thus placed human life at our disposal: suppose they had said, *You may kill a ruffian in your own defense, but you may not enter into a defensive war.* The prohibition would admit, not of *some* exceptions to its application—the exceptions would be so many, that no prohibition would be left; because there is no practical limit to the right of self-defense, until we arrive at defensive war. If one man may kill one, two may kill two, and ten may kill ten, and an army may kill an army: and this is defensive *war*. Supposing, again, the Christian Scriptures had said, *An army may fight in its own defense, but not for any other purpose*. We do not say that the exceptions to *this* rule would be so many as wholly to nullify the rule itself; but we say that whoever will attempt to apply it in practice, will find that he has a very wide range of justifiable warfare; a range that will embrace many more wars than moralists, laxer than we shall suppose him to be, are willing to defend. If an army may fight in defense of their own lives, they may and they must fight in defense of the lives of others; if they may fight in defense of the lives of others, they may fight in defense of their property; if in defense of their property, they will fight in defense of political rights; if in defense of political rights, they will fight in promotion of interests; if in promotion of interests, they will fight in promotion of their glory and their crimes. Now let any man of honesty look over the gradations by which we arrive at this climax, and I believe he will find that, *in practice*, no curb can be placed upon the conduct of an army until they reach it. There is, indeed, a wide distance between fighting in defense of life and fighting to further our crimes; but the steps which lead from one to the other will follow in inevitable succession. I know that the letter of our rule excludes it, but I know the rule will be a letter only. It is very easy for us to sit in our studies, and to point the commas, and semicolons, and periods of the soldier's career; it is very easy for us to say he shall stop at defense of life, or at protection of property, or at the support of rights; but armies will never listen to us—we shall be only the Xerxes of morality throwing our idle chains into the tempestuous ocean of slaughter.

What is the testimony of experience? When nations are mutually exasperated, and armies are levied, and battles are fought, does not everyone know that with whatever motives of defense one party may have begun the contest, both, in turn, become aggressors? In the fury of slaughter, soldiers do not attend, they cannot attend, to questions of aggression. Their business is destruction, and their business they will perform. If the army of defense obtains success, it soon becomes an army of aggression. Having repelled the invader, it begins to punish him. If a war is once begun, it is vain to think of distinctions of aggression and defense. Moralists may *talk* of distinctions, but soldiers will *make* none; and none can be made; it is without the limits of possibility.

But, indeed, what is defensive war? A celebrated moralist [Paley] defines it to be, war undertaken in consequence of "*an injury* perpetrated, attempted, or feared"; which shows with sufficient clearness how little *the assassin* concerns the question, for fear repecting life does not enter into the calculation of "injuries." So, then, if we fear some injury to our purses, or to our "honor," we are allowed to send an army to the country that gives us fear, and to slaughter its inhabitants; and this, we are told, is defensive war. By this system of reasoning, which has happily been called "martial logic," there will be little difficulty in proving any war to be defensive. Now we say that if Christianity allows defensive war, she allows all war—except indeed that of simple aggression; and by the rules of this morality, the aggressor is difficult of discovery; for he whom we choose to "fear" may say that he had previous "fear" of us, and that his "fear" prompted the hostile symptoms which made us "fear" again. The truth is, that to attempt to make any distinctions upon the subject is vain. War must be wholly forbidden, or allowed without restriction to defense; for no definitions of lawful or unlawful war will be, or can be, attended to. If the principles of Christianity, in any case, or for any purpose, allow armies to meet and to slaughter one another, her principles will never conduct us to the period which prophecy has assured us they shall produce. There is no hope of an eradication of war but by an absolute and total abandonment of it.

What then is the principle for which we contend? *An unreasoning reliance upon Providence for defense, in all those cases in which we should violate his laws by defending ourselves.* The principle can claim a species of merit, which must at least be denied to some systems of morality —that of simplicity, of easiness of apprehension, of adaptation to every understanding, of applicability to every circumstance of life.

Charles Sumner
1811–1874

Senator from Massachusetts, chairman of the powerful Foreign Relations Committee, an accomplished orator, a man of learning and culture, Charles Sumner was one of the leading political figures of his day. He was also one of the most disliked. His lumping together of Southern slave holders and Northern cotton manufacturers—"the lords of the lash and the lords of the loom," as he once described them—alienated the powerful, but won him a devoted popular following. His passion for justice brought him much physical suffering. After Sumner had made a long speech denouncing the Kansas–Nebraska Act, in which he spoke of "the rape of a virgin territory" and characterized his opponents as "skunks," an irate politician accosted him in the nearly empty Senate chamber and beat him senseless with a cane, incapacitating him for months.

No less a critic of war—"there can be no peace that is not

honorable . . . no war that is not dishonorable"—he approached this problem as a public man and as a Christian. Although he admitted that human life may be defended at the cost of human life, and that he personally could not rise to the requirements of the Gospel, Sumner remains an outstanding representative of the optimistic pacifism of the nineteenth century. Whereas Dymond and the absolute pacifists interpreted the Gospel as imposing a standard basically at variance with man's natural proclivities, Sumner took the opposite tack. For him, war was discredited precisely because the law of God was confirmed in human nature. Moreover, since wars were the consequence of the predominance of the animal part of our nature, and since the nineteenth century saw the enthronement of science and reason, the time had come for man to abandon his animal self and live in accordance with his divine self.

A good place to start, Sumner affirmed in 1845 in an oration before the Boston city authorities, would be with the vast accumulations of armaments. The Roman proverb *Si vis pacem para bellum* ("If you wish for peace prepare for war") was a damnable heresy. It denied that spark of divine rationality in man, and therefore his true nature, dooming him to an eternal cycle of fear, armament, and war. Sumner's insight has gained rather than lost significance since his own day; for the application of science (hitherto revered) to warfare has lent momentum to the cycle, shortening the time between wars and increasing the ferocity of each succeeding war.

"Si Vis Pacem Para Bellum"

The sentiment, that in time of peace we must prepare for war, has been transmitted from distant ages when brute force prevailed. It is the terrible inheritance, the *damnosa hæreditas,* which painfully reminds the people of our day of their relations with the Past. It belongs to the rejected

From Charles Sumner, The True Grandeur of Nations: An Oration Delivered Before the Authorities of the City of Boston, July 4, 1845 *(Boston, 1845).*

dogmas of barbarism. It is the companion of those harsh rules of tyranny by which the happiness of so many has been offered up to the propensities of the few. It is the child of Suspicion and the forerunner of Violence. Having in its favor the almost uninterrupted usage of the world, it possesses a hold on the common mind, which is not easily unloosed. And yet the conscientious soul cannot fail, on careful observation, to detect its most mischievous fallacy —a fallacy the most costly the world has witnessed, and which dooms nations to annual tributes in comparison with which all that have been extorted by conquests are as the widow's mite by the side of Pharisaical contributions. . . .

Dismissing from our minds, the actual usage of nations on the one side, and the considerations of economy on the other, and regarding preparations for war in time of Peace in the clear light of reason, in a just appreciation of the nature of man, and in the injunctions of the highest truth, . . . they cannot fail to be branded as most pernicious. They are pernicious on two grounds; *first,* because they inflame the people, who make them, exciting them to deeds of violence which otherwise would be most alien to their minds; and *second,* because having their origin in the low motive of distrust and hate, they inevitably, by a sure law of the human mind, excite a corresponding feeling in other nations. Thus they are in fact not the *preservers of peace,* but the *provokers of war.*

In illustration of the *first* of these grounds, it will occur to every inquirer, that the possession of power is always in itself dangerous, that it tempts the purest and highest natures to self-indulgence, that it can rarely be enjoyed without abuse; nor is the power to employ Force in war, or otherwise, an exception to this law. History teaches that the nations possessing the greatest military forces, have always been the most belligerent; while the feebler powers have enjoyed, for a longer period, the blessings of Peace.

The din of war resounds throughout more than seven hundred years of Roman history, with only two short lulls of repose; while smaller states, less potent in arms, and without the excitement to quarrels on this account, have enjoyed long eras of Peace. . . .

The *second* of these grounds is a part of the unalterable nature of man, which was recognized in early ages, though unhappily it has been rarely made the basis of intercourse among nations. It is an expansion of the old Horatian adage, *Si vis me flere, priman flendum est tibi;* if you wish me to weep, you must yourself first weep. So are we all knit together, the feelings in our own bosom awaken corresponding feelings in the bosom of others; as harp answers to harp in its softest vibrations; as deep responds to deep in the might of its passions. What within us is good invites the good in our brother; generosity begets generosity; love wins love; Peace secures Peace; while all within us that is bad challenges the bad in our brother; distrust engenders distrust; hate provokes hate; War arouses War. Life is full of illustrations of this beautiful law. Even the miserable maniac, in whose mind the common rules of conduct are overthrown, confesses its overruling power, and the vacant stare of madness may be illuminated by a word of love. The wild beasts confess it; and what is the interesting story of Orpheus, whose music drew, in listening rapture, the lions and panthers of the forest, but an expression of this prevailing law? . . . Thus, from all quarters . . . ascends the spontaneous tribute to the prevailing power of that law, according to which the human heart responds to the feelings by which it is addressed, whether of confidence or distrust, of love or hate.

It will be urged that these instances are exceptions to the general laws by which mankind are governed. It is not so. They are the unanswerable evidence of the real nature of man. They reveal the Divinity of Humanity, out of which all goodness, all happiness, all true greatness can alone proceed. They disclose susceptibilities which are general, which are confined to no particular race of men, to no period of time, to no narrow circle of knowledge and refinement—susceptibilities which are present wherever two or more human beings come together. It is, then, on the impregnable ground of the universal and unalterable nature of man, that I place the fallacy of that prejudice, in obedience to which, in time of peace we prepare for war.

But this prejudice is not only founded on a misconception of the nature of man; it is abhorrent to Christianity. . . .

. . . Christianity not only preaches the superiority of Love over Force; it positively enjoins the practice of the one, and the rejection of the other. It says, "Love your neighbors"; but it does not say; "In time of Peace rear massive fortification, build the man of war, enlist armies, train the militia, and accumulate military stores to be employed in future quarrels with your neighbors." . . . But its precepts go still further. They enjoin patience, suffering, forgiveness of evil, even the duty of benefitting the destroyer, "as the sandal wood, in the instant of its overthrow, sheds perfume on the axe which fells it." And can a people, in whom this faith is more than an idle word, consent to such enormous sacrifices of money, in violation of its plainest precepts?

The injunction, "Love one another," is applicable to nations as well as individuals. It is one of the great laws of Heaven. And any one may well measure his nearness to God by the degree to which he regulates his conduct by this truth.

In response to these successive views, founded on considerations of economy, of the true nature of man, and of Christianity, I hear the sceptical note of some defender of the transmitted order of things; some one who wishes "to fight for Peace,' saying, these views are beautiful, but visionary; they are in advance of the age; the world is not yet prepared for their reception. To such persons (if there be such) I would say, nothing can be beautiful that is not true; but these views are true; the time has now come for their reception; now is the day and now is the hour. Every effort to impede their progress arrests the advancing hand on the great dial-plate of human happiness. . . . Let us, while we recognize those transcendant ordinances of God, the *Law of Right,* and the *Law of Love*—the double suns which illuminate the moral universe—aspire to the true glory, and what is greater than glory, the great good, of taking the lead in the disarming of the nations. Let us abandon the system of preparation for war, in time of Peace, as irrational, unchristian, vainly prodigal of expense, and having a direct tendency to excite the very evil against which it professes to guard. Let the enormous means thus released from iron hands, be devoted to labors of beneficence. Our battlements shall be schools, hospitals, colleges and churches; our arsenals shall be libraries; our navy shall be peaceful ships on errands of perpetual commerce; our army shall be the teachers of youth, and the ministers of religion. This is indeed, the cheap defense of nations. In such entrenchments what Christian soul can be touched by fear. Angels of the Lord shall throw over the land an invisible, but impenetrable panoply;

> Or if virtue feeble were
> Heaven itself would stoop to her.
>
> [Milton, *Comus*]

At the thought of such a change in policy, the imagination loses itself in the vain effort to follow the various streams of happiness, which gush forth as from a thousand hills. Then shall the naked be clothed and the hungry fed.

Institutions of science and learning shall crown every hilltop; hospitals for the sick, and other retreats for the unfortunate children of the world, for all who suffer in any way, in mind, body or estate, shall nestle in every valley; while the spires of new churches shall leap exulting to the skies. The whole land shall bear witness to the change; art shall confess it in the new inspiration of the canvas and the marble; the harp of the Poet shall proclaim it in a loftier rhyme. Above all, the heart of man shall bear witness to it, in the elevation of his sentiments, in the expansion of his affections, in his devotion to the higher truth, in his appreciation of true greatness. The eagle of our country, without the terror of his beak, and dropping the forceful thunderbolt from his pounces, shall soar with the olive of Peace, into untried realms of ether, nearer to the sun. . . .

William Ellery Channing
1780–1842

Based in the New England and Middle Atlantic states, the American peace crusade in its heyday, from the establishment of the American Peace Society in 1828 (the year *Dymond on War* appeared) to the Civil War, included the lights of the intellectual and religious communities. Among them, none was as respected and honored by his peers as William Ellery Channing, who was also a moving spirit in the development of Unitarianism in the United States.

In a hard-hitting series of lectures and sermons, which were still in print and enjoying a wide circulation sixty years after his death, Channing set out to demolish the prevailing commonplaces about war. Whereas Erasmus, Dymond, and Sumner denounced war for prudential reasons and as contrary to human nature, questioning the validity of self-defense for the Christian, Channing had a peculiarly American (for the 1830's) distrust of institutions and officialdom. Like Huck Finn's father, he was "agin' the guv'mnt." In a tone almost Niebuhrian, he affirmed that, since the collectivity is always and everywhere bound to function on a lower level morally than the individual, the state this side of Utopia and whatever its constitution, will seek to be judge, jury, and executioner in its own cause.

Of particular interest to the twentieth-century reader is the fact that Channing also had a peculiarly American faith in the U.S. Constitution and the republican form of government. When coupled with a Christian sense of injustice, the freedom of speech guaranteed by the Constitution must find expression through the ballot, also constitutionally guaranteed. No brow-beating by the administration or pleas for national solidarity in the face of the foe should be permitted to still the voice of dissent. Only in this way can a free people end an unjust war and check their leaders, of whom Channing said (long before Lord Acton coined his famous aphorism): "Power has ever a tendency to corrupt, to feed an irregular ambition, to harden the heart against the claims and sufferings of mankind."

The State and Individual Duty

The right of war, which is said to belong to sovereignty, not only keeps out of sight the enormous guilt of rulers in almost all national conflicts; it also hides or extenuates the frequent guilt of subjects in taking part in the hostilities which their rulers declare. In this way much of the prevalent insensibility to the evils of war is induced, and perhaps on no point is light more needed. The ferocity and cruelty of armies impress us little, because we look on them as doing a work of duty. The subject or citizen, as we think, is bound to obey his rulers. In his worst deeds as a soldier he is discharging his obligations to the state; and thus murder and pillage, covered with a cloak of duty, excite no deep, unaffected reprobation and horror. . . .

From William Ellery Channing, "Lecture on War" and "The Citizen's Duty in a war Which He Condemns," in Discourses on War, ed., Edwin D. Mead (Boston: Ginn & Co., 1903).

I maintain that the citizen, before fighting, is bound to inquire into the justice of the cause which he is called to maintain with blood, and bound to withhold his hand if his conscience condemn the cause. On this point he is able to judge. No political question, indeed, can be determined so easily as this of war. War can be judged only by plain, palpable necessity; by unquestionable wrongs, which, as patient trial has proved, can in no other way be redressed; by the obstinate, persevering invasion of solemn and unquestionable rights. The justice of war is not a mystery for cabinets to solve. It is not a state secret which we must take on trust. It lies within our reach. We are bound to examine it. . . .

. . . [Yet] the presumption is always against the justice and necessity of war. This we learn from the spirit of all rulers and nations towards foreign states. It is partial, unjust. Individuals may be disinterested; but nations have no feeling of the tie of brotherhood of their race. A base selfishness is the principle on which the affairs of nations are commonly conducted. A statesman is expected to take advantage of the weaknesses and wants of other countries. How loose a morality governs the intercourse of states! What falsehoods and intrigues are licensed diplomacy! What nation regards another with true friendship? What nation makes sacrifices to another's good? What nation is as anxious to perform its duties as to assert its rights? What nation chooses to suffer wrong, rather than to inflict it? What nation lays down the everlasting law of right, casts itself fearlessly on its principles, and chooses to be poor or perish rather than to do wrong? Can communities so selfish, so unfriendly, so unprincipled, so unjust, be expected to wage righteous wars? Especially if with this selfishness are joined national prejudices, antipathies, and exasperated passions, what else can be expected in the public policy but inhumanity and crime? An individual, we know, cannot be trusted in his own cause, to avenge his own wrongs; and the civil magistrate, an impartial umpire, has been substituted as the only means of justice. But nations are even more unfit than individuals to judge in their own cause; more prone to push their rights to excess, and to trample on the rights of others; because nations are crowds, and crowds are unawed by opinion, and more easily inflamed by sympathy into madness. Is there not, then, always a presumption against the justice of war?

The presumption is increased, when we consider the false notions of patriotism and honor which prevail in nations. Men think it a virtuous patriotism to throw a mantle, as they call it, over their country's infirmities, to wink at her errors, to assert her most doubtful rights, to look jealously and angrily on the prosperity of rival states; and they place her honor not in unfaltering adherence to the right, but in a fiery spirit, in quick resentment, in martial courage, and especially in victory; and can a good man hold himself bound to stand prepared to engage in war at the dictate of such a state? . . .

Unhappily, public men under all governments are of all moral guides the most unsafe, the last for a Christian to follow. Public life is thought to absolve men from the strict obligations of truth and justice. To wrong an adverse party or another country is not reprobated as are wrongs in private life. Thus duty is dethroned; thus the majesty of virtue insulted in the administration of nations. . . . Public bodies want conscience. Men acting in masses shift off responsibility to one another. Multitudes never blush. If these things be true, then I maintain that the Christian has not a right to take part in war blindly, confidingly, at the call of his rulers. . . .

It becomes us to rejoice, my friends, that we live under a Constitution one great design of which is to prevent the necessity of appealing to force, to give the people an opportunity of removing without violence those rulers from whom they suffer or apprehend an invasion of rights. This is one of the principal advantages of a republic over an absolute government. . . ; [it] secures to its subjects this immense privilege of confirming to them two most important rights, the right of suffrage and the right of discussing with freedom the conduct of rulers. . . .

From the important place which these rights hold in a republican government you should consider yourselves bound to support every citizen in the exercise of them, especially when an attempt is made to wrest them from any by violent means. It is particularly your duty to guard with jealousy the right of expressing with freedom your honest convictions respecting the measures of your rulers. Without this the right of election is not worth possessing. If public abuses may not be exposed, their authors will never be driven from power. Freedom of opinion, of speech, and of the press is our most valuable privilege, the very soul of republican institutions, the safeguard of all other rights. . . . Nothing awakens and improves men so much as free communication of thoughts and feelings. Nothing can give to public sentiment that correctness which is essential to the prosperity of a commonwealth but the free circulation of truth from the lips and pens of the wise and good. If such men abandon the right of free discussion; if, awed by threats, they suppress their convictions; if rulers succeed in silencing every voice but that which approves them; if nothing reaches the people but what would lend support to men in power—farewell to liberty. The form of a free government may remain, but the life, the soul, the substance is fled.

We have heard the strange doctrine that to expose the measures of rulers is treason. The cry has been that, war being declared, all opposition should therefore be hushed.

A statement more unworthy of a free country can hardly be propagated. If this doctrine be admitted, rulers will have only to declare war, and they are screened at once from scrutiny. At the very time when they have armies at command, when their patronage is most extended and their power most formidable, not a word of warning, of censure, of alarm must be heard. The press, which is to expose inferior abuses, must not utter one rebuke, one indignant complaint, although our best interests and most valuable rights are put to hazard by an unnecessary war! Admit this doctrine, let rulers once know that by placing the country in a state of war they place themselves beyond the only power they dread—the power of free discussion—and we may expect war without end. Our peace and all our interests require that a different sentiment should prevail. We should teach all rulers that there is no measure for which they must render so solemn an account to their constituents as for a declaration of war; that no measure will be so freely, so fully discussed; that no administration can succeed in persuading this people to exhaust their treasure and blood in supporting war unless it be palpably necessary and just. In war, then, as in peace, assert the freedom of speech and of the press. Cling to this as the bulwark of all your rights and privileges.

Menno Simons
1494–1561

Originally a Roman Catholic priest in his native West Friesland, Menno Simons left his pulpit in 1536 to join the Anabaptists, so called because of their practice of rebaptizing adults. The year 1536 was not a good time to be known as an Anabaptist. Hunted as heretics and feared as wild revolutionaries (a tiny segment of this Europe-wide movement did display tendencies toward anarchism and apocalyptic war), the various Anabaptist communities were disorganized and leaderless. For the rest of his life, Menno strove to purge these communities of warlike elements and to weld the brethren of the Netherlands and north Germany into a constructive religious force.

The following excerpt, from his *Reply to False Accusations* (1552), is revealing on several counts. In addition to describing the sufferings of the "Mennonites" (for so they were being called even during his lifetime) and denouncing the true revolutionaries, the instigators of war and persecution, it deals with the doctrines characteristic of sectarian pacifism: the church-world antinomy, scriptural literalism, and total nonresistance. Whatever the price, the Christian is to shun the world and its government as the dominion of Satan; and the price exacted by the world for such independence was even more staggering than Menno indicates. But the Mennonites paid it, and in so doing were instrumental in wringing from the state a concession unheard of until their time, a concession of inestimable value and potential. Wherever in the West conscientious objection to military service has been legally allowed, the law was initially framed with an eye to removing the disabilities of the historic peace churches. The state recognized, in effect, the existence of persons other than clergy in the traditional sense, as well as special areas of human concern, that rightfully stand outside its purview.

Reply to False Accusations

They say that we are seditionists and that we would take cities and countries if we had the power.

ANSWER: This prophecy is false and will ever remain so; and by the grace of God, time and experience will prove

From The Complete Works of Menno Simons, *trans. Leonard Verduin (Scottdale, Penn.: The Herald Press, 1956). Reprinted with special permission.*

that those who thus prophesy according to the Word of Moses are not of God. Faithful reader, understand what I write.

The Scriptures teach that there are two opposing princes and two opposing kingdoms: the one is the Prince of peace; the other the prince of strife. Each of these princes has his particular kingdom and as the prince is so also is the kingdom. The Prince of peace is Christ Jesus; His kingdom is the kingdom of peace, which is His Church; His messengers are the messengers of peace; His Word is the word of peace; His body is the body of peace; His children are the seed of peace; and his inheritance and reward are the inheritance and reward of peace. In short, with this King, and in His kingdom and reign, it is nothing but peace. Everything that is seen, heard, and done is peace. . . .

Such exceeding grace of God has appeared unto us poor miserable sinners that we who were formerly no people at all and who knew no peace are now called to be such a glorious people of God, a church, kingdom, inheritance, body and possession of peace. Therefore we desire not to break this peace, but by this great power by which He has called us to this peace and portion, to walk in His grace and peace, unchangeably and unwaveringly unto death.

Peter was commanded to sheathe his sword. All Christians are commanded to love their enemies; to do good unto those who abuse and persecute them; to give the mantle when the cloak is taken, the other cheek when one is struck. Tell me, how can a Christian defend Scripturally retaliation, rebellion, war, striking, slaying, torturing, stealing, robbing and plundering and burning cities, and conquering countries?

The great Lord Who has created you and us, who has placed our hearts within us knows, and He only knows that our hearts and hands are clear of all sedition and murderous mutiny. By His grace we will ever remain clear. For we truly confess that all rebellion is of the flesh and of the devil.

O beloved reader, our weapons are not swords and spears, but patience, silence, and hope, and the Word of God. With these we must maintain our heavy warfare and fight our battle. Paul says, The weapons of our warfare are not carnal; but mighty through God. With these we must intend and desire to storm the kingdom of the devil; and not with swords, spears, cannon, and coats of mail. For He esteemeth iron as straw, and brass as rotten wood. Thus may we with our Prince, Teacher, and Example Christ Jesus, raise the father against the son, and the son against the father, and may we cast down imagination and every high thing that exalteth itself against the knowledge of God, and bring into captivity every thought in obedience to Christ.

True Christians do not know vengeance, no matter how they are mistreated. In patience they possess their souls. And they do not break their peace, even if they should be tempted by bondage, torture, poverty, and besides, by the sword and fire. They do not cry Vengeance, vengeance, as does the world; but with Christ they supplicate and pray: Father, forgive them; for they know not what they do.

According to the declaration of the prophets they have beaten their swords into plowshares and their spears into pruning hooks. They shall sit every man under his vine and under his fig-tree, Christ; neither shall they learn war any more.

They do not seek your money, goods, injury, nor blood, but they seek the honor and praise of God and the salvation of their souls. They are the children of peace; their hearts overflow with peace; their mouths speak peace, and they walk in the way of peace; they are full of peace. They seek, desire, and know nothing but peace; and are prepared to forsake country, goods, life, and all for the sake of peace. For they are the kingdom, people, congregation, city, property, and body of peace, as has been heard. . . .

In Brabant, Flanders, Friesland, and Gelderland the God-fearing pious hearts are led daily to the slaughter as innocent sheep, and are tyrannically and inhumanly martyred. Their hearts are full of spirit and strength; their mouths flow like rivulets; their conduct savors of holy oil; their doctrine is powerful; and their life is beyond reproach. Neither emperor nor king, fire nor sword, life nor death, can frighten or separate them from the Word of the Lord. And do you suppose that their hearts are even then still ensnared by bitterness, sedition, vengeance, plunder, hatred, and bloodshed? If that were the case, then there has been a lot of suffering for naught.

Oh, no, reader, no! Learn to know what a true Christian is, of whom he is born, how he is minded, what his real intention and ambition is, and you will find that they are not rebels, murderers, and robbers as the learned ones rave, but that they are God-fearing, pious, peaceable people as the Scriptures teach.

The other prince is the prince of darkness, Antichrist, and Satan. This prince is the prince of all tumult and blood. Raging and murder is his proper nature and policy. His commandments and teachings of his kingdom, body, and church are of the same nature. Here we need not much Scripture, for seeing, hearing, and daily experience prove the truth. . . .

The merciful and gracious Lord grant and give you and them wisdom that you may learn to know of what spirit and kingdom you are the children, what you seek, what prince you serve, what doctrine you maintain, what sacraments you have, what fruits you produce, what life you lead, and in what kingdom, body, and church you are incorporated. This is our sincere wish. . . .

Peter Ridemann
1506–1556

Peter Ridemann was born in a country town in Silesia, where he grew up and earned his living as a cobbler. At some time during his early twenties, he gave up his trade to devote his undivided attention to the Hutterite Brethren; indeed, he has been credited with being the second founder of the brotherhood. Named after Jakob Hutter, who was burned at the stake in Innsbruck in 1536, the brotherhood established its settlements in Moravia and Hungary, eventually migrating to Britain and the United States. Essentially like the Dutch Mennonites in theology, it differed from them in economic outlook and communal organization. Whereas the Mennonites were usually town-based artisans and merchants, the Hutterites lived in agricultural communities based on the common ownership of property, a custom largely abandoned by the eighteenth century.

The Hutterites were also more consistent in their peace principles. Whereas some Mennonites had by the seventeenth century become sufficiently prosperous to buy shares in the Dutch East India Company, whose merchantmen were armed with cannon, the Hutterites avoided any occasion for earthly contention. Fully two centuries before the Quaker John Woolman won fame for refusing to pay a Pennsylvania war tax, and four centuries before secular-minded war resisters in the United States began to deduct from their income tax returns the percentage going for military purposes, the Hutterites had incorporated this principle into their basic confession, Ridemann's *Account* of 1545. Beyond tax refusal, the Hutterites even forbade the cutlers in their community workshops to make any implements that could be used exclusively for war. Some professing Christians of the twentieth century, who during the week engage in the research and development of weapons systems and who on Sunday attend church, would undoubtedly have elicited from them a sad shaking of the head.

Huttcrite Principles and Practice

Concerning Governmental Authority

Governmental authority is appointed and ordained by God as a rod of his anger for the discipline and punishment of the evil and profligate nation. Therefore doth Paul name it the servant of God's vengeance, by means of which God will avenge himself on their sins and bring the evil they have done upon their own head, that their wickedness might not continue to spread and that the whole earth might not on their account become blcmished and unclean. . . .

Therefore is one rightly obedient and subject to them [rulers], and the more diligent one is therein, the better it is and the more pleasing to God. For whosoever resisteth this, resisteth the ordinance of God. Where, however, the rulers command and act against God, there one must leave their command undone, and obey God rather than man. For the conscience hath been set free and is reserved for God alone, that he and no human being may be Lord of the same and rule over, teach and direct it withersoever it pleaseth him. Therefore wherever the government presumeth to lay hands upon the conscience and control the faith of man, there it is robbing God of what is his. Therefore it is wrong to obey it in this. Now, since the office of government is an ordinance and establishment of God and because it hath been appointed and ordained by God, within its own limits it is right and good, but where it is abused, this same misuse is wrong. The office, nevertheless, re-

From the Account of Our Religion, Doctrine and Faith, Given by Peter Ridemann of the Brothers Whom Men Call Hutterians *(Rifton, N.Y.: The Plow Publishing House, 1970). Reprinted with special permission.*

maineth as it was ordained. Therefore is the office to be honoured. For, even though godless men fill it, the office is not thereby annulled. And God permitteth this to the godless for the greater punishment of the people. But just as a godless government is given to the nation by God as a punishment, even so is a disobedient nation given to the godless government, that they might tear and devour one another and at last be consumed together. . . .

Concerning Warfare

Now since Christ, the Prince of Peace, hath prepared and won for himself a kingdom, that is a Church, through his own blood; in this same kingdom all worldly warfare hath an end, as was promised aforetime, "Out of Zion shall go forth the law, and the word of the Lord from Jerusalem, and shall judge among the heathen and shall draw many peoples, so that they shall beat their swords into plowshares and their lances or spears into pruning hooks, sickles and scythes, for from thenceforth nation shall not lift up sword against nation, nor shall they learn war any more."

Therefore a Christian neither wages war nor wields the worldly sword to practice vengeance, as Paul also exhorteth us saying, "Dear brothers, avenge not yourselves, but rather give place unto the wrath of God, for the Lord saith, Vengeance is mine; I will repay it." Now if vengeance is God's and not ours, it ought to be left to him and not practised or exercised by ourselves. For, since we are Christ's disciples, we must show forth the nature of him who, though he could, indeed, have done so, repaid not evil with evil. For he could, indeed, have protected himself against his enemies, the Jews, by striking down with a single word all who wanted to make him captive.

But though he might well have done this, he did not

himself and would not permit others to do so. Therefore he said to Peter, "Put up thy sword into its place." Here one can see how our King setteth out with a powerful host against his enemy; how he defeateth the enemy and how he taketh vengeance; in that he taketh Malchus' ear, that had been struck off, and putteth it on again. And he who did this saith, "Whosoever will be my disciple, let him take his cross upon him and follow me."

Now, therefore, Christ desireth that we should act even as he did, so he commandeth us saying, "It hath been said to the men of old, 'An eye for an eye, and a tooth for a tooth,' but I say unto you, that ye resist not evil: but whosoever shall smite thee on thy right cheek, turn and offer to him the other also." Here it is clearly to be seen that one ought neither to avenge oneself nor go to war, but rather offer his back to the strikers and his cheeks to them that plucks off the hair—that is, suffer with patience and wait upon God, who is righteous, and who will repay it. . . .

Concerning Taxation

Since governmental authority is ordained by God and hath its office from him, the payment of taxes for this purpose is likewise ordained and commanded, as Paul saith, "Thus ye must also pay tribute." For this reason we, likewise, willingly pay taxes, tribute or whatever men may term it, and in no way oppose it, for we have learned this from our master, Christ, who not only paid it himself, but also commanded others to do so, saying, "Render unto Caesar what is Caesar's, and to God what is God's." Therefore we, as his disciples, desire with all diligence to follow and perform his command, and not to oppose the government in this.

But where taxes are demanded for the special purpose of going to war, massacring and shedding blood, we give nothing. This we do neither out of malice nor obstinacy but in the fear of God, that we make not ourselves partakers of other men's sins. If one should say, "But ye ought to pay tribute to whom tribute is due, therefore ye do wrong to refuse it," we answer: We do not at all refuse to render tribute to whom it is due, and in the way in which it is due. For God, as is said above, hath ordained that rulers receive taxes, which they have to collect and raise yearly. Therefore we do not refuse to pay the same. But that it followeth from the words of Paul that one should submit to every whim of the ruler is not the case. That this is true is shown by the words of Paul in the same passage, when he saith, "Render therefore to all their dues: tribute to whom tribute is due." He doth not say, "Render whatsoever and however much they want," but, "Render their dues." That is, the yearly taxes which are ordained by God. But what God hath not ordained, what is not regular taxation—that is given, not as a duty and as the ruler's due, but is given because one doth so willingly and because one agreeth thereto, or, in most cases, because one is pressed and coerced to do so.

Therefore the paying of such taxes followeth neither from this word nor from the word of Christ commanding to render to Caesar what is Caesar's. . . .

Concerning the Making of Swords

Since, as hath been said above, Christians should beat their swords into plowshares and take up arms no more—still less can they make the same, for they serve for naught else than to slay, harm and destroy men—and Christ hath not come to destroy men—therefore his disciples, also, refuse to do so; for he saith, "Know ye not of what Spirit ye are the children?" as though he would say, "Doth the

Spirit of grace teach you to destroy, or will ye walk according to the flesh and forsake the Spirit, whose children ye have become? Know ye not that I am not come to destroy men? If ye will be my disciples, ye must let my Spirit rule over you and not walk after the flesh. For he who obeyeth the flesh cannot please God."

Now, since Christians must not use and practice such vengeance, neither can they make the weapons by which such vengeance and destruction may be practiced by others, that they be not partakers of other men's sins. Therefore we make neither swords, spears, muskets nor any such weapons. What, however, is made for the benefit and daily use of man, such as bread knives, axes, hoes and the like, we both can and do make. Even if one were to say, "But one could therewith harm and slay others," still they are not made for the purpose of slaying and harming, so there is naught to prevent our making them. If any should ever be used to harm another, we do not share the harmer's guilt, so let him bear the judgment himself.

The Anabaptists

Because they were constantly harassed and charged with being bad citizens, the Anabaptists tended in their confessions of faith to be fuller in their treatment of civil government than were other Protestant bodies. The confession presented here, addressed "to the children of light . . . scattered everywhere," represents the position of the Swiss Brethren. It was composed in February, 1527, by Michael Sattler, a leader of early Anabaptism who was martyred under horrible circumstances shortly thereafter. The first Anabaptist confession of faith, it consists of seven articles dealing for the most part with doctrinal matters; the sixth and longest article deals with the sword. As used here, the term "sword" means more than just the weapon. It means also the magistrate and the power vested in him by God for the governance of the world; and for precisely this reason it is "outside the perfection of Christ" and prohibited to those who would follow Him.

The Schleitheim Confession

SIXTH [ARTICLE]: We are agreed as follows concerning the sword: The sword is ordained of God outside the perfection of Christ. It punishes and puts to death the wicked, and guards and protects the good. In the Law the sword was ordained for the punishment of the wicked and for their death, and the same [sword] is [now] ordained to be used by the worldly magistrates.

In the perfection of Christ, however, only the ban is used for a warning and for the excommunication of the one who has sinned, without putting the flesh to death, simply the warning and the command to sin no more.

Now it will be said by many who do not recognize [this as] the will of Christ for us, whether a Christian may or should employ the sword against the wicked for the defense and protection of the good, or for the sake of love.

Our reply is unanimously as follows: Christ teaches and commands us to learn of Him, for He is meek and lowly in heart and so we shall find rest to our souls. Also Christ says to the heathenish woman who was taken in adultery, not that one should stone her according to the law of His Father (and yet He says, As the Father has commanded me, thus I do), but in mercy and forgiveness and warning, to sin no more. Such [an attitude] we also ought to take completely according to the rule of the ban.

Secondly, it will be asked concerning the sword, whether a Christian shall pass sentence in worldly dispute and strife such as unbelievers have with one another. This is

From William L. Lumpkin (Ed.), Baptist Confessions of Faith (Chicago: Judson Press, 1959). Reprinted by special permission.

our united answer: Christ did not wish to decide or pass judgment between brother and brother in the case of the inheritance, but refused to do so. Therefore we should do likewise.

Thirdly, it will be asked concerning the sword, Shall one be a magistrate if one should be chosen as such? The answer is as follows: They wished to make Christ king, but He fled and did not view it as the arrangement of His Father. Thus we shall do as He did, and follow Him, and so shall we not walk in darkness. For He Himself forbids [the employment of] the force of the sword saying, The worldly princes lord it over them, etc., but not so shall it be with you. Further, Paul says, Whom God did foreknow He also did predestinate to be conformed to the image of His son, etc. Also Peter says, Christ has suffered (not ruled) and left us an example, that ye should follow His steps.

Finally, it will be observed that it is not appropriate for a Christian to serve as a magistrate because of these points: The government magistracy is according to the flesh, but the Christians' is according to the Spirit; their houses and dwelling remain in this world, but the Christians' citizenship is in heaven; the weapons of their conflict are carnal and against the flesh only, but the Christians' weapons are spiritual, against the fornication of the devil. The worldlings are armed with steel and iron, but the Christians are armed with the armor of God. In brief, as is the mind of Christ toward us, so shall the mind of the members of the body of Christ be through Him in all things, that there may be no schism in the body through which it would be destroyed. For every kingdom divided against itself will be destroyed. Now since Christ is as it is written of Him, His members must also be the same, that His body may remain complete and united to its own advancement and upbuilding.

George Fox
1624–1691

George Fox was born to working class parents in Leicestershire, England. Apprenticed to a shoemaker, at the age of nineteen he underwent a spiritual crisis and, obeying the promptings of his heart, set forth on a solitary quest for spiritual enlightenment. After some years of wandering, during which time he experienced the "Inner Light" (the divine light in the hearts of men), he began preaching and gathering the first congregations of Friends.

During all this time the English Civil War was raging. Perhaps because their sufferings, though severe, never approached those of the Anabaptists, perhaps also because their doctrine of the Inner Light led them into closer communion with their fellow men, the Quakers easily accommodated themselves to the world. They even went so far as to found colonies and accept nearly all the responsibilities of citizenship, including service on the judicial bench. Nor was their peace witness clear-cut from the outset. Although Fox himself seems always to have been a pacifist, many of his followers served in the army under Oliver Cromwell and entertained thoughts of apocalyptic war. When they were expelled from the army (under protest), it was rarely on account of their pacifism, but because the Inner Light induced them to excesses of indiscipline, such as shouting during religious services and refusing "hat honour," a normal sign of deference toward superiors.

Not until the 1660's was Fox able to impress his pacifism on his brethren. From then on, the Quakers' objection to war has rested less on scriptural texts than on the conviction that the Inner Light, by making a man new through allowing him to join spiritually with Christ, removes the ground of contention and points to a better way. Yet, consistent with the peace-church tradition, Quakers have never branded as evil or denied fighting in a just cause to those who have not undergone inward transformation, a position Gandhi later reaffirmed.

The following selection clearly presents the Quaker position. During the first years of the Restoration, when innocent Quakers were imprisoned following an abortive uprising by the Fifth Monarchy Men, millennarian fanatics, Fox and other leaders sent to King Charles II this declaration of principle.

Presented to the King Upon the 21st Day of the 11th Month, 1660

A Declaration from the harmless and innocent people of God, called Quakers, against all seditious plotters, and fighters in the world: for the removing the ground of jealousy and suspicion from both magistrates and people in the kingdom, concerning wars and fightings.

Our principle is, and our practices have always been, to seek peace and ensue it; to follow after righteousness and the knowledge of God; seeking the good and welfare, and doing that which tends to the peace of all. We know that wars and fightings proceed from the lusts of men as James 4:1-3, out of which the Lord hath redeemed us, and so out of the occasion of war. The occasion of which war, and war itself (wherein envious men, who are lovers of themselves more than lovers of God, lust, kill, and desire to have men's lives or estates) ariseth from lust. All bloody principles and practices, as to our own particulars, we do utterly deny; with all outward wars and strife and fightings with outward weapons, for any end, or under any pretense whatsoever, this is our testimony to the whole world. . . .
. . . [We say, as] Christ said to Peter, "Put up thy sword in his place." . . . And further, Christ said to Pilate,

From The Journal of George Fox, *ed. Wilson Armstead (London, 1852). The date 1660 is according to the old calendar then in use; according to the reformed calendar, the date would be January, 1661.*

"Thinkest thou, that I cannot now pray to my Father, and he shall presently give me more than twelve legions of angels?" . . . And so Christ's kingdom is not of this world, therefore do not his servants fight, as he told Pilate, the magistrate who crucified him. And did they not look upon Christ as a raiser of sedition? And did not he pray, "Forgive them?" But thus it is that we are numbered amongst transgressors and numbered amongst fighters, that the Scriptures might be fulfilled.

That the spirit of Christ, by which we are guided, is not changeable, so as once to command us from a thing as evil and again to move unto it; and we do certainly know, and testify to the world, that the spirit of Christ, which leads us into all truth, will never move us to fight and war against any man with outward weapons, neither for the kingdom of Christ [i.e., to wage apocalyptic war] nor for the kingdoms of this world.

First:

Because the kingdom of Christ God will exalt, according to his promise, and cause it to grow and flourish in righteousness, "Not by might, nor by power (of outward sword), but by my Spirit, saith the Lord" (Zech. 4:6). So those that use any weapons to fight for Christ, or for the establishing of his kingdom or government, their spirit, principle, and practice we deny.

Secondly:

. . . We do earnestly desire and wait, that, by the Word of God's power, and its effectual operation in the hearts of men, the kingdoms of this world may become the kingdoms of the Lord, and of his Christ, that he may rule and reign in men by his Spirit and truth; that thereby all people, out of every profession, may be brought into love and unity with God, and with one another; and that they may all come to witness the prophet's words who said, "Nation shall not lift up sword against nation, neither shall they learn war any more" (Isa. 2:4; Mic. 4:3). . . .

. . . This we can say to all the world, we have wronged no man; we have used no force nor violence against any man, we have been found in no plots, nor guilty of sedition. When we have been wronged, we have not sought to revenge ourselves; we have not made resistance against authority, but wherein we could not obey for conscience sake, we have suffered the most of any people in the nation. We have been accounted as sheep for the slaughter, persecuted and despised, beaten, stoned, wounded, stocked, whipped, imprisoned, haled out of synagogues, cast into dungeons and noisome vaults, where many have died in bonds, shut up from our friends, denied needful sustenance for many days together, with other the like cruelties.

And the cause of all these our sufferings is not for any evil, but for things relating to the worship of our God and in obedience to his requirings. For which cause we shall freely give up our bodies a sacrifice, rather than disobey the Lord; for we know, as the Lord hath kept us innocent, so he will plead our cause, when there is none in the earth to plead it. So we, in obedience unto his truth, do not love our lives unto death, that we may do his will, and wrong no man in our generation, but seek the good and peace of all men. He who hath commanded us that we shall not swear at all (Matt. 5:34), hath also commanded us that we shall not kill (Matt. 5:21), so that we can neither kill men, nor swear for nor against them. This is both our principle and practice, and has been from the beginning; so that if we suffer, as suspected to take up arms, or make war against any, it is without any ground from us; for it neither is, nor ever was in our hearts, since we owned the truth of God; neither shall we ever do it, because it is contrary to the spirit of Christ, his doctrine, and the practices of his apostles; even contrary to him, for whom we suffer all things, and endure all things. . . .

Therefore consider these things, ye men of understanding; for plotters, raisers of insurrections, tumultuous ones, and fighters, running with swords, clubs, staves, and pistols one against another; these, we say, are of the world, and hath their foundation from this unrighteous world, from the foundation of which the Lamb hath been slain; which Lamb hath redeemed us from the unrighteous world, and we are not of it, but are heirs of the world of which there is no end, and of a kingdom where no corruptible thing enters. Our weapons are spiritual, and not carnal, yet mighty through God, to the plucking down of the strongholds of sin and Satan, who is the author of wars, fighting, murder, and plots. Our swords are broken into plowshares, and spears into pruning-hooks, as prophesied of in Micah 4. Therefore we cannot learn war any more, neither rise up against nation or kingdom with outward weapons, though you have numbered us amongst the transgressors and plotters. The Lord knows our innocency herein, and will plead our cause with all people upon earth, at the day of their judgment, when all men shall have a reward according to their works. . . .

O, Friends! offend not the Lord and his little ones, neither afflict his people; but consider and be moderate. Do not run hastily, but consider mercy, justice, and judgment; that is the way for you to prosper, and obtain the favor of the Lord. Our meetings were stopped and broken up in the days of Oliver, under pretense of plotting against him; in the days of the Committee of Safety we were looked upon as plotters to bring in King Charles; and now our peaceable meetings are termed seditious. Oh! that men should lose their reason, and go contrary to their own conscience; knowing that we have suffered all things, and have been accounted plotters from the beginning, though we have declared against them both by word of mouth and printing, and are clear from any such thing! We have suffered all along, because we would not take up carnal weapons to fight, and are thus made a prey, because we are the innocent lambs of Christ, and cannot avenge ourselves! These things are left on your hearts to consider; but we are out of all those things in the patience of the saints, and we know, as Christ said, "He that taketh the sword shall perish with the sword" (Matt. 26:52; Rev. 13:10).

William Penn
1644–1718

Son of Sir William Penn, who was an admiral of the Royal Navy and a friend of the Duke of York (the future James II), the younger Penn came to the Friends during his student days at Oxford. Despite his frequent quarrels with his father, who thought his radicalism was ruining his chances for worldly advancement (a not uncommon contemporary phenomenon), and his jail sentences for violating the laws restricting religious dissent, Penn received from the King a grant of land in the New World in consideration of a debt owed his family.

The following letter, read by his commissioners to the Delaware Indians, contains the key to Penn's success as a colonizer: as children of God the Indians had in them the divine spark; and he treated them accordingly, refusing to make war on them or to debauch them with "firewater."

The First Letter to the Indians

London, 18th of 8th Month, 1681

My Friends—There is one great God and power that

From Samuel Hazard, ed., Annals of Pennsylvania, from the Discovery of the Delaware, 1609-1682 *(Philadelphia: Hazard and Mitchell, 1850).*

hath made the world and all things therein, to whom you
and I, and all people owe their being and well-being, and
to whom you and I must one day give an account for all
that we do in the world; this great God hath written his law
in our hearts, by which we are taught and commanded
to love and help, and do good to one another, and not to
do harm and mischief one to another. Now this great God
hath been pleased to make me concerned in your parts of
the world, and the king of the country where I live hath
given unto me a great province, but I desire to enjoy it
with your love and consent, that we may always live together as neighbors and friends, else what would the great
God say to us, who hath made us not to devour and destroy
one another, but live soberly and kindly together in the
world? Now I would have you well observe, that I am
very sensible of the unkindness and injustice that hath
been too much exercised towards you by the people of these
parts of the world, who sought themselves, and to make
great advantages by you, rather than be examples of justice
and goodness unto you, which I hear hath been matter of
trouble to you, and caused great grudgings and animosities,
sometimes to the shedding of blood, which hath made the
great God angry; but I am not such a man, as is well known
in my own country; I have great love and regard towards
you, and I desire to win and gain your love and friendship,
by a kind, just and peaceable life, and the people I send are
of the same mind, and shall in all things behave themselves
accordingly; and if in any thing any shall offend you or
your people, you shall have a full and speedy satisfaction
of the same, by an equal number of just men on both sides,
that by no means you may have just occasion of being
offended against them. I shall shortly come to you myself,
at which time we may more largely and freely confer and
discourse of these matters. In the meantime, I have sent my
commissioners to treat with you about land, and a firm

league of peace. Let me desire you to be kind to them and the people, and receive these presents and tokens which I have sent to you, as a testimony of my good will to you, and my resolution to live justly, peaceably, and friendly with you.

I am your loving friend,

WILLIAM PENN

Adin Ballou
1803–1890

A New England clergyman who during his lifetime preached some nine thousand sermons and wrote about five hundred articles, Adin Ballou is one of the unsung heroes of American social reform and of the peace movement. His Universalist faith, whose principal tenet is that an infinitely good God must have decreed salvation for all men, may have inclined him toward socialism; he published a book on this subject, *Practical Christian Socialism,* in 1854. Earlier, he had founded the Hopedale Community in Milford, Massachusetts, with the object of establishing "an order of human society based on the sublime ideas of the Fatherhood of God and the brotherhood of man, as taught and illustrated by the Gospel of Jesus Christ." Hopedale was a true sect-type community, its members binding themselves to abstain from murder, hatred, unchastity, alcohol, and the obligations of civil society.

This striving after Christian perfection led Ballou into the emerging peace movement as a founder, in 1838, of the New England Non-Resistance Society and the author of *Christian Non-Resistance* (Philadelphia, 1846 and 1910), a rare volume useful for its illustrations of nonviolence in action. His memory as a pacifist has been kept alive by Tolstoy, and understandably so, for they were kindred spirits. Ballou to some extent and Tolstoy much more so were both religious anarchists who abhorred government as inherently coercive and therefore hostile to life. Ballou is of interest today for two reasons: (1) From the purely historical standpoint, he is a bridge connecting several traditions: the scriptural pacifism and aloofness from government of the historic peace churches; the Quaker doctrine that love, expressed through nonviolent resistance, is a weapon against evil that removes the occasion for violence; the pacifist elements contained within Christian socialism; and, later, the Social Gospel and the *Satyagraha* doctrine of Gandhi. (2) On a theoretical level, he turns one of the main criteria of the just war into an argument for nonviolence. Nonviolent resistance to evil is simply more practical, less costly in every way, than war; as a device for spreading this ideal, he gives prime place to the gradual leavening influence of a small, determined minority.

The following selection, from his *Catechism of Non-Resistance*, has an interesting history. Possibly the rudimentary outline of a major work, the original text has been lost, surviving only in the lengthy fragment Ballou sent to Tolstoy and which Tolstoy later published in *The Kingdom of God Is within You.*

The Catechism of Non-Resistance

Q. What does the word [non-resistance] denote?

A. It denotes a lofty Christian virtue, commanded by Christ.

Q. Are we to understand the word non-resistance in its broad sense, that is, as meaning that one should offer no resistance to evil whatsoever?

A. No; it should be understood literally as Christ taught it—that is, not to return evil for evil. Evil should be resisted by all lawful means, but not by evil.

Q. From what does it appear that Christ gave that meaning to non-resistance?

From Leo Tolstoy, *"The Kingdom of God Is Within You," in* The Complete Works of Lyof N. Tolstoi *(New York: Thomas Y. Crowell, 1899), IX.*

A. From these words which he used on that occasion. He said: "Ye have heard that it hath been said, An eye for an eye, and a tooth for a tooth. But I say unto you, That ye resist not evil: but whosoever shall smite thee on thy right cheek, turn to him the other also. And if any man will sue thee at the law, and take away thy coat, let him have thy cloak also" [Matt. 5:39]....

Q. To what laws did Christ allude in the words: "Ye have heard"?

A. To those in which Noah, Moses, and other prophets grant the use of personal violence against those who commit it, for the purpose of punishing and destroying evil deeds. . . . Noah, Moses, and the prophets taught that he who murders, mutilates, or tortures his neighbor doeth evil. In order to combat and destroy this evil, the evil-doer must be chastened by death, mutilation, or some personal torture. Transgressions are to be avenged by transgressions, murder by murder, torture by torture, evil by evil. Thus Noah, Moses, and the prophets. But Christ forbids this. . . .

Q. Did the teaching of the Ancients admit of resisting transgression by transgression?

A. Yes; but Christ forbade it. A Christian has no right in any case to take the life of, or to offend against, the evil-doer.

Q. May he not kill or wound another in self-defense?

A. No.

Q. May he enter a complaint to the magistrates for the purpose of chastising the offender?

A. No. For that which he does through others, he practically does himself.

Q. May he fight in the army against foreign or domestic enemies?

A. Certainly not. He can take no part in war, or in the preparation thereof. He cannot make use of weapons. He cannot resist one transgression by another, whether he is alone or in company, either personally or through other agents.

Q. May he voluntarily select or drill soldiers for the government?

A. He cannot do this, if he wishes to be *faithful* to the law of Christ.

Q. May he voluntarily contribute money to assist a government which is supported by military power, executions, and violence in general?

A. No; unless the money is to be used for some special purpose justifiable in itself, where the object and the means employed are good.

Q. May he pay taxes to such a government?

A. No; he should not pay taxes on his own accord, but he should not resist the levying of a tax. A tax imposed by the government is levied independently of the will of the citizens. It may not be resisted without recourse to violence, and a Christian should not use violence; therefore he must deliver his property to the forced damage caused by the authorities.

Q. May a Christian vote at elections and take part in courts of law or in the government?

A. No. To take part in elections, courts of law, or in the administration of government is the same thing as a participation in the violence of the government.

Q. What is the chief significance of the doctrine of non-resistance?

A. To show that it is possible to extirpate evil from one's own heart, as well as from that of one's neighbor. This doctrine forbids men to do that which perpetuates and multiplies evil in this world. He who attacks another, and does him an injury, excites a feeling of hatred, the worst of all evil. To offend our neighbor because he has offended us, with ostensible motive of self-defense, means but to repeat the evil act against him as well as against ourselves—it means to beget, or at least to let loose, or to encourage the Evil Spirit whom we wish to expel. Satan cannot be driven out by Satan, falsehood cannot be purged by falsehood, nor can evil be conquered by evil. True non-resistance is the only real method of resisting evil. It crushes the serpent's head. It destroys and exterminates all evil feeling.

Q. But admitting that the idea of the doctrine is correct, is it practicable?

A. As practicable as any virtue commanded by the law of God. Good deeds cannot be performed under all circumstances without self-sacrifice, privations, suffering, and, in extreme cases, with the loss of life itself. But he who prizes life more than the fulfillment of God's will is already dead to the only true life. Such a man, in trying to save his life, will lose it. Furthermore, wherever non-resistance costs the sacrifice of one's life, resistance costs thousands of such sacrifices.

Non-resistance preserves; resistance destroys.

It is much safer to act justly than unjustly; to endure an offense rather than resist it by violence; safer even in regard to the present life. If all men refused to resist evil, the world would be a happy one. . . .

Hence, if all were to follow the commandment of non-resistance, there would manifestly be neither offense nor evil-doing. If even the majority were composed of such men they would establish the rule of love and good-will even toward the offenders, by not resisting evil by evil nor using violence. Even if such men formed a numerous minority, they would have such an improving moral influence over society that every severe punishment would be revoked, and violence and enmity would be replaced by peace and good-will. If they formed but a small minority, they would rarely experience anything worse than the contempt of the world, while the world, without preserving it or feeling grateful therefore, would become better and wiser from its latent influence. And if, in the most extreme cases, certain members of the minority might be persecuted unto death, these men, thus dying for the truth, would have left their doctrine already sanctified by the blood of martyrdom.

Peace be with all ye who seek peace; and may the all-conquering love be the imperishable inheritance of every soul who submits of its own accord to the law of Christ. *Resist not evil by violence.*

ADIN BALLOU

Leo Tolstoy
1812–1910

With the publication of *Anna Karenina* in 1877, Tolstoy abandoned his artistic career, embarking upon a course leading ultimately to his excommunication from the Russian Orthodox Church—no disaster, he thought. As a layman with theological pretensions, he resurrected heresies long extinguished. Claiming to be teaching the Gospel message shorn of later corruptions, he denied the centrality to the Christian faith of such doctrines as the Resurrection, the Atonement, the Trinity, and the divinity of Christ. The Decalogue he reduced to five entirely new commandments based on his reading of the Sermon on the Mount: namely, sexual purity, wrongfulness of oaths, love of enemies, nonresistance, and the incompatibility of civic office with the Christian profession.

His religious views were naturally connected with his social theory and pacifism. Though he was regarded in his own day and since as something of a scatterbrained eccentric, nevertheless, it is through this Russian prophet that the old radical sect-idea of realizing the Sermon on the Mount in the world again came to the forefront in the West. Here, as in religion, Tolstoy shunned compromise. Since, as the title of his major religious work indicates, *The Kingdom of God Is Within You* (1893), every social system is wicked, because it is coercive. His Christain anarchism led him to deny absolutely that the righteous man could have anything to do with the state. To Dr. Eugen Schmitt, the editor of a Budapest anarchist newspaper, he stated his theory with the certainty of an algebraic equation: "Government is violence, Christianity is meekness, non-resistance, love. And, therefore, a man who wishes to be a Christian must not serve government. Government cannot be Christian. A Christian cannot serve government. Government cannot . . . [and so on]." He could see only one way out of the dilemma of violence, a way leading to the establishment of the Kingdom of Heaven in the world. The more individuals loved one another, the more evil would be extinguished, and the Kingdom of God would be advanced that much closer. What happens to others was not for Tolstoy the immediate question. The immediate question was, "Is an act right, regardless of the consequences?" Hence he could reject violence even against a maniac killing or outraging a child, because such force would only increase the amount of evil in the world, thereby retarding the coming of the Kingdom.

Included here are excerpts from two little-known works. The undated "Letter to a Non-Commissioned Officer" is unique for its quasi-Marxist tone. All wars, the writer holds, result from a series of interlocking plots by rich laymen and their ecclesiastical lackeys to enslave the poor. The rich, to keep their property, need armies; but since the Gospel prohibits killing, the people must, so to speak, be made "stupid." To dull the people's faculties from childhood so that they will become pliable instruments in their rulers' hands is the function of perverted religion and, going further, of all ideologies. The "Advice to a Draftee" was written in 1899 to a young pacifist named Ernest Schramm. Schramm was in an unenviable position. A candidate for conscription into the Hessian army, he was well aware that evasion meant death. Tolstoy's reply was predictable; and Schramm evidently resolved his dilemma by changing countries, a practice not uncommon among draftees of today.

Letter to a Non-Commissioned Officer

You are surprised that soldiers are taught that it is right to kill people in certain cases and in war, while in the books admitted to be holy by those who so teach, there is nothing like such a permission, but, on the contrary, not only is murder forbidden, but all insulting of others is forbidden also, and we are told not to do to others what we do not wish done to us. And you ask, is not this a fraud? And if it is a fraud, then for whose sake is it done?

Yes, it is a fraud, committed for the sake of those accustomed to live on the sweat and blood of other men, and who have therefore perverted, and still pervert, Christ's teaching, which was given to man for his good, but which has now, in its perverted form, become the chief source of human misery.

The thing has come about in this way:

The government, and all those people of the upper classes that are near the government, and that live by the work of others, need some means of dominating the workers, and this means they find in their control of the army. Defense against foreign enemies is only the excuse. The German government frightens its subjects about the Russians and the French, the French government frightens its people about the Germans, the Russian government frightens its people about the French and the Germans, and that is the way with all governments. But neither the Germans, nor the Russians, nor the French, desire to fight their neighbors and other people; but, living in peace, they dread war more than anything else in the world. The government and the upper governing classes, to excuse their domination of the laborers, behave like a gipsy who whips his horse be-

From The Complete Works of Lyof N. Tolstoi (New York: Thomas Y. Crowell, 1899), VIII.

fore he turns a corner and then pretends he cannot hold it in. They provoke their own people and some foreign government, and then pretend that for the well-being or for the defense of their people they must declare war, which again brings profit only to generals, officers, functionaries, merchants, and, in general, to the rich. In reality war is an inevitable result of the existence of armies; and armies are only needed by governments in order to dominate their own working-classes.

The thing is a crime, but the worst of it is that the government, in order to have a plausible basis for its domination of the people, has to pretend that it holds the highest religious teaching known to man (i.e., the Christian), and that it brings up its subjects in this teaching. That teaching, however, is in its nature opposed not only to murder, but to all violence, and, therefore, the governments, in order to dominate the people and to be considered Christian, had to pervert Christianity and to hide its true meaning from the people, and thus deprive men of the well-being Christ brought them.

This perversion was accomplished long ago, in the time of that scoundrel the Emperor Constantine, who for doing it was enrolled among the saints [of the Eastern Church]. All subsequent governments, especially our Russian government, do their utmost to preserve this perverted understanding, and not to allow the people to see the real meaning of Christianity; because, having seen the real meaning of Christianity, the people would perceive that the governments, with their taxes, soldiers, prisons, gallows, and false priests, are not only not the pillars of Christianity they profess to be, but are its greatest enemies. . . .

The people are oppressed, robbed, poor, ignorant, dying of hunger. Why? Because the land is in the hands of the rich; the people are enslaved in mills and in factories, obliged to earn money because taxes are demanded from them, and the price of their labor is diminished while the price of things they need is increased.

How are they to escape? By taking the land from the rich? But if this is done, soldiers will come and will kill the rebels or put them in prison. Take the mills and factories? The same will happen. Organize and support a strike? But it is sure to fail. The rich will hold out longer than the workers, and the armies are always on the side of the capitalists. The people will never extricate themselves from the want in which they are kept, as long as the army is in the hands of the governing classes.

But who compose those armies that keep the people in this state of slavery? Who are these soldiers that will fire on the peasants who take the land, or at the strikers who will not disperse, and at the smugglers who bring in the goods without paying taxes, that put in prison and there guard those who refuse to pay taxes? The soldiers are these same peasants who are deprived of land, the same strikers who want better wages, these same taxpayers who want to be rid of these taxes.

And why do these people shoot at their brothers? Because it has been instilled into them that the oath they were obliged to take on entering the service is binding, and that, though it is generally wrong to murder people, it is right to do so at the command of their superiors. That is to say that that fraud is played off upon them which has occurred to you. But here we meet the question: How is it that sensible people—often people who can read, and even educated people—believe in such an evident lie? However little education a man may have, he cannot but know that Christ did not sanction murder, but taught kindness, meekness, forgiveness of injuries, love of one's enemies, and therefore he cannot help seeing that on the basis of Christian teaching he cannot pledge himself in advance to kill all whom he may be ordered to kill.

The question is: How can sensible people believe, as all now serving in the army have believcd and still believe, such an evident fraud? The answer is that it is not this one fraud by itself that takes people in, but they have from their childhood been deprived of the proper use of their reason by a whole series of frauds, a whole system of frauds, called the Orthodox Faith, which is nothing but the grossest idolatry. In this faith people are taught that God is triple, that besides this triple God there is a Queen of Heaven, and besides this queen there arc various saints whose corpses have not decayed, and besides these saints there are ikons of the Gods and of the Queen of Heaven, to which one should offer candles and pray with one's hands; and that the most important and holy thing on earth is the pap, which the parson makes of wine and white bread on Sundays behind a railing; and that after the parson has whispered over it, the wine is no longer wine, and the white bread is not white bread, but they are the blood and flesh of one of the triple Gods, etc. . . .

All this is so stupid and senseless that it is quite impossible to understand what it all means. And the very people who teach this faith do not tell you to understand it, but only tell you to believe it; and people trained to it from childhood can believe any kind of nonsense that is told them. And when men have been so befooled that they believe that God hangs in the corner [as an ikon], or sits in a morsel of pap which the parson gives him out of a spoon; that to kiss a board or some relics, and to put candles in front of them, is useful for life here and hereafter, they are called on to enter the military service, where they are humbugged to any extent, being made to swear on the Gospels (in which swearing is prohibited) that they will do just what is forbidden in those Gospels, and then taught that to kill people at the word of those in command is not a sin, but to refuse to submit to those in command is a sin. So that the fraud played off on soldiers, when it is instilled into them that they may without sin kill people at the wish of those in command, is not an isolated fraud, but is bound up with a whole system of fraud, without which this one fraud would not deceive them.

Only a man who is quite befooled by the false faith called Orthodoxy, palmed off upon him for the true Christian faith, can believe that there is no sin in a Christian entering the army, promising blindly to obey any man who ranks above him in the service, and, at the will of others, learning to kill, and committing that most terrible crime forbidden by all laws.

A man free from the pseudo-Christian faith called Orthodoxy will not believe that. . . .

. . . The will of God is not that we should fight and oppress the weak, but that we should acknowledge all men to be our brothers, and should serve one another.

These are the thoughts your letter has aroused in me. I shall be very glad if they help to clear up the questions you are thinking about.

Advice to a Draftee

In my last letter I answered your question as well as I could. It is not only Christians but all just people who must refuse to become soldiers—that is, to be ready at another's command (for this is what a soldier's duty actually consists of) to kill all those one is ordered to kill. The question as you state it—which is more useful, to become a good teacher or to suffer for rejecting conscription?—is falsely stated. The question is falsely stated because it is wrong for us to determine our actions according to their results, to view actions merely as useful or destructive. In the choice of our

From The Atlantic Monthly, *February, 1968. Reprinted with the special permission of The Houghton Library, Harvard University.*

actions we can be led by their advantages or disadvantages only when the actions themselves are not opposed to the demands of morality.

We can stay home, go abroad, or concern ourselves with farming or science according to what we find useful for ourselves or others; for neither in domestic life, foreign travel, farming, or science is there anything immoral. But under no circumstance can we inflict violence on people, torture or kill them because we think such acts could be of use to us or to others. We cannot and may not do such things, especially because we can never be sure of the results of our actions. Often actions which seem the most advantageous of all turn out in fact to be destructive; and the reverse is also true.

The question should not be stated: which is more useful, to be a good teacher or to go to jail for refusing conscription? but rather: what should a man do who has been called upon for military service—that is, called upon to kill or to prepare himself to kill?

And to this question, for a person who understands the true meaning of military service and who wants to be moral, there is only one clear and incontrovertible answer: such a person must refuse to take part in military service no matter what consequences his refusal may have. It may seem to us that this refusal could be futile or even harmful, and that it would be a far more useful thing, after serving one's time, to become a good village teacher. But in the same way, Christ could have judged it more useful for himself to be a good carpenter and submit to all the principles of the Pharisees than to die in obscurity as he did, repudiated and forgotten by everyone.

Moral acts are distinguished from all other acts by the fact that they operate independently of any predictable advantage to ourselves or to others. No matter how dangerous the situation may be of a man who finds himself in the power of robbers who demand that he take part in plundering, murder, and rape, a moral person cannot take part. Is not military service the same thing? Is one not required to agree to the deaths of all those one is commanded to kill?

But how can one refuse to do what everyone does, what everyone finds unavoidable and necessary? Or, must one do what no one does and what everyone considers unnecessary or even stupid and bad? No matter how strange it sounds, this strange argument is the main one offered against those moral acts which in our times face you and every other person called up for military service. But this argument is even more incorrect than the one which would make a moral action dependent upon considerations of advantage.

If I, finding myself in a crowd of running people, run with the crowd without knowing where, it is obvious that I have given myself up to mass hysteria; but if by chance I should push my way to the front, or be gifted with sharper sight than the others, or receive information that this crowd was racing to attack human beings and toward its own corruption, would I really not stop and tell the people what might rescue them? Would I go on running and do these things which I knew to be bad and corrupt? This is the situation of every individual called up to military service, if he knows what military service means.

I can well understand that you, a young man full of life, loving and loved by your mother, friends, perhaps a young woman, think with a natural terror about what awaits you if you refuse conscription; and perhaps you will not feel strong enough to bear the consequences of refusal, and knowing your weakness, will submit and become a soldier. I understand completely, and I do not for a moment allow myself to blame you, knowing very well that in your place

I might perhaps do the same thing. Only do not say that you did it because it was useful or because everyone does it. If you did it, know that you did wrong.

In every person's life there are moments in which he can know himself, tell himself who he is, whether he is a man who values his human dignity above his life or a weak creature who does not know his dignity and is concerned merely with being useful (chiefly to himself). This is the situation of a man who goes out to defend his honor in a duel or a soldier who goes into battle (although here the concepts of life are wrong). It is the situation of a doctor or a priest called to someone sick with plague, or a man in a burning house or a sinking ship who must decide whether to let the weaker go first or shove them aside to save himself. It is the situation of a man in poverty who accepts or rejects a bribe. And in our times, it is the situation of a man called to military service. For a man who knows its significance, the call to the army is perhaps the only opportunity for him to behave as a morally free creature and fulfill the highest requirement of his life—or else merely to keep his advantage in sight like an animal and thus remain slavishly submissive and servile until humanity becomes degraded and stupid.

For these reasons I answered your question whether one has to refuse to do military service with a categorical "yes" —if you understand the meaning of military service (and if you did not understand it then, you do now) and if you want to behave as a moral person living in our times must.

Please excuse me if these words are harsh. The subject is so important that one cannot be careful enough in expressing oneself so as to avoid false interpretation.

LEO TOLSTOY
April 7, 1899

Mohandas K. Gandhi

1869–1948

Regarded as a saint by his followers and as a "naked fakir" by his critics, Mahatma Gandhi might seem out of place here, among Christians and Westerners. Yet he has had a profound impact on contemporary thought; for, as Martin Luther King, Jr., said in *Stride Toward Freedom,* "Gandhi was probably the first person in history to lift the love ethic of Jesus above mere interaction between individuals to a powerful and effective social force on a large scale."

Gandhi's methods of militant nonviolence were dictated in part by objective realities and by his innermost convictions. Dominated, humiliated, and exploited by foreigners for centuries, the ancient civilizations of Asia by 1919 were experiencing an upsurge of nationalism. But as a practical matter, for India to succeed in expelling the British through revolution was impossible without incalculable suffering. Drawing upon his own Hindu tradition augmented by his reading of Ruskin, Tolstoy, Thoreau, and the Sermon on the Mount, Gandhi had also come to the realization that nonviolence must be the law of our species—nonviolence, but not nonresistance to evil, as with the Anabaptist churches. *Satyagraha,* literally, "clinging to truth," meant for him resistance to evil in the name of God, unto death, if need be; but because it was nonviolent, appealing rather to the heart and to the reason, *Satyagraha* put an end to evil by converting the evildoer.

Throughout his writings Gandhi affirmed, moreover, that true nonviolence was not a resource of the weakling or the coward. It must spring instead from inner strength, from "disciplined, controlled rage," as Erik H. Erikson describes it in *Gandhi's Truth;* hence his praise for the Rishis, incomparable warriors who deliberately cast away their weapons. Yet nonviolent resistance is not without risks. Gandhi knew full well that the failure and frustration concomitant with a partial realization of goals and only a partial acceptance of nonviolence might find vent in senseless violence; admitting a "Himalayan blunder," he suspended his 1919 civil disobedicnce campaign for precisely that reason. The recent experiences of moderate civil rights leaders in the United States have borne him out fully. After capturing the imagination of men of goodwill everywhere, Dr. King found reform either too slow or not forthcoming at all in certain areas. Because of this, he and other moderates were gradually overshadowed by more violent spokesmen and, in several instances, avowed revolutionaries.

"The Doctrine of the Sword" explains in some detail Gandhi's position in 1920.

The Doctrine of the Sword

Such being the hold that the doctrine of the sword has on the majority of mankind, and as success of Non-cooperation depends principally on absence of violence during its pendency, and as my views in this matter affect the conduct of a large number of people, I am anxious to state them as clearly as possible.

I do believe that, where there is only a choice between cowardice and violence, I would advise violence. Thus when my eldest son asked me what he should have done, had he been present when I was almost fatally assaulted in 1908, whether he should have run away and seen me killed or whether he should have used his physical force which he could and wanted to use, and defended me, I told him that it was his duty to defend me even by using violence. Hence it was that I took part in the Boer War, and the so-called Zulu rebellion and the late War. Hence also do I advocate training in arms for those who believe in the method of violence. I would rather have India resort to arms in order to defend her honour than that she should

From Young India, *August 11, 1920. Reprinted with the special permission of the Navajivan Trust, Ahmedabad, India.*

in a cowardly manner become or remain a helpless witness to her own dishonour.

But I believe that non-violence is infinitely superior to violence, forgiveness is more manly than punishment. Forgiveness adorns a soldier. But abstinence is forgiveness only when there is the power to punish: it is meaningless when it pretends to proceed from a helpless creature. A mouse hardly forgives a cat when it allows itself to be torn to pieces by her. I therefore appreciate the sentiment of those who cry out for the condign punishment of General Dyer[1] and his ilk. They would tear him to pieces if they could. But I do not believe India to be helpless. I do not believe myself to be a helpless creature. Only I want to use India's and my strength for a better purpose.

Let me not be misunderstood. Strength does not come from physical capacity. It comes from an indomitable will. An average Zulu is any way more than a match for an average Englishman in bodily capacity. But he flees from an English boy, because he fears the boy's revolver or those who will use it for him. He fears death and is nerveless in spite of his burly figure. We in India may in a moment realize that one hundred thousand Englishmen need not frighten three hundred million human beings. A definite forgiveness would therefore mean a definite recognition of our strength. . . . It matters little to me that for the moment I do not drive my point home. We feel too downtrodden not to be angry and revengeful. But I must not refrain from saying that India can gain more by waiving the right of punishment. We have better work to do, a better mission to deliver to the world.

I am not a visionary. I claim to be a practical idealist. The religion of non-violence is not meant merely for the

1. In 1919, Brigadier-General R. E. H. Dyer ordered his troops to fire into a crowd of demonstrators, thus perpetrating the Amristar massacre.—Ed.

Rishis and saints. It is meant for the common people as well. Non-violence is the law of our species as violence is the law of the brute. The spirit lies dormant in the brute and he knows no law but that of physical might. The dignity of man requires obedience to a higher law—to the strength of the spirit.

I have therefore ventured to place before India the ancient law of self-sacrifice. For Satyagraha and its offshoots, non-cooperation and civil resistance, are nothing but new names for the law of suffering. The Rishis, who discovered the law of non-violence in the midst of violence, were greater geniuses than Newton. They were themselves greater warriors than Wellington. Having themselves known the use of arms, they realized their uselessness and taught a weary world that its salvation lay not through violence but through non-violence.

Non-violence in its dynamic condition means conscious suffering. It does not mean meek submission to the will of the evil-doer, but it means the putting of one's whole soul against the will of the tyrant. Working under this law of our being, it is possible for a single individual to defy the whole might of an unjust empire to save his honour, his religion, his soul and lay the foundation for that empire's fall or its regeneration.

And so I am not pleading for India to practice non-violence, because it is weak. I want her to practice non-violence being conscious of her strength and power. No training in arms is required for realization of her strength. We seem to need it, because we seem to think that we are but a lump of flesh. I want India to recognize that she has a soul that cannot perish and that can rise triumphant above every physical weakness and defy the physical combination of the whole world. What is the meaning of Rama, a mere human being, with his host of monkeys, pitting himself against the insolent strength of ten-headed Ravan surrounded in supposed safety by the raging waters on all sides of Lanka? Does it not mean conquest of physical strength by spiritual strength? However, being a practical man, I do not wait until India recognizes the practicability of the spiritual life in the political world. India considers herself to be powerless and paralyzed before the machine-guns, the tanks and the aeroplanes of the English. And she takes up Non-cooperation out of her weakness. It must still serve the same purpose, namely, to bring her delivery from the crushing weight of British injustice, if a sufficient number of people practise it.

I isolate this Non-cooperation from Sinn Feinism,[2] for, it is so conceived as to be incapable of being offered side by side with violence. But I invite even the school of violence to give this peaceful Non-cooperation a trial. It will not fail through its inherent weakness. It may fail because of poverty of response. Then will be the time for real danger. The high-souled men, who are unable to suffer national humiliation any longer, will want to vent their wrath. They will take to violence. So far as I know, they must perish without delivering themselves or their country from the wrong. If India takes up the doctrine of the sword, she may gain momentary victory. Then India will cease to be the pride of my heart. I am wedded to India, because I owe my all to her. I believe absolutely that she has a mission for the world. She is not to copy Europe blindly. India's acceptance of the doctrine of the sword will be the hour of my trial. I hope I shall not be found wanting. My religion has no geographical limits. If I have a living faith in it, it will transcend my love for India herself. My life is dedicated to service of India through the religion of non-violence which I believe to be the root of Hinduism.

2. An Irish revolutionary movement of the nineteenth century that resorted to terrorism.—Ed.

The Pacifism of the Social Gospel

A uniquely American movement, the Social Gospel, which flourished in the sixty-odd years following the Civil War, was at once a manifestation of the revulsion against industrial capitalism in its predatory stage and the interpenetration in liberal Protestantism of religious and social thought. In the hands of its prophets, men like Walter Rauschenbusch, Shailer Matthews, and Charles A. Ellwood, this type of Christianity was distinguished by its confidence in human potentialities and its optimism that human happiness could be attained within historical time. As a program of social regeneration, the Social Gospel was vastly different from the idealism of, say, English Christian Socialism, with its emphasis on moral suasion, or Tolstoyan anarchism, or the millenarianism of the sects. It involved, rather, an insistence upon the mission of the Church to utilize the state as the instrument to reform society and to build the Kingdom of God *on earth*.

This stress on the pre-eminence of the state as the agency of social uplift presupposes a willingness to use coercion. In domestic affairs, there was never any question that the possessing classes should be made to do what is right. In international affairs, at least in international affairs before 1919, exponents of the Social Gospel were equally aggressive, supporting the crusade against Kaiserism that would make the world safe for democracy. Yet, by the early thirties, it was evident that the world had not been made safe for democracy: dictatorships had been spawned throughout Europe, and the Depression boded ill for the survival of democracy in the United States. The Social Gospel now turned pacifist. Its pacifism, however, which drew the fire of Christian "realists" of the caliber of Reinhold Niebuhr, was non-scriptural in the sense that the pacifism of the Mennonites relies on the Sermon on the Mount. Instead it gathered up, modified, and enlarged diverse elements: the Social

Gospel itself, pragmatism, utilitarianism, Gandhi's teachings, Socialism, and theological liberalism. From this "pacifist" standpoint, war was simply the wrong way to go about building the Kingdom.

Although the selection included here does not deal with war per se, it touches upon the broader issue of coercion and social justice within the framework of Christian ethics and expounds the ideal of redemptive love as understood by modern pacifism. The work of Kirby Page (a minister who was also editor of *The World Tomorrow,* the first publication of the Fellowship of Reconciliation, an interdenominational pacifist organization), the selection was written specifically to combat communist teaching on class war and revolution. Page's justification of coercion, even of nonviolent revolution, to achieve social justice is, it will be noted, in striking contrast to Luther's condemnation of revolution and Knox's justification of revolution for religious objectives.

Love, Coercion, and Nonviolent Revolution

Is compulsion necessarily a violation of the law of love? Is it impossible to exercise coercion in the spirit of active goodwill? Does forcible restraint necessarily mean a departure from the principle of mutuality? Does loyalty to the Golden Rule lead to acquiescence in the face of evil or at most to *passive* resistance? Do the two Great Commandments forbid all kinds of social coercion?

Here is a fundamental problem of this age. If an affirmative answer is given to these questions, a logical consequence will be the withdrawal of religionists from active participation in the class struggle, on the one hand, and, on the other, the repudiation of religion as a practical and

Condensed from Kirby Page, "Is Coercion Compatible with Religion?" and "Class War and Religion," in The World Tomorrow *(March 1 and 8, 1933). Reprinted with special permission.*

beneficent factor under present circumstances by persons who consider forcible restraint and coercion as absolutely essential to social justice. . . .

But we are not impaled upon the horns of this dilemma, the rejoinder will be made from certain quarters. To withhold approval from the use of restraint or compulsion is not necessarily to be neutral or inactive. It is still possible to be unrestrained in condemnation of evil and untiring in the endeavor to convert and transform wrongdoers. And this response requires us to consider two fundamental questions: Have we reason to believe that conversion of the present owners of property will produce the necessary social changes required in order that justice may be secured by the victims of the existing economic system? Is there available a supplementary method which is both ethically justifiable and socially effective? My own opinion can be put in few words: Persuasion by itself will *not* suffice; and fortunately ethical forms of effective coercion are available. . . .

We must now face the vital question of whether or not religion is practicable under present conditions. If compulsion is absolutely incompatible with love toward one's neighbor, then the conclusion is inescapable that truly religious persons cannot function as citizens of complex modern communities, and if consistent must withdraw to ascetic colonies. But was Tolstoy justified in interpreting the Sermon on the Mount in anarchistic terms? The answer cannot be found in isolated texts or combinations thereof, but rather in a consideration of the basic elements which together constitute the religion of Jesus. He himself summed up his message as a twofold obligation of love toward God and love toward all men, including enemies. The Golden Rule of conduct was phrased in terms of mutuality; "do unto others as you would have them do unto you." The true criterion of every thought and deed must, therefore, be found in its effects upon human personality, human relations, and communion between man and God.

Perhaps we may gain illumination from a consideration of the way true love may legitimately express itself in the home. Does deep affection on the part of a father rule out all forcible restraint or compulsion of a son? Or is it true to say that under certain circumstances love just because it is love will coerce the loved one? Consider this situation: a son in a fit of rage seizes a chair and is about to kill his sister. The father is near at hand and quickly reaches the conclusion that nothing short of physical restraint will save his daughter's life. Will the use of force against his son constitute a violation of the spirit of love? The only ethical answer is an emphatic negative. Love toward son and love toward daughter alike demand the prevention, by ethical means, of a terrible crime.

The central problem here involved may be evaded by saying that if the son had received proper training such a situation would never have arisen, or that other means than forcible restraint are open to the father. But the crucial question for those of us who live in a wicked and sinful generation is this: If failure on the father's part to use force would cost the daughter's life, would such restraint be incompatible with genuine love toward the son? By no means. On the contrary, for the father to permit a crime which he could prevent would itself constitute a base betrayal of affection for the boy. That is to say, there is no inherent irreconcilability between love and coercion, but rather the reverse; under some circumstances love ceases to be love if it fails to use moral means of restraint. . . .

. . . [But] is physical restraint of a son by a father the same thing in principle as would be the taking of the boy's life? No, emphatically no, is my answer. The deliberate killing of a son to protect a daughter raises a fundamentally different question. Forcible coercion is not necessarily a violation of the law of love, but I find it impossible to reconcile the intentional slaughter of any human being with the religious principle of reverence for personality, that is, respect for the personality of the dead man. Nor does active goodwill or the principle of mutuality justify the willful taking of human life.

But what is demanded by the principle of respect for the personality of the daughter? Is the life of her brother more sacred than her own? Here we are confronted with the all-important question of an ethical strategy on the part of the innocent in dealing with the guilty. The opinion has been almost universal and is still widespread that, in order to protect helpless people, the killing of criminal men is not only ethically justifiable but actually obligatory. Indeed the entire protective and penal system of modern society at present is founded upon this assumption.

This basic concept seems to me to be wholly at variance with the religion of Jesus. He summed up his way of life in the language of the two pre-eminent commandments, and sought to erect the Divine Society—the Family of God— upon the foundations of the fatherhood of God and the brotherhood of man. Every person is a child of God and a brother of man. Therefore personality is the supreme value, and should be regarded as an end and not merely as a means to an end. Brother should act toward brother in ways that are consistent with brotherhood. If coercion of every kind is an inherent denial of the family spirit, then it is immoral. But if certain types and degrees of compulsion represent true expressions of brotherly affection, coercion may ennoble personality. If the killing of a brother is an act which in its very essence is alien to and destructive of the family bond, then it is ethically unjustifiable.

From the perspective of high religion, the authorization of the police to kill a fleeing thief is a grossly immoral procedure. Property is elevated above personality. And if the observation be made that the inviolability of private property is necessary to the enrichment of personality in general, and that the refusal to kill robbers would encourage thieving and thus jeopardize all property, the rejoinder may be offered that the society which can protect its property only by shooting or hanging its offenders stands morally condemned. Before a just society can be established the property system and the penal code of such a social order must be radically transformed.

If the principle is accepted that killing in defense of property and life is valid and mandatory, armed preparedness for war follows automatically. In an endeavor to safeguard the inviolability of property rights and human life on the high seas, the United States entered the [First] World War, and to this day millions of patriotic citizens believe that our loss of 100,000 soldiers and the expenditure of 25 billion dollars was not only justifiable but unavoidable. That the navy is maintained at its present level for the purpose of protecting our sea-borne traffic and safeguarding our property in foreign lands, far more than for the purpose of keeping our shores from being invaded and our fellow citizens from being murdered, is an argument that runs like a crimson thread through the literature of armed preparedness.

Emphasis upon the social menace of the doctrine of defensive killing does not, however, excuse us from the necessity of facing squarely this supremely significant question: If a father is confined within the limits of the alternatives of taking his son's life or witnessing the death of his daughter at the hands of his son, what would be his religious duty? If non-killing fails to protect property and life, what is the way out for society? For me the answer of religion is clear: Seek to protect the innocent by reliance upon methods which are consistent with deep reverence for the personality of the wrongdoer; resort to that kind and degree of restraint or compulsion which is warranted by this principle; run the consequent risks and accept whatever penalties are thereby imposed.

And if you say that such a policy would result in suffering and death for many innocent persons, I will make a triple rejoinder. The struggle between innocence and guilt necessarily results in misery and loss of life regardless of the methods and weapons used. Second, the existing penal code and the war system of armed preparedness to slaughter the guilty, and the eventual resort to armed hostilities, produce far more pain and cause more deaths among the innocent than would be the case if the doctrine of defensive killing were abandoned. Third, it is morally preferable for the innocent to die at the hands of the guilty than to save their own lives by slaying the offenders. Retaliatory killing is provocative and tends to be self-perpetuating. The willingness of the innocent to die rather than to kill may be redemptive. . . .

Must class conflict necessarily assume the form of violent class war if it is to free the workers from the yoke of exploitation? Here we come to the parting of the ways for Communists and Socialists; perhaps one should say Socialists like Norman Thomas and the leaders of the Socialist Party of the United States, as well as those who dominate the British Labor Party. Communists believe that privilege and power cannot be wrested from the owning class without a violent combat and the resort to armed hostilities, while Socialists accept the class conflict as a reality, but reject violent class war, putting their reliance instead in economic and political coercion. . . .

Realism at this point seems highly imperative. Much loose talk has been going the rounds to the effect that, while violence is unethical, the revolution cannot be ushered in without a "final push"[1] of armed force. Let us be clear as to what is involved. If this "final push" is to make possible the seizure of power, it must be executed with weapons that are equal to or superior to those used by the owning class. Hasty improvisations for the final battle would merely result in ghastly slaughter of the workers. Even a general strike, accompanied by rioting and street fighting, would not dispossess the present holders of economic power. Successful seizure of power requires a disciplined revolutionary army which is equipped with modern weapons of battle and supported with adequate quantities of munitions and other military supplies. This means that revolutionary violence can be made effective only by years of armed preparedness. The notion that the workers can overthrow capitalism by a last minute "final push" is utter nonsense. Lenin repeatedly pointed out that seizure of power will remain impossible as long as the army continues loyal to the old regime.

Moreover, the social consequences of prolonged civil war in a highly industrialized nation would be devastating beyond imagination. The degree of interdependence of the people in an urban civilization and the destructiveness of chemical and aerial warfare would transform congested areas into infernos. The demolition and dislocation of an infinitely complex productive and distributive system would quickly produce hunger and starvation on an appalling scale in metropolitan communities. . . .

The ethical and religious case against revolutionary violence is made even more conclusive when we recognize the part played by hatred in Communist tactics. Not class solidarity alone, but class hatred is deliberately engendered as necessary to effective hostility against the owning class. Communist literature abounds with direct incitations to hatred and every effort is made to infuriate the workers into armed rebellion against their oppressors. Class emnity must take the form of suppressing all opposition. "Under the dictatorship [of the proletariat]," writes William Z. Foster, Communist candidate for President of the United States, "the capitalist parties—Republican, Democratic, Progressive, Socialist, etc.—will be liquidated, the Communist Party functioning alone as the party of the toiling masses." That virulent hatred and enmity are irreconcilable with high religion seems obvious beyond dispute.

My conclusion, then, is that the Socialist program of persuasion and social coercion through economic and political pressure is more consistent with religious idealism than any other method which offers hope of building a just social order; and that the Communist strategy of violent class war is pragmatically indefensible and morally unjustifiable.

And now a concluding question must be faced: What should be the attitude of truly religious persons toward the workers, if in desperation they resort to armed action in an endeavor to secure justice? My own answer is clear and unequivocal. I am on the side of the victims of exploitation and injustice, and make no pretense of being neutral in the class conflict. I have been endeavoring to make my position clear that under no circumstances will I participate in armed warfare, whether it be international or class warfare. Moreover, I will never sanction or approve any kind of armed hostilities. But this must not be interpreted as meaning that I will forsake the exploited masses. I am on their side, even if they follow the fatal example of their oppressors and resort to retaliatory violence. . . . Likewise, it is possible for a non-violent revolutionist to refrain from participating in or sanctioning armed hostilities, without abandoning his loyalty to the workers. Being convinced that all armed warfare is ineffective and unethical, a radical religious pacifist should refrain from hatred and murder, and should depend utterly on persuasion and ethical forms of coercion, being willing to run risks and accept consequences while cooperating to the utmost with a loving and suffering God, who through the ages has been endeavoring to create a just and harmonious Fellowship of Kinsmen.

1. This phrase is, of course, a prime instance of the secularized apocalypticism of the Marxists and other revolutionaries.—Ed.

Conscientious Objection to Military Service —Pro and Con

Conscientious objection, broadly defined as the refusal by an individual on grounds of innermost conviction to participate in an activity required by society, has a long history. Insofar as it concerns the rejection of military service on Christian principles, it goes back to the pre-Constantinian Empire. The first COs were, like Maximilianus, martyrs for their faith. Conscientious objection, however, did not become a serious problem for governments until the wars of the twentieth century made it necessary to call on all segments of the population for military service.

The term "conscientious objector" itself is fairly recent. Coined in England during World War I, it described those exempted from the Conscription Act of 1916 because of "a conscientious objection to the undertaking of combatant service." A new pejorative term, usually shortened to "conchie," had entered the language. Since then, the number of COs has grown in the democratic countries of the West (the U.S. had 50,000 in World War II), albeit not without a great deal of suffering. They were harassed, discriminated against, and imprisoned under the nastiest conditions. The French COs received the harshest treatment of all: during World War I—when even clergymen were conscripted into combat units—many objectors were shot as deserters and their next-of-kin sent a curt notice to the effect that So-and-So had "died a coward."

Of the selections included in this section, the first, from the recollections of Thomas Lurting, is a fascinating picture of the development of a man's inner life. Impressed at the age of fourteen into service in the Irish wars, then into the wars against the Dutch and the Spaniards, Lurting eventually rose to the rank of boatswain's mate. Converted to Quakerism while serving on the frigate *Bristol,* he continued a fighter until moved to pacifism in a stunning flash of insight. So intense was his new-found aversion to war that he became an "absolutist," refusing even to assist the ship's doctor in mending the wounded. His stand is not unique. In the midst of every modern war individuals have suddenly come to see the incompatibility of war with a higher duty. The experiences of Captain Howard Levy, a doctor convicted of refusing to train Green Beret medics for Vietnam, parallel those of Lurting.

The second selection comes from the 1941 trial in the U.S. District Court for Eastern Pennsylvania of Arle Brooks, a social worker, a minister in the Disciples of Christ, and a pacifist who refused to register for the draft. It is a valuable document in many ways, for in addition to revealing the powerful personalities involved, it deals with a basic problem of ethics and politics, a problem involving ultimately the survival of the state itself: to what extent is a minority bound by the decisions of the majority in a democracy? Brooks's defense and the reasons given by the judge (a Quaker) for imprisoning him illustrate what can happen when one party feels compelled by conscience to disobey the law, while the other feels compelled to uphold the conscience of the laws.

Finally, by way of rebuttal to the COs, we have Karl Barth, who volunteered for the Swiss home guard during World War II. Barth's views assumed added significance when President Nixon announced support for abolishing the draft and substituting a professional, all-volunteer army. Barth would have disagreed with this proposal, for he believed it is the individual's responsibility to decide whether a war is just, and that any philosophy presuming to decide this for him in advance, or any measure shielding him from the ultimate consequences of his decision, is wrong. Only conscription forces each individual to make a decision on the righteousness of the national course. Each war must be judged separately, on its own merits—or demerits, as is more likely the case. A negative decision once taken, however, the objector must be prepared to suffer as prescribed by law, content in the knowledge that his rebelliousness is in reality the highest, though for the moment an unappreciated, form of patriotism.

Adventures of a Seventeenth-Century Conscientious Objector

Now I shall a little hint at the first Rise of the People called *Quakers* in our Ship. There was some Soldiers put on Board us, and one of them had been at a Meeting in *Scotland,* of the aforesaid People; and there was two young Men in the Ship, who had some Converse with him, but he was taken away from the Ship in a little Time, but the two young Men made little appearance of any Conviction of Convincement, until about six Months after, the first thing observable was, they refused to hear the Priest, or put off their Hats to the Captain, for which they called them *Quakers.* These two Men often met together in Silence, and their so meeting caused a serious Enquiry among others, and their Number increased, and as they increased, so Persecution increased against them; and the Captain was sore troubled and disturbed at their Increase, himself being a *Baptist Minister.* The Priest that officiated in our Ship was cruel and bitter against them; crying out thus to me, *O Thomas, an honest Man, and a good Christian! Here is a dangerous People on Board . . . a blasphemous People, denying the Ordinances and Word of God.* The which made me as cruel as himself, and I gave them many a

From The Fighting Sailor Turn'd Peaceable Christian, Manifested in the Convincement and Conversion of Thomas Lurting *(London, 1724). The punctuation has been altered slightly.*

hearty Blow, and I was violent upon them, and a great Persecutor of them. . . . [But] the Lord wrought so much upon me, that I could no more beat any of the People called *Quakers,* and in a little Time the Lord gave me a true Sight of the Priest; for when I could not do his Work, and beat and abuse the said People, then I was accounted neither an *honest Man* nor *good Christian* by him. So I began to look upon the said People with a single Eye, for good. . . . After some Time, I desired to be much alone, and in my still and quiet Retirements, the Lord was very good to me, and gave me many a heavenly Visitation, and though I was in Judgment, yet that was my Portion, and I patiently bore them, and came to love his Judgements and Visitations, and they became to me very sweet and pleasant, and of more value than *Rubies,* and was my great Delight, and with them I was very well pleased, because they brought me into much tenderness, for the which I loved them at my very Heart. For it was Heart-work; and many Times alone the Lord would break in upon me, by the inshining of his glorious Light in my own Heart, meted me, and modified me: Yea, so powerfully many Times, that I could not contain, or forbear crying out, *O Lord!* . . . With this Exercise and many more, I continued about six Months, being taken off all outward Concerns, and being alone, some said I was mad, others I was distracted; and so wrote home to *England.* . . .

. . . We being now at *Leghorn,* were ordered to go to *Barcelona,* to take or burn a *Spanish* Man of War; and our station was to lie against a Castle to batter it, the which we did; and one Corner of the Castle played some Shot into our Ship, and I was for bearing down that Corner. And we, called Quakers, fought with as much Courage as any, seeing then no farther; and for my Part, I was stripped into my Waistcoat, (every one in fighting Habit) and went to it in Earnest, and with as much Courage as ever; and I went into the Fore-castle, and levelled the Guns; *but,* said I, *Fire not till I go out to see where the Shot lights, that we may level higher or lower:* and here I was as great a fighter as most. But he that hath all Men's Hearts in His Hand, can turn them at his Pleasure, yea, he in a Minute's Time so far changed my Heart, that in a Minute before, I needing my whole Strength and Rigour to kill and destroy Men's lives, and in a Minute after I could not kill or destroy a Man, if it were to gain the World. For as I was coming out of the Fore-castle Door, to see where the Shot fell, the Word of the Lord ran through me, *how if I had killed a Man;* and it was with such Power, that for some Time I hardly knew whether I was in the Body or out of it. But when I came to see, and felt what it was, I turned about, and put on my Clothes, and walked on the Deck, as though I had never seen a Gun fired, under a great Exercise of Mind; and some asked me, *If I was hurt?* I answered, *No; but under some Scruple of Conscience on the account of Fighting,* although I had not heard that the *Quakers* refused to fight. And when Night came, we went out of the Castle-shot, and I much desired to know what the Friends would say to this. I sent for two of them . . . and I queried much with them about Fighting, to which they gave me little Answer; but said, *If the Lord sent them well home, they would never go to it again.* My answer to them was, with a Dread and Fear upon me, *That if I stood honest to that, of God in my Conscience, and if we came to it Tomorrow that with the Lord's Assistance I would bear my Testimony against it.* For this I plainly saw, that inasmuch as we had been such great Actors in it, now we must bear our Testimony against Fighting; not doubting that way will be made for our Delivery; but if not, the Will of God be done. . . . Some Time after, a Friend went to the Captain to be cleared [released?]; he asked the Reason: His Answer was, *He could fight no longer.* Then said the

Captain, *He that denies to fight in time of Engagement, I will put my Sword in his Guts.* Then, said the *Friend, thou wilt be a Manslayer, and guilty of shedding Blood;* for which the Captain beat him sorely with his Cane and Fist, although he was a *Baptist Preacher.* . . .

Some time after (about the Year 1655) we were at *Leghorn,* and we were ordered to go a Cruizing; and one Morning, we espied a great Ship bearing down upon us, which we supposed to be a *Spanish* Man of War, with whom we had Wars. So Order was given to make the Ship clear to Fight. *Now comes a trying Time to prove every one's Foundation.* . . . So then I went down [into the hold], with a Dread upon me, and spoke to two or three of [the Friends]. . . . I declared to them how Things was with me, and that Things seemed very dark and cloudy . . . yet my Hopes and Belief was in the Lord, and that I had not the least Scruple, but that the Lord would deliver me, and not me only, but all such as were of my Faith and belief; adding *I lay not this as an Injunction upon any one, but leave you all to the Lord, to do as he shall direct you; yet one Thing I advise you of, that you be not ensnared. In a little Time they will call you to your Quarters; which if you go, you shew yourselves Men for their Turns. And further, I must advise you, that the Captain puts great Confidence in you, therefore let us be careful that we give him no just Occasion. Therefore, all that are of my Mind, let us meet in the most publick Place upon the Deck, in the full View of the Captain, that he may not say we deceived him, in not telling him that we would not fight; that he might have put others in our room or Place.* . . . And when I went upon the Deck, I set my Back against the Gear-Capstan, with my Face towards the Captain, where he had a full View of me. Standing there a-while, I turned my Head to see who was coming after me, and when I saw my Friends there behind me, my very Heart leaped for Joy, and I was overcome with the Sight of them. For to me they were the loveliest that I ever beheld, and my very Bowels rowled within me for them, and my Life was given up freely for them, to see them given up as innocent Lambs, ready for the Slaughter, standing all together. In a little Time comes the Lieutenant, and says to one of them, *Go down to thy Quarters;* his Answer was, *I can fight no more:* The which was what he looked for; for he was our Great Enemy. Then he goes to the Captain and makes the worst of it, saying, *Yonder the Quakers be all together, and I do not know but they will mutiny, and one says he cannot fight.* Then [the Captain] asked his Name, and came down. He first heaved his Hat over-board, and took hold of his Collar, and beat him with a large Cane, and then dragged him down to his Quarters. Then the Captain goes upon the Half-Deck again, and called his Man to bring him his Sword; which done, he drew it in as much Fury and Indignation as I ever saw Sword drawn; for Passion had overcome him. No sooner was his Sword drawn, but the Word of the Lord ran through me like Fire, saying, *The Sword of the Lord is over him: And if he will have a Sacrifice, proffer it him.* And this Word was so powerful in me that I greatly quivered and shook, though endeavoured the contrary, fearing they should think I was afraid of the Sword, but I was not. . . . Then watching the Captain, as he came forward with his drawn Sword in his Hand, I fixt my Eye upon him, and he furiously looked on me, to have daunted me; but I was carried above all his furious Looks. I had about five Paces and six Steps upon the Quarter-Deck before I came to him, in much Dread, and stepped the five Paces, and on the third Step, his Countenance changed pale, and he turned himself about from me, and went off, and called to his Man to take away his Sword. I, standing there a while, said to my Friend, *The Captain is gone, let us return to our Friends;* who received us very kindly, and were glad to see how we were delivered. In a little Time, the Ship we all thought to fight withal, proved a *Genoese,* our Friend; and before Night, the Captain sent the Priest to me, to desire me not to be angry with him, for it was in his Passion. My Answer, by the Priest, was to the Captain, *That I had nothing but good will to him, and all Men living;* and bid him tell the Captain, *That he must have a Care to such Passions; for if he killed a Man in his Passion, he might seek a place for Repentance, and might not find it.* And ever after this, the Captain was very kind and respective to me. . . .

At another Time (in the Year 1662), going to *Harwich* laden with Corn, and no sooner we came to Anchor, but a Press-Boat came on Board us; and the first Man they laid Hands on was me, saying *You must go with us. I hope not so,* said I. Then they swore that I was a lusty Man, and should go. Then they laid Hands on me, and lifted me into their Boat, and carried me on Board the Ship *Mary,* one *Jeremiah Smith,* Commander, who was a very loose and wicked Man. . . . The next Day the Steward came to me to know my Name. I asked him for what? He replied, That I might have my Victuals. I told him, it was Time enough when I came for my Victuals. So I continued without any Food *five Days,* only at Times a Draught of Water; for I was sensible, if I had eat of their Victuals, they would have kept me. . . . On the Sixth Day . . . the Captain, having most of his Officers about him, sent for me by his Man. . . . *I hear so,* said the Captain, . . . *that thou hast had a Command, and so thou shalt have here; or else thou shalt stand by me, and I will tell thee what I will have done, and thou shalt call the Men to do it; or else thou shalt stand by the Fore-Braces, and I will call to thee to do so and so; and this is not killing a man, to hale a Rope.* I answered, *But*

I will not do that. Then, he said, *thou shalt be with the Coopers, to hand Beer for them, there is a great occasion for it.* I answered, *But I will not do That.* Then, said he again, *I have an Employment for thee, which will be a great Piece of Charity, and a saving of Men's Lives. Thou shalt be with the Doctor, and when a Man comes that hath lost a Leg or an Arm, to hold the Man while the Doctor cuts it off; this is not killing Men, but saving Men's Lives.* I answered, *But I will not do That, for it's all an Assistance.* Then he said, *I will send thee to Prison.* I answered, *I am in thy Hand, thou may'st do with me what thou pleasest. But,* said the Captain, *I hear thou wilt starve thyself. Not so,* said I, *for I have money in my pocket, and if thou wilt sell me any Victuals, I will eat before thee.* The Captain said, *I cannot sell the King's Victuals.* I answered, *Nor I cannot do the King's Work, therefore cannot eat the King's Victuals.*

In a little Time after, I was called to go into the Boat, expecting to be sent to Prison, but when we came on Shore, contrary to my Expectations, the Captain bade me, *Go which Way I would.* . . .

These and many more like Experiences, hath the Lord carried me through, too long here to mention; for the which I bless his worthy Name. For he was always, in the greatest Straits, ready to assist me, as I was willing to give up to him, and to be nothing of my self.

THOMAS LURTING

The Trial of a Conscientious Objector (1941)

From The United States *vs* Arle Brooks *(Philadelphia: American Friends Service Committee, 1941). Reprinted with special permission. The Judge was George A. Welsh; the lawyer, W. C. Longstreth; the U. S. Attorney, Edward A. Kallick.*

Opening of the Court

THE COURT: Arle Brooks: on December 5 you stood mute before the Court when asked how you pleaded, and the Court directed a plea of not guilty to be entered. You are charged in this indictment with failing to register in accordance with the provisions of the Selective Service and Training Act of September 16, 1940. How say you now?

MR. BROOKS: *Nolo contendere.*

THE COURT: You plead *nolo contendere.*

MR. KALLICK: Now, if the Court pleases, I ask that on the basis of that plea, that a verdict of guilty be entered.

THE COURT: Very good. Now, before I make any disposition of this case, I see Mr. Longstreth here, and I would like to have the benefit of anything you would like to say, and I would like to hear from Arle, if he doesn't mind. . . . Arle, will you take the stand, please.

Direct Examination

BY THE COURT: . . .

Q. . . . I want you to feel free to express yourself in your own way and tell us exactly how you feel about it, if you will, please.

A. Yes. I appreciate your sympathetic consideration. My conscience forbade me to register under the Selective Service Training Act of 1940.

The present wars are the natural product of our economic system and our way of living. Preparation for war is easier than going through the painful process of reconstructing our social and economic system and improving our own way of living.

Wars destroy human lives. Individuals have the right to give their lives for a cause. They have no right to take the life of another. Wars are futile, destructive, and immoral. Wars have failed to solve the basic problems of the world. Participation in war to settle international and national differences does not do justice to man's intelligence.

The people of America are filled with fear of an invasion. Are we so morally weak that the power of one man could control one hundred and thirty million free people? Free people cannot be enslaved unless they will it. Are we too lethargic to find a better method for solving international affairs? The people of India have almost won their freedom from Great Britain without firing a shot. They have been willing to give their lives, but have refused to take the lives of the British soldiers.

Democracy does not mean blindly following the will of the majority. In a democracy the minority has a right and a duty to follow its ideals. Sometimes the ideals of the minority have eventually been adopted by the majority. Gandhi said, "We are sunk so low that we fancy that it is our duty and our religion to do what the law lays down. If man will only realize that it is unmanly to obey an unjust law, no man's tyranny will enslave him. . . . It is a superstition and an ungodly thing to believe that an act of a majority binds a minority." . . .

Conscription is a denial of the democracy for which I have worked. Under conscription the individual is required blindly to obey his superior officer, even though his superior officer is wrong. Hitler could not have waged his wars if the people of Germany had not granted him the power to enslave them. The United States is adopting a system of conscription which may produce tyranny instead of freedom.

I cannot agree with those who believe that registration is a mere census. Registration is the first and necessary step for conscription. My conscience will not permit me to take that first step.

As a minister I could have received complete exemption. I felt it my moral duty to do all within my power to protest against conscription which will eventually weaken and destroy democracy. I am not evading the draft. I am opposing it. I am defending democracy.

Thank you. . . .

Q. . . . Would [you] be willing to do any work that would be for humanity's welfare except that of performing any kind of military service, even though that work would be hazardous?

A. Oh, yes, certainly. . . .

Q. Would the question of the hazard of the work make any difference in influencing you in coming to a conclusion as to what work you would take?

A. No, that, I believe, would not enter into it.

Q. Would not enter into it.

MR. KALLICK: May I ask a question, also?

THE COURT: Yes.

Cross-Examination

BY MR. KALLICK:

Q. Mr. Brooks, have you ever counselled others between the ages of 21 and 36 not to register and do as you have done?

A. I believe each person should follow his conscience.

Q. Will you just answer yes or no.

A. Yes. No, I have not told anyone not to register. . . .

BY THE COURT:

Q. You feel that would be interfering with another man's conscience, do you?

A. That's right.

THE COURT: So do I. All right, Arle, will you go down there. . . .

Mr. Longstreth, I would be very glad to have an expression from you. I have known you for a good many years.

MR. LONGSTRETH: Your Honor . . .

. . . Arle Brooks is no draft dodger. He wrote a letter which was received by the Draft Board on the day of registration which set forth his age, his address and his name and why he could not register. And this Draft Act gave him the choice of either registering or being punished for not registering. And he has elected that latter alternative as a protest against a statute which he feels is evil.

Arle Brooks has never injured any fellow man, and his sole crime is that he is unwilling to enroll himself among those who may be called upon to learn to kill their fellow man.

Now, on the walls of the Capitol in Harrisburg hangs a painting by Violet Oakley in honor of an Englishman who openly broke the British Conventicle Acts which forbade any religious services except those according to the Church of England. And today we are honoring that man, William Penn, for breaking a law that he felt was contrary to his conscience.

The Romans threw to the lions the early Christians who refused to burn a pinch of incense on the altar to Caesar. Those early Christians would rather be torn limb from limb than do homage to Caesar. And it was the blood of those Christians that caused the Christian Church to wax strong.

Men are won on higher ideals by seeing idealists willing to suffer for their ideal.

Today we regard as barbaric that British age that imprisoned men for worshipping God according to the dictates of their conscience, and we revere the province of Pennsylvania because it was tolerant to all forms of religion.

Now, future generations will gauge the degree of civilization that we today have attained, according to the tolerance that we show men that differ from us.

THE COURT: Thank you.

MR. KALLICK: If the Court please . . . I must ask the Court that a substantial sentence be imposed. It would be unthinkable, to my way of looking at the problem, if each and every one of the one hundred and thirty million people in this country would have the right to say which law they shall obey and which law they shall not obey. What the judgment of the next generation will be of us who are the officers of this Court, we can't allow to interfere with our course of duty as we see it today. I believe that if this defendant or any of the others were permitted, without any action by the Government, to just go along in their way and not register, we would have a terrible condition in this country in a very short time. We have an example of that during the days of Prohibition, when we had judges on the Bench who refused to enforce that Act because of their personal views. I again reiterate that so far as the democracy as we know it today is concerned, the laws passed by the majority should be upheld by the minority, as well as the majority.

I, therefore, ask that Your Honorable Court fix sentence at this time.

I might say one more thing, if the Court please. I talked with Mr. Brooks like I have with most of the others, and personally we have gotten to be pretty good friends. His conscientious objections to this Act are so deep-seated and rooted that he told us that even if there were an armed invasion of the country, this country, there would be no defense by him or the others in his group to counteract that invasion; they would offer passive resistance, as they have in India. . . .

THE COURT: That shows that he is really motivated by conscience.

Well, Arle, I know that you have thought over this subject for some time. I am convinced that your action here is not precipitous, and you must in the quiet solitude of your own closet have tried to wrestle with the question as to what you should do. Feeling as you do, that, of course, was a real battle, because a conscientious man—and I believe you to be entirely conscientious—would be torn in a situation of this kind between two loyalties: the loyalty to the Supreme Being that you have been trying to serve for a number of years in a very active, practical way, and loyalty to the Government that gives you physical protection and opportunity even to exercise your right of conscience. And to a young man of your age, educated, and refined, and with a spiritually open eye, you must have been torn. I can remember exactly when I was your age, and I know just how you feel. I want you to know that. It was not such a long time, either.

But America is not normal today—and you must be charitable with the rest of us. Now, here is where you have got to exercise some charity. Those ideals that you have expressed are more deep-rooted in our people than you think. I believe countless millions in the United States feel just as you feel. And I believe right in this court room with this mixed audience we are all of one mind. I think right in the very hearts of all of us here, we are in complete harmony with your objective. And I am not here to pay any compliments or throw any bouquets. I am going to sentence you; it is hard for me to do it, but it is my duty, and I feel like Pontius Pilate. I have got to obey the law, and that law commands me, and I would obey it if it meant my life—never mind my feelings, but that is the law, and I have got to live within the law and uphold the law, and I have got to sentence you, as a Judge. But as a man, with sons of my own (who don't take your particular viewpoint, I will say that), but as a man who is interested in young men, as I have been for thirty-odd years, I can't help but say that I admire the strength of character that causes you to take this choice when you believe it is the right view for you to take. Now, there are millions who do not believe that it is necssary, that your view is necessary or wise just now, but you do, and I would not argue with you at all. And as I said the other day, you cannot, and ought not to argue with a brother man on a matter of conscience. This is your conscience, and it is your duty to obey it, even if it brings physical pain or death, when it comes to a real matter of conscience.

Now, there are millions of us who can't conceive that this would be such a vital matter of conscience, taking this as just a preliminary step, when you could be excused under the wise provision of the law. I really think if this had been foreseen, those men who drafted that law and who had full and proper regard for the conscientious objector, might have made it possible for the registration officer to register you anyhow upon the receipt of a letter such as you wrote, and then let you come forward under the regular provisions of the Act, but they haven't done it, and you stand as having defied that law, and that law carries a compulsion, and I am going to give you *a year and a day*[1] ... and then see what the future has in store.

I know you won't be discouraged over this; and the battle that you will have to fight now will be one of a little bit of resentment, feeling that possibly in spite of all that you have tried to do among the sharecroppers and among the West Side of Chicago, that you should find yourself wearing stripes in a prison cell. It seems hard for a boy to understand that his ideals can be stricken down so. Here is where you have got to exercise a little charity for us. There is no thought of harming you, but there is a great law that has got to be uniform for millions of our people. Now, you have run afoul of it in your aspirations and your hopes and in your conscience, and I have got to give you this sentence to carry out my obligations as a Judge, that I swore to protect that Flag and to protect the Constitution; and I am sure of this: that the physical punishment and inconvenience that you have will not cost you, when your soul is striving, as yours evidently is striving, for the expression of its highest duty. And just consider that I am your father, for the time being, and say that if you were my son, I would not feel differently about it.

1. No easy sentence, as a prison term of a year and a day automatically deprives one of his citizenship, making him, if born in the United States, a stateless alien.—Ed.

The Responsibilities of Conscientious Objection

The pacifist demand for the abolition of conscription is short-sighted. For conscription has the salutary effect of bringing home the question of war. War is an affair of the state and therefore of the totality of its subjects, not of a minority or majority of volunteers or militarists. All citizens share responsibility for it both in peace and war. They thus share the burden of this responsibility, and must themselves face the question whether it is right or wrong. This fact is given due expression and brought right home by conscription, whereas it is glossed over in every other type of military constitution. To make military service once again something for mercenary or volunteer armies would be to absolve the individual from direct responsibility for war and to leave both war and the resultant "moral odium" . . . to others. . . . If anything is calculated to perpetuate war, it is this Pharisaic attitude. Conscription, however, has the in-

From Karl Barth, Church Dogmatics, III/4, 466-469. Reprinted with special permission.

valuable advantage of confronting both the prudent and the stupid, both the peace-loving and less peace-loving, with the problem of the belligerent state as their own personal problem, and conversely of compelling them to express their own personal attitude to war in their responsibility as citizens of the state instead of treating it merely as a matter of private opinion. If the state makes participation in war obligatory upon all, the individual must face the question whether as a citizen he can approve and cooperate in war, i.e., every war as such, or whether as a citizen he must resist and evade it. The abolition of conscription would take the edge off this decision for those not personally affected. It would make it merely political rather than both political and personal. This could not possibly contribute to the serious discussion or solution of the problem of war. Pacifists, therefore, should be the very last to call for the abolition of conscription.

The dignity of an absolute divine command cannot, of course, be ascribed to military service. . . . The state is not God, nor can it command as He does. No compulsory duty which it imposes on the individual, nor urgency with which it presses for its fulfillment, can alter the fact that the attitude of the individual to all its decisions and measures, and therefore to this too, is limited and defined by his relationship to God, so that, although as a citizen he is committed to what is thought right and therefore resolved by the government or the majority, he is not bound by it finally and absolutely. . . .

Two formal presuppositions are essential if . . . refusal of military service by one or more individuals is to be accepted as imperative and therefore legitimate. The first is that the objector must accomplish his act of insubordination in the unity of his individual and personal existence with his existence as a citizen. There can be no question of calming his private conscience by binding his civic conscience. His relationship to God will not absolve him from his obligation to the state; it will simply pose it in a specific way, which may perhaps be this way. Quite apart from less worthy motives, it cannot be merely a matter of satisfying his own personal abhorrence of violence and bloodshed, of keeping his own hands clean. His refusal of military service can have nothing whatever to do with even the noblest desertion of the state, and certainly not with anarchy. He must be convinced and assured that by his opposition he stands and acts for the political community as willed and ordained by God, not denying the state but affirming it in contrast to the government, the majority, the existing law and constitution. His refusal of military service must have the meaning and character of an appeal from the badly informed state of the present to the better informed state of the future. Therefore, notwithstanding all appearances to the contrary, it must be intended and executed as an act of loyalty to the state.

Second, the man who objects to military service must be prepared to accept without murmur or complaint the consequences of the insubordinate form of his national loyalty, the hostility of the government or majority to which he may be exposed, and the penalty for his violation of the existing law and constitution. He cannot demand that the state which in his view is badly informed should treat him as though it were already what he hopes it will be, namely, the better informed state of tomorrow. He cannot ask, therefore, for considerate exceptions in the administration of valid decrees, or even for protective laws of exemption, in the case of those likeminded with himself. He should certainly not try to be drafted to the medical or pioneer corps instead of the infantry. He should not ask for the impossible, claiming on the one hand to act as a prospective martyr, and on the other to be spared from martyrdom after all, or at least to have it made easier for him. He must act honestly and consistently as a revolutionary, prepared to pay the price of his action, content to know that he has on his side both God and the better informed state of the future, hoping to bear an effective witness to it today, but ready at least to suffer what[ever penalties] his insubordination must now entail. If these two presuppositions are not present, there can be no question of true conscientious objection, i.e., of the objection which is commanded and therefore legitimate.

There is also a material error in conscientious objection, however, if it rests on an absolute refusal of war, i.e., on the absolutism of radical pacifism. In such a case, it is no less rebellion against the command of God than the affirmation of war and participation in it on the basis of radical militarism, i.e., of the superstition of the inevitability of war, or the view that it is an element in the divine world order and an essential constituent of the state. If we are genuinely ready to obey the command of God, we cannot go so far either to the right or to the left as to maintain such absolute ethical tenets and modes of action in loyalty to Him. On the contrary, we shall have to take account of the limitation of even the best human views, principles, and attributes. In the national loyalty which is always required, conscientious objection is possible only if it is relative and not absolute, and therefore if it is not tainted by the idea that the state is utterly forbidden in any circumstances either to wage war or to prepare for it. . . .

On the other hand, conscientious objection may well be necessary and legitimate in a situation in which one or more persons cannot fail to see that the cause for which the state is arming or waging war is concretely an evil one, that the war in which they are asked to participate is one of the many unjust and irresponsible wars which are not risked out of a genuine emergency but planned and embarked upon deliberately. It is not to be expected that in

such a situation this recognition will be a general one, or
that it will take a specific form among the people at large.
It may often be current as an obscure premonition on the
part of many, and official propaganda will naturally do all
it can to prevent it breaking through. But in such a situation
it will certainly obtrude upon certain individuals in such
a definite form that in spite of all official propaganda they
cannot conceal the fact, but are taught by the divine command, that they must protest against this war not only in
thought and word but also by conscientious objection. This
does not mean that they will be released from their responsibility to the state. It means that they will have to
discharge this responsibility in such a way that they refuse
to fulfil the duty of military service, not in principle, but
in relation to the concrete military action now demanded.
. . . It is thus strange that even Schleirmacher should dare
to make the statement: "To exclude oneself from participation in war, if one does not consider it to be just, is rebellion." This is surely wrong as a general proposition. An
individual may hold an erroneous opinion as to whether a
war is just. And the man who in answering this question
thinks that he should act on his objection must realize that
he may be mistaken, that he may not really have the command of God on his side at all, and that he thus runs the
risk of being a rebel. Nevertheless this does not alter the
fact that the question of responsibility for war and warlike
preparation must always be heard and answered by individuals. . . . The government or majority in any state has
to reckon with the fact that individuals cannot spare themselves but have necessarily to put the personal question of
responsibility for the specific war at issue, and that it may
happen that they will have to return a negative answer to
the question even in practice. It would be a great gain for
peace if all governments or majorities in all states knew
they had actually to take this into account.

IV

THE BOMB AND AFTER

"No more war, war never again."

—Pope Paul VI at the United Nations

Helmut Gollwitzer

1908–

Author, lecturer, and professor of theology at the University of Bonn, Helmut Gollwitzer is also a leading exponent of what has come to be called "nuclear pacifism." An imprecise term at best, "nuclear pacifism" has nothing in common with the pacifism and nonresistance of the historic peace churches. It does not reject all war. As Gollwitzer told the 1966 Geneva Conference on Church and Society: "The answer given by Christian pacifists leaves to non-Christians that very secular task which requires the greatest love and unselfishness, namely, the use of force. . . ." The "pacifist" element in his thought (and it is as absolute and uncompromising as can be imagined) enters only with the prospect of nuclear war. For nuclear pacifism applies consistently and rigorously the old teaching on the just war to the new weapons of mass destruction. As with the Schoolmen, its key words are "proper disposition," "proportionality," and the rest. Since nuclear war can, in their opinion, have none of these characteristics, therefore the Christian's duty consists in refusing cooperation to any state undertaking such a conflict, regardless of the provocation.

In "The New Pacifism," which first appeared in the German theological journal *Die Stimme der Gemeinde,* Gollwitzer examines the responsibilities of the Church in light of the scientific transformation of the traditional means of warfare.

The New Pacifism

In 1526 Martin Luther published his famous pamphlet, "Can soldiers be in a state of grace?" This title expresses a question which the Church cannot evade. It is an inevitable consequence of the Christian message that people who hear it and are influenced by it come to the Church, which preaches this message to them, and ask: "If it is true—this

From Fellowship, *September 1, 1961. Reprinted with the special permission of the Fellowship of Reconciliation.*

message of God's reconciliation with the world, of His self-sacrifice on the Cross for man whom He loved and has lost, and if His commandment is true that we are to love our neighbor and even our enemy—can we still participate in the use of force in the many forms customary in human society, and without which this society cannot subsist, because there is so much sin and evil in the world? Can we still continue to be judges, policemen, government officials, government ministers, statesmen and soldiers?" The Church should not evade the duty of answering these questions, and it always has evaded them. . . .

Why did the churches avoid committing themselves? Why did Christians avoid facing the question whether one can participate in atomic warfare and still remain in a state of grace? I think their hesitation was due to political and theological reasons. Atomic weapons were first discovered in the West and were developed in order to avert the menace first of yellow, then of red, totalitarianism. Today their existence serves to maintain the balance of power between West and East, and it is hoped through them to prevent the further spread of communist dictatorship; they act as a mutual deterrent against atomic warfare, which might break out more easily if one side were stronger than the other. Freedom of speech exists in the West, but not in the East. Anyone who refuses to participate in the use of atomic weapons therefore weakens the West and increases the danger of our being overwhelmed by Bolshevism. He makes it more difficult for the governments of the West to maintain an order based on freedom and justice, and plunges soldiers and politicians into insoluble conflicts of conscience. . . .

How can one obey the Christian message about loving God and one's neighbor, when one has to use force or even kill other people to maintain order and justice? This is where the conflict of conscience arises. Hitherto all the great Christian confessions have given the same answer (for different theological reasons but with the same result in practice). The classic formulation of this answer is found in the *Declaration* made by the Confessing Church of Germany at Barmen in 1934: "In the world which is not yet redeemed in which the Church exists, the State has been entrusted by God with the task of maintaining justice and peace, as far as is humanly possible, by using (or threatening to use) force." It is therefore the duty of every Christian to assist the state in this task. Just as the police are essential for the maintenance of justice and peace at home, so the army is essential to maintain justice and peace outside. As long as the state uses the army to defend justice, the Christian acts rightly in helping the state as a policeman, soldier or munitions worker, even if this involves having to kill those who threaten his country with armed force. . . .

. . . Theological ethics [then] regarded the basic problem as solved: whether in certain cases a soldier can still be in a state of grace. They therefore did not ask themselves whether the development of modern technical weapons and military methods did not completely transform the nature of war to such an extent that it was high time for the Church to protest. So we slid blindly into the age of total war, clinging to formulas which may have been applicable in earlier times. That is why people often ask us today whether the CBR [i.e., chemical, biological, radiological] weapons are really essentially different from the atrocities committed during the Second World War, and whether the Church, which hitherto has never radically opposed participation in war, should do so now. There is only one answer: the Church ought probably to have refused to participate in war much sooner; at any rate, this is its very last chance to do so, because the new weapons of mass destruction have brutalized warfare so completely that participation in it is completely incompatible with the will of God. The weapons which Paul, Augustine and Luther had in mind could still be adapted to use in a war fought in defense of justice. Once the decision had been taken to apply force in the cause of justice, then the use of a rifle or a culverin was as justifiable as the use of a sword or a catapult. Although all lethal weapons are terrible in themselves, it could not be affirmed that such weapons "misused God's gifts, blasphemed against God's goodness, and betrayed man who is made in God's image" any more than did the sword spoken of by Paul, in face of the still more terrible reality of evil in the world and the need for adamant resistance to it.

The official reports and articles in the technical military periodicals today, describing the diabolical inventions of perverted science and strategy, give one the impression that they were written by madmen. It suffices to read a few of them; they make it superfluous to give any lengthy explanations as to whether modern methods of mass destruction are different in quality from the weapons of earlier times. The very question is an insult to the honorable weapons formerly used, which were carried openly, and which it would have been considered dishonorable and treacherous to employ against an unarmed man.

Those arms were a token of a virile concern to defend justice and to protect the weak against exploitation and wrong; the man who used them had personal control of them, so that he could use his discretion. There was therefore some sense in giving him advice about the distinctions between a Christian soldier and a common assassin. Today it has become impossible to draw any such distinction—and this is the primary reason for our refusal to participate in war today.

By their very nature these weapons eliminate all distinction between combatants and non-combatants. It is true earlier types of weapons (from the axe to the bomb) could also be used against non-combatants; but this was an illegitimate way of using them; it was not determined by their very nature. The new instruments of warfare completely abolish all distinction between combatants and civilians; in fact, their very purpose is to decimate the population of the enemy country. By their very nature these weapons are blind. . . .

. . . All this changes also the character of the deterrence which is the purpose of armament in peacetime. Hitherto the purpose of armaments was to deter the enemy from aggression by threatening him with armed resistance. The present methods of intimidation, on the other hand, are really threats to take reprisals on hostages. Intimidation by nuclear weapons is a threat to proceed to a terrible retribution; if millions of innocent citizens, adults and children, are wiped out indiscriminately, the same fate will be inflicted on the population of the enemy; it may even be undertaken as a preventive measure. This clearly means the end of the partial humanization of war which existed in the past—just as there can no longer be any mutually respected Red Cross, and no code of ethics for the soldier. When a soldier is trained to massacre thousands of civilians at once, he cannot be expected to respect the life of an individual non-combatant. The new weapons have sounded the death-knell of all military ethics; and this places the army chaplain in an entirely new position. These weapons destroy all connection between war and justice, on which the analogy between war and police work was formerly based. The analogy made it quite clear that a war undertaken in defense of justice could not resort to "any methods whatsoever," any more than a murderer can be menaced by "any methods whatsoever" in order to deter him from crime. If a kidnapper has kidnapped a child and threatens to murder it, the police cannot kidnap his own child and threaten to murder it. When Hitler announced, in January

1939, that he intended to "liquidate" all the Jews in Europe if war was declared, the Western powers could not retaliate by threatening to kill an expatriated German for every Jew.

Certain methods and certain threats destroy the very justice which they are trying to safeguard. For threats are effective only if one is prepared to carry them out. Hence the limitations of the police, who cannot have recourse to "any methods whatsoever," as the criminal does. But they accept these limitations in the name of the justice which they exist to defend, and endeavor to be stronger than the criminal while confining themselves to legitimate methods, i.e., methods which respect the difference between guilty and innocent persons. The same applies to international relations; war can no longer be said to safeguard justice when the methods which it employs, or threatens to employ, are in themselves crimes.

The Christian ethic concerning war was, moreover, based on the assumption that the purpose of the war was to conclude a just peace with the enemy who, through the use of force, has been obliged to abandon his unjust intentions and to accept a new phase of peaceful co-existence—just as the police use force not in order to kill the offender but in order to disarm him. And the modern theory of the just war recognized the enemy's right to life, and to exist as a sovereign state. The rules of warfare and the weapons used were in accordance with this theory; so were the hostilities which were always preceded by warnings, by a solemn declaration of war, and in which battles alternated with periods of repose so that diplomacy was never completely paralyzed and there was always opportunity for contacts, negotiations, and for the official intervention of neutrals.

The new weapons, on the other hand, have only one purpose: to take the enemy by surprise and annihilate him. And they insist on nothing less than unconditional surrender. They correspond to a mentality which refuses to recognize the enemy's right to live and which is blind to any relationship except that of friend-and-foe. It refuses to recognize any *human* relation to the enemy or any responsibility toward him, and regards it as treason even to think that the antagonism may be relative. It is the mentality of the person who thinks he is the only person fit to live and who therefore wants to destroy everything outside his own "world." . . . One can even say more: not only do these weapons correspond to this mentality; they condition it and impose it. They can only be used (in fact or in threat) if we are prepared to stop at nothing, to inflict every kind of disaster on those who touch our property, to stop at no injustice in order to defend our own rights, to destroy the lives and health of millions of people in town and country, including women and children and even the lives of future generations, in order to maintain our Western freedoms and privileges (or, on the other side, in order to maintain Socialism).

These new weapons turn us all into murderers in our mentality; for that is the only mentality which can produce and use such weapons. The older weapons left us the choice of how they should be used, so that there was still some purpose in urging people to use them rightly; the new weapons, on the other hand, cannot be used except for indiscriminate mass murder. Anyone who uses them is forced into the mentality of a murderer. A Church which recognizes its fellow men as barriers appointed by God against our own sinful tendency to pride and self-glorification, and which realizes that it is the Body of Christ extending over all frontiers (and that this is not merely an empty phrase), a Christian Church which recognizes that in the enemy camp there are also men whom God loves and who are members of the Body of Christ, might still consider it possible to participate in the former struggles between combatants, owing to its own existence within the secular orders. But if the Church were to participate in an atomic war of annihilation it would destroy itself spiritually, even more than externally. . . .

Our analysis of the transformation in warfare brought about by the new weapons can lead us to only one conclusion: there must never be an atomic war, and that there never *will* be an atomic war as far as it depends on us Christians, on Christian politicians, on you and me. "You and I will not have anything to do with these inventions of the devil"—that is the Christian message which the pastor must pass on to his congregation—"We shall not participate, even in case of reprisals." Christians cannot participate, because the only circumstance in which it ever was permissible for them to think of taking up arms was in order to defend justice. But when the authorities urge a Christian to participate in these preparations for universal massacre, there is only one answer he can give: *Si omnes, ego non* ("Even if everyone else consents, I refuse!").

A. J. Muste
1885–1967

Dutch-born Abraham Johannes Muste (called "Foxy Grandpa" by a youthful follower) was for fifty years a crusader for peace and social justice. An ordained minister in the Dutch Reformed Church of America, during World War I, he resigned his pulpit in Newtonville, Massachusetts, rather than betray his pacifist convictions through preaching a holy war against the Germans. Throughout the twenties and thirties, he was active in the labor movement, helping to found the Brookwood Labor College and to organize strikes in the rubber and auto industries: it was during a Muste-led strike in 1936 that the technique of the sit-down was first employed. Although he abandoned Christian pacifism in the early thirties and became a Marxist-Leninist revolutionary, he returned to the faith after a very short time. From 1940 until his death, he was the moving spirit in innumerable peace undertakings: the Fellowship of Reconciliation, the War Resisters League, the Committee for Non-Violent Action, Peacemakers, the campaign against the Polaris-carrying submarine, and, in his last years, the agitation against the Vietnamese war. A prolific writer, he published in 1952 his most widely read work, *Of Holy Disobedience,* urging noncooperation with the state's preparations for war.

The following selection, expressive of the shame felt in peace circles at the atomic bombing of Japan and the onset of the Cold War, contains his formula for peace. Muste held that since mankind seems trapped in a vicious circle of violence and counterviolence, the only way to break the cycle is by unilateral disarmament of a superpower willing to become a martyr, a veritable Christ of the nations, for the sake of redeeming the world. There is much food for thought in this essay, especially since its main theme has been taken up of late by nonpacifists and the nonreligious, including Sir Stephen King-Hall, a retired Commander in the Royal Navy. There are also several questions that might be asked:

1) By announcing in advance that the U.S. is willing to undergo martyrdom, does this not in effect tempt the other side to bring the evil to pass in a kind of self-fulfilling prophecy in reverse?

2) Such radical action would require national unanimity; but where hundreds of millions of people are concerned, there is bound to be a sizeable minority in opposition. What happens to them? Does the majority have the right to compel their martyrdom?

3) Would national martyrdom indeed heal the world, or might it not condemn other innocent nations to war and tyranny by removing their shield?

A Plea for Unilateral Disarmament

If ever in its long history mankind has stood in need of

From *A. J. Muste,* Not by Might *(New York: Harper & Row, Inc. 1947), pp. 111-123, 128-129. Reprinted with special permission.*

a nation capable of leading it to a radically new adaptation to an unprecedented situation, it is now. If ever, in the providence of God, there was need for a nation willing to assume the burden of being a "spiritual Israel," seized as a whole with a transcendant idea and for its sake willing to renounce power, it is now. . . .

What would it mean, then, for the United States in the present crisis to assume the role of a nation seeking to apply the law of good will, love and self-sacrifice?

We suggest that it would involve three main courses of action. First, the United States would renounce warmaking as a national policy for any purposes and under any circumstances. War is violence in its most irrational, outrageous and futile form, and a nation seeking to follow a Christian or pacifist course simply could not any longer have anything to do with it. As evidence that the United States was through with warmaking it would disband its armed forces, scrap its guns and bombers, stop making atomic bombs and the weapons of germ warfare and destroy such atomic and biological weapons as it already has on hand. In other words, it would disarm unilaterally —at once—regardless of what other nations might be willing to do.

Secondly, the nation would launch navies and air forces on great missions of mercy to starving, sick and homeless peoples everywhere. It would spend the billions it would save by scrapping its war establishment, and perhaps a good many more billions, on rehabilitating the sick and broken-down economies of the world. . . .

Thirdly, the United States would propose to participate in building the necessary world organizations both in the cultural, the economic and the political field, including probably some kind of federal world government along some such lines as those of our federal union.

Obviously the key to these proposals, and their most

controversial element, is that the United States should disarm. It is for this reason—and not because the proposals for rehabilitation and world organization are not immensely important—that we shall devote our attention primarily to the disarmament question. . . .

We need not dwell at length . . . upon the point that, if men only exercised a little sense, fear of the effects of atomic war and other prudential, common-sense considerations might lead a nation just to have done with war. Fear may in certain circumstances and up to a point have salutary effects, as when fear of epidemics leads people to build a pure water supply system. As someone has said, when a man is pursued by a bull, he can run faster than he ever thought possible. But beyond a certain point fear leads either to the endless lashing about of the panic-stricken, or to paralysis. On the other hand, men try today to persuade themselves that the atomic bomb is not so bad: It is not "the ultimate weapon," certain experts solemnly assure us; if it is a really big city it might take several bombs to wipe it out. So men go about their eating and drinking, marrying and giving in marriage. On the other hand, they say to themselves: "This thing is so bad that it is now more than ever necessary to keep ahead in the race. We must do everything possible to ensure that we suffer a little less and the others a whole lot more." Fear cannot solve our problem, since mutual fear is our problem: how to break that electric circuit running between Russia and the United States which becomes daily more heavily charged as the fear in each stimulates fear in the other? . . .

. . . As things stand, neither Russia nor the United States will make a gesture to restore genuine confidence, some such gesture as the suspension of the production of atomic weapons by the United States. Bargains may conceivably be made which in the opinion of both parties will leave each in the same relative power position, but that solves nothing. It does not constitute a move toward peace but simply a move in the ongoing hidden war. For the rest, the United States dare not make a move which might actually weaken its relative power position: How can it be sure that the Russians will not take advantage of it? How indeed be sure that at that very moment the Russians may not perfect a weapon which will radically alter the balance and render the United States utterly "defenseless"? If, on the other hand, the United States—or Russia—makes a move which is only an apparent and not a real concession, the realists on the other side will, of course, recognize it for what it is and be accordingly unimpressed. Finally, there is the question: Suppose a nation, the United States, for example, recognizing how desperate is the need for preventing another war and, therefore, of resolving "the crisis of confidence," made some genuine concessions, risked its power position. Suppose these measures failed to "work," that Russia just "took advantage" of them. Would the United States then—too late perhaps—conclude that it had made a grave error and get back into the armaments race or would it persist in the path of reconciliation by self-sacrifice? Plainly, a nation which is not prepared to make the latter decision would be under the suspicion that it was in the final analysis bluffing and that would be decisive in determining its effect on another nation and on the total situation. Furthermore, a nation which was not prepared to make the decision indicated would be psychologically incapable of embarking on a course of reconciliation. . . .

When we do turn our eyes inward upon ourselves we shall see that the basic issue is not how we can prevent others from waging war against us, but we should be purged of the guilt of the obliteration bombing [of Germany] and the guilt of Hiroshima and Nagasaki. When we see ourselves, we shall smite our breasts and cry, "God, be merciful unto us sinners."

We shall not need to be told that there is only one true cure for the malady which afflicts us as well as other peoples. That cure is repentance. And repentance always means unilateral action, though that may well stimulate multilateral action by means of example and contagion. No one can repent of other men's or nation's sin. And when one repents he does not wait to see whether someone else stops sinning before deciding that he must quit. We shall, therefore, as a nation renounce the sin of war-making, and that will mean disarming whether anyone else does or not, divesting ourselves of the means to wage war. What use has the converted sinner for the paraphernalia of crime? . . .

The course we have sketched is the course a Christian, a pacifist, nation would follow. What would happen if it did?

If such a savior-nation appeared—rather we should say, if the United States became such a nation, because on this plane action has to be unilateral; no nation can ask another to accept such a role—then it is most likely that other nations would acclaim us and would follow our example. Is it likely that other nations would attack and devour a nation which alone among the nations might conceivably have been able to conquer them all and which now came armed with food, clothing, medicine, machines, skills, instead of with atomic bombs and germ weapons? Is it likely they would hate the nation which had broken the tension, so largely caused by its own hideous weapons, that had held the world in its awful grip? Did you hate your mother who came to you in the dark when you were shrieking in the torment of a nightmare and took you in her arms and comforted you?

Surely people who think that if a nation such as ours were to give up the way of violence other nations would go right ahead and bomb and kill anyway are assuming that the law of cause and effect has been suspended. I assume that it operates. War comes because two nations pursue certain policies. It is the inevitable result of those policies. Then one nation radically changes its course. Will the other not be affected by that? The cause is fundamentally changed: will the results, the effect, remain the same? I do not think so. The trouble with the world is that men do not reap what they sow but rather that, having sown the wind, they are too surely to reap the whirlwind. We shall not reap another kind of harvest until we sow another kind of seed. But if we do sow another kind of seed, though it be in tears, we shall presently reap in joy another kind of harvest. . . .

A word should be said at this point about a question based on a distinction between the Russian people and their rulers, which troubles many people. "Granted," they say, "that the Russian people are the same as other folks and may be expected to respond normally to fair and generous treatment, is it not true that the men in the Kremlin are totalitarians with vast power and may be expected not to relinquish that power without a bitter fight?" One possible answer to that question is that they do indeed have a vast apparatus of power and wield it ruthlessly, but that they have often demonstrated that they are realists. Being realists, they do not take our present inadequate and largely phony "peace" proposals seriously. By the same token, if they were faced with proposals which really made peace and the peaceful development of their own country possible, they would respond in kind. Thus democratic life might revive or be born in Russia. Critical as I have been of Stalinist leaders over many years, I do not believe that this possibility can be dismissed as simply silly. . . .

. . . If Stalin and the Russian people were to be confronted with the true revolutionary spectacle of a Christian nation actually practicing the faith it professed, taking the way of the Cross—of good will, reconciliation and self-sacrifice—in this unutterably tragic hour, I cannot but believe they would be impressed. I think they would know they were in the presence of power—real power—power against which neither Russia nor the gates of hell could prevail. Does the reader doubt that? When professing Christians say they doubt it, is it because they really do, deep down in their hearts, or because they are not ready to meet the demands which their faith makes upon them, including that of being willing to be deemed foolish by men in order that as little children they may accept and live by the wisdom of God? . . .

[Yet], if Western civilization has reached the point of disintegration where a nation which followed the redemptive course we have described was subjected to attack and perhaps crucifixion, it would mean that in any event only four choices are now open to this nation and its people:

1. The first possibility is that the United States would be destroyed along with other nations in the general holocaust of an atomic war.

2. A second possibility is that the United States, with the guilt of first launching atomic warfare on its hands, would be defeated by Russia or some other nation in the coming war. Thus it would lose both in a material and in a spiritual sense. . . .

3. A third possible outcome is that the United States would emerge as the so-called victor in such a war. . . . It would still remain that spiritually [as well as economically] the nation would suffer incalculable loss and utter defeat. It would have the guilt on its hands of having first launched atomic war in 1945. The United States of the American Dream would finally disappear and the nation would "harden into bitter empire." The rest of the world would lie prostrate and mangled at its feet. Having visited this havoc on mankind in order to secure its own survival and dominance, this nation would be hated and des-

pised as no other nation in all history has been. It would have the task, which no other empire has succeeded in achieving, of trying to rule the world. Does any sane person believe that it would succeed? What shall a man, or a nation, gain if it wins the whole world and loses its own soul? What shall be said of a nation which loses its soul and the whole world as well?

4. The fourth and final choice is the one we are discussing, namely, that the nation, having assumed a redemptive mission, having by accepting suffering washed the stain of Hiroshima and Nagasaki from its soul, would be defeated, would suffer terribly, would perhaps lose its existence as a nation-state. We must not yield to any disposition to minimize the horrors this might involve. But on no ground that I can think of is it clear that this outcome would be substantially worse than the others. Whatever course the nation now takes, its national existence is at stake. The only live option remaining has to do with the cause for which we stake that existence. And surely no one who believes in the Judaeo-Christian world-view can doubt for a moment that such a savior-nation would be honored and loved more than any other in all history by the generations to come—as men have always loved the prophets and pioneers and martyrs, though in their lifetime they crucified them, and have understood well enough that the ultimate victory rested with the sons of God.

The sickness of our age is such that there is no longer any cure for it except that which might be wrought by a nation prepared to give its life in order that the nations might be healed and return to God. There is, of course, no nation which is not subject to the moral law, including the command to love. But if there be a nation on which a special responsibility rests, it is surely the United States. In any event, moral responsibility calls, as we have seen, for unilateral action. What we who live in this land have to do is to see to it that this nation heeds the call of God and of distressed humanity.

The Popes and Peace

The Roman Catholic response to the nuclear menace has been as emphatic as the Protestant, but with this difference: whereas the diffuse nature of Protestantism has tended to blunt its appeals, the popes and the councils speak with a more authoritative voice. The documents included in this section have been selected to illustrate the evolution of papal thought from the early stages of the nuclear arms race to the point where the world now stands on the eve of doomsday. They are noteworthy in that, whereas they deal with the most up-to-date issues, their arguments pro and con all gather around a common pole: the traditional just war.

In the first statement, from an address to the Eighth Congress of the World Medical Association, in Rome, September 1954, Pope Pius XII raises the question of the moral responsibility of the man of science for the uses to which others put the creations of his genius. Pius's definition of the scientist's role harkens back to Aquinas's discussion of the duties of the priest in a just war. Although he may encourage others to fight, it is contrary to his profession for him to take part in the bloodshed himself. Ordinarily the same would apply to the scientist, except that in an atomic war of self-defense, acknowledged by Pius as a real possibility, the scientist would have to weigh his duty in accordance with "just war" norms.

John XXIII's encyclical *Pacem in Terris (Peace on Earth)* goes beyond his predecessor's statement in denying that justice can ever have recourse to atomic war, and by setting forth in broad principles a peace program derived from the natural law, involving negotiation, the recognition of the rights of others, and disarmament.

"The Fostering of Peace and the Promotion of a Community of Nations," the fifth chapter of the Second Vatican Council's 1965 *Pastoral Constitution on the Church in the Modern World,* is probably the most comprehensive Roman pronouncement on war in modern times. It is at once an explication of new facts in terms of traditional concepts and a departure from traditional views. As regards peace, it is "Augustinian," reaffirming that peace can never be achieved permanently on earth, but is something that must be constantly striven for and won anew. It is also valuable as a guide in current problems because it condemns absolutely a total nuclear war for "peace" and the individual who commits genocide "under orders," extends the just war to cover guerrilla war, and recognizes for the first time the legitimacy of a qualified pacifism and conscientious objection.

The Immorality of ABC Warfare

Has not the doctor . . . a role to play in producing, perfecting and increasing the methods of modern warfare, in particular the methods of ABC [atomic, biological, chemical] warfare? One cannot answer this question without having first resolved this other one: Is modern "total war," especially ABC warfare, permissible in principle? There can be no doubt, particularly in view of the horrors and immense sufferings caused by modern warfare, that to unleash it without just cause (that is to say, without its being forced upon one by an obvious, extremely serious and otherwise unavoidable injustice) constitutes a "crime."

One cannot even in principle pose the question of the lawfulness of atomic, bacteriological and chemical warfare except in the case where it must be judged as indispensable in order to defend oneself under the circumstances pointed out above. Even then, however, one must strive to avoid it by all possible means through international understandings

From Pope Pius XII, "War and Peace," in Henry W. Flannery, ed., Patterns for Peace: Catholic Statements on International Order *(Westminister, Md.: Newman Press, 1962). Reprinted with special permission.*

or to impose limits on its use that are so clear and rigorous that its effects remain restricted to the demands of defense. When, moreover, putting this method to use involves such an extension of the evil that it entirely escapes from the control of man, its use must be rejected as immoral. Here there would no longer be a question of "defense" against injustice or a necessary "safeguarding" of legitimate possessions, but the pure and simple annihilation of all human life within the radius of action. This is not permitted for any reason whatsoever.

Let us return to the doctor. If ever, within the compass of the limits already indicated, a modern ABC war can be justified, the question of the morally lawful collaboration of the doctor can then be raised. But you will be in agreement with Us: one prefers not to see the doctor occupied with a task of this sort. It is in too great a contrast to his basic duty: to give aid and cure, not to do injury or kill.

. . . The doctor is the enemy of war and the promoter of peace. And he is ready to heal the wounds of war, once they already exist, so should he do all he can to prevent them.

Mutual good will always allows states to avoid war as the final means of settling differences between themselves. Several days ago We again expressed Our desire that any war be punished at the international level if [it] is not absolutely necessary for the self-defense of a community seriously threatened by an injustice that cannot be prevented in any other way. Even such a war, however, must be waged at the risk of giving a free hand in international affairs to brute violence and lack of conscience. It is not enough, therefore, to have to defend oneself against just any injustice in order to justify resorting to the violent means of war. When the damages caused by war are not comparable to those of "tolerated injustice," one may have a duty to "suffer the injustice."

What We have just discussed applies especially to ABC warfare—atomic, biological and chemical. As to the question of knowing whether it [ABC warfare] can become clearly necessary in *self-defense* against ABC warfare, let it suffice for Us to have posed it here. The answer can be deduced from the same principles which are today decisive for permitting war in general [i.e., the principles of the just war] . . . .

Pacem in Terris

The following excerpts from Pacem in Terris, *taken from the English version issued by the Paulist Press, come from the Introduction; part III, on the relations between states; and, lastly, from the concluding prayer for peace. The italicized headings, not in the original text, have been added to lend continuity to the excerpted portions. Reprinted with special permission.*

The Natural Law

How strongly does the turmoil of individual men and peoples contrast with the perfect order of the universe! It is as if the relationships which bind them together could be controlled only by force. But the Creator of the world has imprinted in man's heart an order which his conscience reveals to him and enjoins him to obey. . . . But fickleness of opinion often produces this error, that many think that the relationships between men and states can be governed by the same laws as the forces and irrational elements of the universe, whereas the laws governing them are of quite a different kind and are to be sought elsewhere, namely, where the Father of all things wrote them, that is, in the nature of man. By these laws men are most admirably taught, first of all how they should conduct their mutual dealings among themselves, then how the relationships between the citizens and the public authorities of each state should be regulated, then how states should deal with one another, and finally how, on the one hand, individual men and states, and on the other hand, the community of all peoples, should act towards each other, the establishment of such a world community of peoples being urgently demanded today by the requirements of universal common good. . . .

The Moral Law of Nations

Our Predecessors have constantly maintained, and We join them in reasserting, that political communities are subjects of rights and duties. This means that their relationships also must be harmonized in truth, in justice, in a working solidarity, in liberty. The same moral law which governs relations between individual human beings, serves also to regulate the relations of political communities with one another. . . .

Political communities have the right to existence, to self-development and to the means necessary for this. They have the right to play the leading part in the process of their own development and the right to their good name with due honors. From which it follows as a simultaneous consequence that they have also the corresponding duty of respecting those rights in others and of avoiding an act of violation. Just as an individual man may not pursue his own interests to the detriment of other men, so, on the international level, one State may not develop itself by restricting or oppressing other States. St. Augustine rightly says, *What are kingdoms without justice but bands of robbers?*

Not only can it happen, but it usually does happen that the advantages and conveniences which nations strive to acquire for themselves become objects of contention; nevertheless, the resulting disagreements must be settled, not by force, nor by deceit or trickery, but rather in the only manner which is worthy of the dignity of man, i.e., by a mutual assessment of the reasons on both sides of the dispute, by a mature and objective investigation of the situation, and by an equitable reconciliation of differences of opinion. . . .

Disarmament

On the other hand, it is with deep sorrow that We note the enormous stocks of armaments that have been and still are being made in the more economically developed countries with a vast outlay of intellectual and economic resources. And so it happens that, while the people of these countries are loaded with heavy burdens, other countries as a result are deprived of the collaboration they need in order to make economic and social progress.

The production of arms is allegedly justified on the grounds that in present-day conditions peace cannot be preserved without an equal balance of armaments. And so, if one country increases in armaments, others feel the need to do the same. And if one country is equipped with nuclear weapons, other countries must produce their own, equally destructive.

Consequently, people live in constant fear lest the storm that threatens every moment should break upon them with dreadful violence. And with good reason, for the arms of war are ready at hand. Even though it is difficult to believe that anyone would deliberately take the responsibility for the appalling destruction and sorrow that war would bring in its train, it cannot be denied that the conflagration may be set off by some uncontrollable and unexpected chance. And one must bear in mind that, even though the monstrous power of modern weapons acts as a deterrent, it is to be feared that the mere continuance of nuclear tests, undertaken with war in mind, will have fatal consequences for life on earth.

Justice, right reason and humanity, therefore, urgently demand that the arms race should cease; that the stockpiles which exist in various countries should be reduced equally and simultaneously by the parties concerned; that nuclear weapons should be banned; and that a general agreement should eventually be reached about progressive disarmament and an effective method of control. . . .

We believe that this can be brought to pass, and We consider that it is something which reason requires, that it is eminently desirable in itself and that it will prove to be the source of many benefits.

In the first place, it is an objective demanded by reason. There can be, or at least there should be, no doubt that relations between states, as between individuals, should be regulated, not by force of arms, but by the light of reason, by the rule, that is, of truth, of justice and of active and sincere co-operation.

Secondly, We say that it is an objective earnestly to be desired in itself. Is there anyone who does not ardently yearn to see war banished, to see peace preserved and daily more firmly established?

And finally, it is an objective which will be a fruitful source of many benefits, for its advantages will be felt everywhere—by individuals, by families, by nations, by the whole human family. The warning of Pius XII still rings in our ears: *Nothing is lost by peace; everything may be lost by war.* . . .

Fearfulness and Hope in the Contemporary World

Men are becoming more and more convinced that disputes which arise between states should not be resolved by recourse to arms, but rather by negotiation.

It is true that on historical grounds this conviction is based chiefly on the terrible destructive force of modern arms. And it is nourished by the horror aroused in the mind by the very thought of the cruel destruction and the immense suffering which the use of those armaments would bring. And for this reason it is hardly possible to imagine that in the atomic era war could be used as an instrument of justice. . . .

There is reason to hope, however, that by meeting and negotiating men may come to discover better bonds—deriving from the human nature which they have in common—that unite them, and that they may learn also that one of the most profound requirements of their common nature is this: that between them and their respective peoples it is not fear which should reign but love, a love which tends to express itself in collaboration that is loyal, manifold in form and productive of many benefits.

Concluding Prayer for Peace on Earth

May He banish from the hearts of men whatever might endanger peace; may He transform them into witnesses of truth, justice, and brotherly love. May He enlighten the rulers of peoples so that in addition to their solicitude for the proper welfare of their citizens, they may guarantee and defend the great gift of peace. May He enkindle the wills of all, so that they may overcome the barriers that divide, cherish the bonds of mutual charity, understand others, and pardon those who have done them wrong. By virtue of His action, may all peoples on earth become as brothers, and may the most longed for peace blossom forth and reign always between them. . . . Finally, upon all men of good will to whom this encyclical letter is also addressed, we implore from Almighty God health and prosperity. . . .

The Fostering of Peace and the Promotion of a Community of Nations

Introduction

In our generation when men continue to be afflicted by acute hardships and anxieties arising from the ravages of war or the threat of it, the whole human family faces an hour of supreme crisis in its advance toward maturity. Moving gradually together and everywhere more conscious already of its unity, this family cannot accomplish its task of constructing for all men everywhere a world more genuinely human unless each person devotes himself to the cause of peace with renewed vigor. Thus it happens that the Gospel message, which is in harmony with the loftier strivings and aspirations of the human race, takes on a new luster in our day as it declares that the artisans of peace are blessed "because they will be called the sons of God" (Matt. 5:9). . . .

The Nature of Peace

Peace is not merely the absence of war; nor can it be reduced solely to the maintenance of a balance of power between enemies; nor is it brought about by dictatorship. Instead, it is rightly and appropriately called an enterprise of justice (Is. 32:7). Peace results from that order structured into human society by its divine Founder, and

From *Second Vatican Council,* Pastoral Constitution on the Church in the Modern World *(Washington, D.C.: National Catholic Welfare Conference, 1965); the subtitles have been added. Reprinted with special permission.*

actualized by men as they thirst after ever greater justice. The common good of humanity finds its ultimate meaning in the eternal law. But since the concrete demands of this common good are constantly changing as time goes on, peace is never attained once and for all, but must be built up ceaselessly. Moreover, since the human will is unsteady and wounded by sin, the achievement of peace requires a constant mastering of passions and the vigilance of lawful authority.

But this is not enough. This peace on earth cannot be obtained unless personal well-being is safeguarded and men freely and trustingly share with one another the riches of their inner spirits and their talents. A firm determination to respect other men and peoples and their dignity, as well as the studied practice of brotherhood are absolutely necessary for the establishment of peace. Hence peace is likewise the fruit of love, which goes beyond what justice can provide.

That earthly peace which arises from love of neighbor symbolizes and results from the peace of Christ which radiates from God the Father. For by the Cross the Incarnate Son, the Prince of Peace, reconciled all men with God. By thus restoring all men to the unity of one people and one body, He slew hatred in His own flesh; and, after being lifted on high by His resurrection, He poured forth the spirit of love into the hearts of men.

For this reason, all Christians are urgently summoned to do in love what the truth requires (Eph. 4:15), and to join with all true peacemakers in pleading for peace and bringing it about.

Motivated by this same spirit, we cannot fail to praise those who renounce the use of violence in the vindication of their rights and who resort to methods of defense which are otherwise available to weaker parties too, provided this can be done without injury to the rights and duties of others or to the community itself.

Insofar as men are sinful, the threat of war hangs over them, and hang over them it will until the return of Christ. But insofar as men vanquish sin by a union of love, they will vanquish violence as well and make these words come true: "They shall turn their swords into plow-shares, and their spears into sickles. Nation shall not lift up sword against nation, neither shall they learn war any more" (Isa. 2:4).

Curbing the Savagery of War

In spite of the fact that recent wars have wrought physical and moral havoc on our world, war produces its devastation day by day in some part of the world. Indeed, now that every kind of weapon produced by modern science is used in war, the fierce character of war threatens to lead the combatants to a savagery far surpassing that of the past. Furthermore, the complexity of the modern world and the intricacy of international relations allow guerrilla warfare to be carried on by new methods of deceit and subversion. In many cases the use of terrorism is regarded as a new way to wage war.

Contemplating this melancholy state of humanity, the Council wishes, above all things else, to recall the permanent binding force of universal natural law and its all-embracing principles. Man's conscience itself gives ever more emphatic voice to these principles. Therefore, actions which deliberately conflict with these same principles, as well as orders commanding such actions, are criminal, and blind obedience cannot excuse those who yield to them. The most infamous among these are actions designed for the methodical extermination of an entire people, nation or ethnic minority. Such actions must be vehemently condemned as horrendous crimes. The courage of those who fearlessly and openly resist those who issue such commands merits the highest commendation.

On the subject of war, quite a large number of nations have subscribed to international agreements aimed at making military activity and its consequences less inhuman. Their stipulations deal with such matters as the treatment of wounded soldiers and prisoners. Agreements of this sort must be honored. Indeed they should be improved upon so that the frightfulness of war can be better and more workably held in check. All men, especially government officials and experts in these matters, are bound to do everything they can to effect these improvements. Moreover, it seems right that laws make humane provisions for the case of those who for reasons of conscience refuse to bear arms, provided however, that they agree to serve the human community in some other way.

Certainly, war has not been rooted out of human affairs. As long as the danger of war remains and there is no competent and sufficiently powerful authority at the international level, governments cannot be denied the right to legitimate defense once every means of peaceful settlement has been exhausted. Government authorities and others who share public responsibility have the duty to conduct such grave matters soberly and to protect the welfare of the people entrusted to their care. But it is one thing to undertake military action for the just defense of the people, and something else again to seek the subjugation of other nations. Nor, by the same token, does the mere fact that war has unhappily begun mean that all is fair between the warring parties.

Those too who devote themselves to the military service of their country should regard themselves as the agents of security and freedom of peoples. As long as they fulfill this

role properly, they are making a genuine contribution to
the establishment of peace.

Total War

The horror and perversity of war is immensely magnified
by the increase in the number of scientific weapons. For
acts of war involving these weapons can inflict massive
and indiscriminate destruction, thus going far beyond the
bounds of legitimate defense. Indeed, if the kind of instruments which can now be found in the armories of the
great nations were to be employed to their fullest, an almost
total and altogether reciprocal slaughter of each side by
the other would follow, not to mention the widespread
devastation that would take place in the world and the
deadly aftereffects that would be spawned by the use of
weapons of this kind.

All these conditions compel us to undertake an evalua-
tion of war with an entirely new attitude. The men of our
time must realize that they will have to give a somber
reckoning of their deeds of war, for the course of the future
will depend greatly on the decisions they make today.

With these results in mind, this most Holy Synod makes
its own the condemnation of total war already pronounced
by recent popes, and issues the following declaration:

Any act of war aimed indiscriminately at the destruction
of entire cities or extensive areas along with their population
is a crime against God and man himself. It merits unequivocal and unhesitating condemnation.

The unique hazard of modern warfare consists in this:
it provides those who possess modern scientific weapons
with a kind of occasion for perpetrating just such abomina-
tions; moreover, through a certain inexorable chain of
events, it can catapult men into the most atrocious decisions. That such may never happen in the future, the

bishops of the whole world gathered together, beg all men, especially government officials and military leaders, to give unremitting thought to their responsibility before God and the entire human race.

The Arms Race

Scientific weapons, to be sure, are not amassed solely for use in war. Since the defensive strength of any nation is considered to be dependent upon its capacity for immediate retaliation, this accumulation of arms, which increases each year, likewise serves, in a way heretofore unknown, as a deterrent to possible enemy attack. Many regard this as the most effective way by which peace of a sort can be maintained between nations at the present time.

Whatever be the facts about this method of deterrence, men should be convinced that the arms race in which an already considerable number of countries are engaged is not a safe way to preserve a steady peace, nor is the so-called balance resulting from this race a sure and authentic peace. Rather than being eliminated thereby, the causes of war are in danger of being gradually aggravated. While extravagant sums are being spent for the furnishing of ever new weapons, an adequate remedy cannot be provided for the multiple miseries afflicting the whole modern world. Disagreements between nations are not really and radically healed; on the contrary, they spread the infection to other parts of the earth. New approaches based on reformed attitudes must be taken to remove this trap and to emancipate the world from its crushing anxiety through the restoration of genuine peace.

Therefore, we say it again: the arms race is an utterly treacherous trap for humanity, and one which ensnares the poor to an intolerable degree. It is much to be feared that if this race persists, it will eventually spawn all the lethal ruin whose path it is now making ready. Warned by the calamities which the human race has made possible, let us make use of the interlude granted us from above and for which we are thankful, to become more conscious of our own responsibility and to find means for resolving our disputes in a manner more worthy of man. Divine Providence urgently demands of us that we free ourselves from the age-old slavery of war. If we refuse to make this effort, we do not know where we will be led by the evil road we have set upon. . . .

The Morality of Nuclear War: A Medieval Disputation

The following disputation was held at the invitation of the National Peace Council at Caxton Hall, London, on January 30, 1956, and broadcast on the Third Programme of the B.B.C. Although its subject could hardly be of more contemporary concern, it is "medieval" in the sense that its procedure has its origin in the exercises of the medieval universities. To this day, the disputation is a required weekly exercise in the theological colleges of the Order of Preachers (Dominicans).

The disputation differs fundamentally from the debate: whereas the debater seeks to score points through appealing to passion, pity, political advantage, and the like, participants in the disputation are bound absolutely by the rules of logic. The procedure is quite uncomplicated. The defendant poses a thesis, explains its terms of reference, and indicates his course of argumentation. The objector then proceeds to attack his thesis in strict logical form. And so the disputation proceeds, like a graceful ballet of the intellect, until either party admits the fallaciousness of his position.

In the disputation before us, the defender of the thesis, Father Ian Hislop, O.P., of Vaughan College, Leicester, and the objector, Father Laurence Bright, O.P., formerly a research student in atomic physics at Oxford and now lecturer in philosophy in the Dominican House of Studies, Hawkesyard, develop the case against nuclear war along the lines of the preceding documents, going more fully into the question of the nondiscriminatory nature of these devices and the immorality of testing and keeping them as a "deterrent."

The Disputation

FR. IAN HISLOP: Since this is your subject, Laurence, perhaps you would describe the meaning of the term "nuclear warfare" for us.

FR. LAURENCE BRIGHT: I think we had better take the term "nuclear warfare" quite generally at first so as to cover every possible use of the new weapons, from the small atomic fission bombs that might be used against limited objectives, such as a ship at sea, to the gigantic hydrogen or fusion-fission bomb capable of devastating large areas of [a] continent. I hope we shall eventually be able to discriminate between their different uses and decide which, if any, can be morally justified and which not. This means we shall have to consider the three effects which all these weapons produce, and which I want briefly to mention at this point. There is first of all the direct destruction of life and property by blast from the explosion and fire due to intense heat. This differs in degree only, not in kind, from the destruction caused by the so-called conventional weapons. But nuclear weapons have two effects peculiar to themselves and due to the intense radiation they spread over a far wider area. A heavy dose of radiation may lead to death within a few weeks. And those who survive may have

From "The Morality of Nuclear War: A Medieval Disputation," in Blackfriars, A Monthly Review (March, 1956). Reprinted with special permission.

suffered genetic changes which can affect their offspring, perhaps only after many generations. I think that our method of disputation will allow us to consider the moral consequences of these three effects separately and in their correct order.

DEFENDANT: Thank you. I must now put forward a preliminary statement of my thesis, which will serve as a basis for discussing the points you have raised. And since the normal assumption would seem to be that nuclear weapons can be justified, more or less as other weapons in the past have been, I shall, for the purposes of argument, put the thesis in a negative form, and maintain:

That nuclear warfare is not immoral.

OBJECTOR: Nuclear warfare is immoral. Therefore your thesis is false.

DEFENDANT: . . . Will you please prove that statement?

OBJECTOR: Yes;
That which of its nature is destructive is immoral.
But nuclear warfare is of its nature destructive.
Therefore nuclear warfare is immoral.

DEFENDANT: . . . First I shall distinguish the major premise.
That which is of its nature uncontrollably destructive is immoral: I affirm.
That which is of its nature controllably destructive is immoral: I deny.
Next I shall distinguish the minor premise in the same sense.
Nuclear warfare is of its nature controllably destructive: I affirm.

It is of its nature uncontrollably destructive: I deny.

I therefore deny that the argument follows and will explain my distinction.

The distinction I have made concerns the very nature of these weapons, for on this depends the possibility of distinguishing between moral and immoral ways of using them. A weapon must be of its nature controllable if its use is to be kept within justifiable limits. To use a weapon whose destructive force escapes one's control is morally evil since it will not only destroy those who are engaged in unjust aggression but also the innocent. This seems to me like shooting down a crowd of persons with machine-gun fire because several guilty men are hiding in the crowd. If nuclear weapons can be used in such a way as to select purely military targets, for example a fort or a tank group, it would appear that their use could be justified; but if not, then they must be rejected. Perhaps you can help me again on this matter of fact?

OBJECTOR: I will try and do so. In this first objection we are restricting our attention to the effects of blast wave and heat flash. Now it is possible to make an atomic weapon whose destructive power, so far as these effects are concerned, is not vastly greater than the destructive power of conventional weapons. It could be used as a tactical weapon against limited military objectives. On the other hand, atomic bombs of very much greater destructive power are now being made, and the destructive power of hydrogen bombs is, so far as I know, necessarily greater still. You cannot make—or at least no one would want to make —a small hydrogen bomb; it is intended to destroy a target the area of a large city. So on the basis of direct effects only, it seems that you have ruled out all use of hydrogen and large atomic bomb[s], since these are only intended for indiscriminate use against cities, but you will allow the tactical use of small atomic weapons. I should now like to see whether further restrictions have to be made if we go on to consider the radiation effects. From this standpoint I shall affirm the minor premise in the form you have just rejected, and shall say that nuclear warfare is of its nature uncontrollably destructive.

DEFENDANT: . . . Will you please prove your new statement?

OBJECTOR: Yes. Something whose effects spread far beyond the target area is of its nature uncontrollably destructive.

But nuclear warfare has effects which spread far beyond the target area.

Therefore nuclear warfare is of its nature uncontrollably destructive.

DEFENDANT: . . . I shall first distinguish the major premise.

Something whose effects spread far beyond the target area without assignable limits is of its nature uncontrollably destructive: I agree.

Something whose effects spread far beyond the target area within assignable limits is of its nature uncontrollably destructive: I deny.

I shall next distinguish the minor premise in the same sense.

Nuclear warfare has effects which spread far beyond the target area, within assignable limits: I agree.

Which spread far beyond the target area without assignable limits: I deny.

I therefore deny that the argument follows and will explain my distinction.

You maintain that the effects of nuclear weapons spread far beyond the target area and therefore their use is immoral. The distinction I have used in reply is again spatial in character. If spatial limits can be assigned to the effects of the bomb it is not impossible that its use might be justified, due warning having been given, in order to neutralize an area of military importance. The whole distinction hinges around the question whether such limits can be assigned. What do you think?

OBJECTOR: We have agreed that spatial limits can be assigned to the direct effects of small atomic weapons. But when a nuclear explosion occurs at ground level radioactive fragments of earth, etc., are carried up into the atmosphere and slowly descend over a wide area causing what is known as radiation sickness in men and animals. Anyone who receives more than a certain dose of radiation, whether directly or through eating contaminated food, is likely to die within a few weeks. A hydrogen bomb may contaminate many thousands of square miles in this way. But even with the tactical use of smaller bombs, which is our present concern, a somewhat unpredictable area will be contaminated. You maintain that this area must be limited so as to exclude non-combatants. No doubt this is possible, but it would certainly not be easy under war conditions to ensure that the explosion occurs in the air rather than on the ground. Moreover, such limitation depends on weather conditions over which we have little control. When testing the bomb long delays were often necessary in order to have the right wind conditions. During actual combat rather greater impatience might be felt. But even if these radiation effects do not rule out such restricted use of atomic weapons as you are prepared to admit, I believe that the genetic effects are decisive in doing so, and this is the basis of my third objection. I shall therefore affirm the minor premise of the last objection in the form you have just rejected, and shall say that nuclear warfare produces effects which are without assignable limits.

DEFENDANT: . . . Will you please prove that statement?

OBJECTOR: Yes. That which produces genetic damage has effects which are without assignable limits.
But nuclear warfare produces genetic damage.
Therefore nuclear warfare produces effects which are without assignable limits.

DEFENDANT: . . . I first distinguish the major premise.
That which produces unpredictable genetic damage has effects which are without assignable limits: I agree.
That which produces predictable genetic damage has effects without assignable limits: I deny.
I shall next distinguish the minor premise in the same sense.
Nuclear warfare produces predictable genetic damage: I agree.
Produces unpredictable genetic damage: I allow to pass.
This final objection I find most powerful. I have managed to find a distinction that enables me to escape, for the moment, from the fast-closing jaws of your logic. You have argued that nuclear warfare has effects that are without assignable limits because it produces genetic damage. I have replied that if you can predict the damage you are enabled to exercise some control; on the other hand, if the damage is unpredictable, then only a person who was quite irresponsible would make use of these nuclear weapons. I suspect that I have really conceded the argument because, as applied to the minor premise, the only prediction that can be made is that it will produce unpredictable genetic damage. Is that the case?

OBJECTOR: I think so. The third effect of a nuclear explosion lies in the genetic changes, in the majority of cases harmful, which result from comparatively small amounts of radiation, even very far away from the original target, falling on the human reproductive organs. These changes do not, as is sometimes thought, produce dramatically obvious effects, such as the birth of monsters. Many generations may elapse before anything observable occurs. But inevitably, sooner or later, some descendant will either die prematurely or be made sterile. Now there is one sense in which these effects can be predicted. It will eventually be possible to calculate the number of casualties due to a given dose of radiation; even now it can be shown that the number of these delayed casualties which will occur down the years will be of the same order of magnitude as the number due to the direct effects of the bombing. But in another sense this effect is quite unpredictable because at the time it operates its victims will not yet be born. Clearly they at least cannot be said to share in the guilt for which they suffer. And I feel bound to add that every atomic test which is made produces its yet unknown victims as a result of this effect. No doubt it will be said that these tests are responsible for fewer deaths than the natural radiation continually present on earth, about which nobody worries, or than the radiation used legitimately in medicine and industry; that these deaths are an occupational hazard that we must put up with for the sake of the greater good. Personally I do not see how such known evil consequences, even if in a sense unintentional, can fail to change the morality of the situation; we cannot ignore them, much as we may be tempted to. . . . I should [also] like to say a little more about a point which lay behind a good deal of our discussion: the indiscriminate nature of these new weapons. I believe it is legitimate to kill soldiers who have taken up arms in an unjust cause if there is no other way of bringing about a just peace. But there must be many blameless people even among the members of the aggressor nation. How can we impute blame to small children "who know not how to distinguish between their right hand and their left"? Yet they will certainly be among the victims if a city is hit by a nuclear bomb or if a cloud of radioactive dust drifts in their direction; and what of those yet unborn, who will suffer from genetic damage caused many years before, perhaps to people who lived far away from the scene of conflict and took no part in it?

DEFENDANT: Your objection reduces to the statement that nuclear warfare is immoral because it is indiscriminate. Here the principle to guide us is that punishment may only be exacted from those who are in some way responsible for, or who help to maintain, the wrong. It may be difficult in practice to be exact about who does or does not fall under this description, but it is quite clear that the use of a weapon that is indiscriminately destructive on a large scale makes it impossible to exclude from its range those who cannot on any view be said to be responsible either for the wrong or for maintaining it. Further, if the effects of the nuclear bombs are as far-reaching as you have indicated, it is wrong to use them because they imply the destruction of those civilized ways of life that are the highest product of man's creative reason. Their use then implies, at a critical level, the use of reason to negate reason. One is not maintaining that atomic research is irrational, only stating that its use for war is irrational and therefore immoral.

Objections from the Audience

HUGH DELARGY, MEMBER OF PARLIAMENT: The possession of the hydrogen bomb exposes this island, vulnerable and densely populated as it is, to dangers which no responsible government should allow its people to have to risk. It is therefore morally wrong to manufacture the bomb, because to do so exposes the nation to the certain annihilation that would follow its use by an enemy. Far from being a deterrent, it is in fact an *invitation* to an enemy possessing nuclear weapons to destroy this country. And that is morally indefensible for a government that is bound to protect its people.

FR. IAN HISLOP: I am glad this question has been raised as it seems to me to be one that every citizen must face. If the manufacture of the hydrogen bomb exposes the nation —or for that matter the civilized peoples of the earth—to annihilation if it is used, is it moral to make it as a deterrent? A deterrent is only for *use*, if its *use* is contemplated even if only as a last resort; and for this one has to be *willing* to make use of it. If the effects of using the hydrogen bomb are as far-reaching as we have suggested, it is the kind of weapon which it is wrong to use and, therefore, wrong to be willing to use. Hence its use as a deterrent is wrong. One can go further than that, I think, and say that if it is wrong to use the hydrogen bomb, it is wrong to manufacture it. The primary responsibility, here, falls on those who direct, either governmentally, scientifically or administratively, the process of manufacture, but those who engage in the manufacture also share the responsibility, as does, too, the citizen of a democratically governed people.

If it is argued that the bomb is only used as a deterrent against systems that appear as inhuman, it must be very carefully considered whether their inhumanity is greater than the possibility of the removal of all civilized human existence, to put it at its lowest, involved in the use of the bomb.

Once one considers the possible results of the use of this weapon the conclusion forces itself that war, as a method of resolving disputes, cannot be regarded as having a place in a scientifically ordered world, unless that world is prepared to destroy itself. The conclusion is clear. Social consciousness—at parochial, urban, trade union, national and international levels—of the implications of the presence of the bomb in our society must be both deepened and enlarged in order that the tardy evolution of international institutions for dealing with disputes may be hastened. Such a development seems to me to be the one way out of the impasse we have created for ourselves.

DAME KATHLEEN LONSDALE, F.R.S.: Nuclear war is immoral because it attempts compulsion by efficient, scientific torture. But can physical force afford to be inefficient, of its kind? The moral alternative is surely complete disarmament and entire reliance on spiritual force, on persuasion and redemption by unselfish goodwill and Christ-like love.

FR. IAN HISLOP: Thank you. I agree with you, that where large groups are concerned, and serious disputes involved, physical force cannot afford to be inefficient. It is a fairly safe conclusion, from experience, that, in the heat of warfare, moral sensitivity diminishes and that the opposing forces slip into the state of mind that victory justifies anything. As the pernicious tag has it: "My country right or wrong."

I agree, too, that reliance on spiritual force is of immense importance. As much reliance as possible should be put on it, but it would be "starry eyed" to expect mere reliance to solve everything. I do not think, however much these qualities may be admired, that most people including myself are unselfish or full of Christ-like love—in the sense that they are able to give social expression to these virtues. We have not yet found, in our society, institutional forms to express and support our rather vague humanitarian desires —for instance, our relation to foreigners. We may be willing enough some of the time, but most of us are capable of behaving like maladjusted children, some are quite insensitive to spiritual considerations, and practically everybody is at the mercy of undeveloped international traditions. As long as this situation obtains, it is necessary, provided the motive is good, and the means proportionate, to restrain (for example by police action) certain people from injuring their fellow-citizens. . . .

On the other hand, as has been stressed, I think, in the disputation, the use of force must not be excessive. When an evil is inescapable, and we are unable to overcome it, because resistance to it would involve an excessive and immoral use of force, one has no choice but to refuse to acquiesce, even to the point of losing one's own life in what is from one point of view a hopeless struggle. . . .

Thomas Merton
1915–1968

Until his accidental death in 1968, Thomas Merton, a monk of the Order of the Cistercians of the Strict Observance (Trappists), was among the most indefatigable advocates of peace. The author of numerous works of prose and poetry about the religious life and nonviolence, among them *The Seven Story Mountain, Seeds of Contemplation,* and *Emblems of a Season of Fury,* Father Merton was also the founder of the Catholic Peace Fellowship, one of the fourteen religious affiliates of the Fellowship of Reconciliation.

Published as a leaflet for the Fellowship, *Red or Dead, the Anatomy of a Cliché* takes up a theme mentioned by Father Hislop in the *Disputation;* namely, that however diabolical we may envision the system we are opposing, it is not worth destroying if in so doing we risk the near certainty of destroying humanity as well. His most pointed barbs, however, are reserved for the Dr. Strangeloves, the "think-tank" theoreticians of computerized annihilation, who, like Herman Kahn in his 1960 book *On Thermonuclear War,* hold that the birth in subsequent generations of a few million deformed babies is an acceptable price to pay "if that means not giving up Europe to Soviet Russia."

Red or Dead, the Anatomy of a Cliché

When an issue of incredible gravity can be made to depend on an insane half truth, it becomes important to analyze the so-called "thinking" that is involved.

The whole world is in the grip of pathological war preparations—all initiated in order to "preserve peace"—and we find men who are considered sane, seriously resolving the whole problem into the alternative: "Red or dead." Either you survive and become a Communist, or else risk annihilation in the act of destroying communism. For the latter, the destruction of communism has become the one all-important aim of life, more important than the survival of civilization, crucial enough to risk the annihilation of the entire human race.

To put it coldly and bluntly, the policy of nuclear deterrence which the majority of Americans, Christian and non-Christian alike, seem to have implicitly accepted, at least in a general, tacit way by not protesting against it, depends on a readiness to annihilate completely without warning, the great civilian population centers of the enemy country, together with their military installations. It is for this end that we are paying taxes. It is from the preparations for nuclear war that a very significant percentage of the popula-

Reprinted with the special permission of the Fellowship of Reconciliation.

tion is deriving its income either directly or indirectly. It is on these preparations that the whole economy of the country rests.

In these circumstances I wonder if the cliché about being Red or dead does not acquire a sinister hidden meaning. I wonder if, after all, without quite realizing the fact, we are beginning to feel that our inner contradictions are beyond solution, and are beginning to sense the climax of despair which they have prepared for us.

From the moment you take the "Red or dead" cliché as the expression of a realistic alternative, from the moment you pretend to base serious discussion upon this alternative, you are implicitly admitting the following propositions, which I for one find completely untenable.

1. You are saying that the very survival of democracy is bound up with total nuclear war. That without recourse to the threat of total nuclear war, without the readiness to wage such a war, without the ability to annihilate the enemy by a "first strike," the survival of democracy, freedom and Western civilization are no longer conceivable.

2. In other words, you are saying that it is not possible for democracy, for Western civilization, to survive by peaceful means. That we have exhausted the resources of humanity and reasonableness which would make negotiation thinkable except on a basis of terror.

3. You are saying that if we of the West survive at all, we can only survive as Communists. That it is a choice of surviving and becoming a Communist, or dying in defense of the ideals of democracy, the capitalist economy, freedom, the American Way of Life. If you push this far enough you are simply implying that the American Way of Life cannot survive except by war, but that communism can survive without recourse to total nuclear war.

4. You are saying that since for the Communists survival

automatically means victory, they must be prevented at all cost from surviving. That since for the West survival without nuclear war practically means defeat, then to reject nuclear war in order to survive is purely and simply to admit defeat.

5. The last assumption is at once the most horrible, the most absurd and the most revealing. It is purely and simply that if we are reduced to a choice between the survival of the Communists and the destruction of the entire human race, then the brave, noble, heroic and even *Christian* course is to choose the destruction of the human race. This is of course not frankly admitted, because their reasoning always leaves a kind of irrational loophole for "survival." There is always a *chance* that some "fifty million on our side" might be left standing after everyone else had been blown up. No one seems to consider the possibility that such survival might be at once culpable, subhuman and infernally awful.

To my mind this whole line of "reasoning" is purely and simply insane, if not actually demonic. For all its gestures of conquest it is a mentality of defeat. It is nothing but appeasement in reverse—it does not grovel, but it destroys itself, assuming there is no alternative between groveling and destruction. Such an assumption is a pure surrender to irrationality and to hysteria. Nothing could be more directly contrary to the spirit of liberty, and of reasonable initiative characteristic of the American tradition.

1. This kind of thinking represents a *mentality of defeat*. All down the line it presumes that democratic values are not strong enough to prevail by peaceful means. All down the line it accepts the arguments which Marx long ago drew up against the capitalist system: *that it could not survive except by recourse to war,* and that it *would resort to any extreme* in order to crush opposition. . . .

2. It represents a mentality of *despair*. While claiming to believe in democratic ideals, in freedom, in the creativity supposedly inherent in our way of life, it admits in reality a *radical doubt of all those values*. It has no practical faith in them because it cannot believe that they have retained enough power to overcome the opposition raised by nuclear communism. Only nuclear weapons can do the trick. This attitude is the result of the secularist, irreligious, pragmatic spirit which has actually undermined the whole moral structure of the West. It springs from the emptiness, the resentment, the sense of futility and meaninglessness which gnaw secretly at the heart of Western man.

3. It is finally nothing else than a *mentality of suicide*. It is the self-destructive, self-hating resentment that follows the accumulated petty humiliations, repeated errors, reiterated blunders and stupidities with which we have continually lost face before those whom we secretly despised. In order to release the pent-up and desperate pressures of our self-hate we are now ready to destroy ourselves and the whole world with us in one grand explosion. And we justify ourselves by claiming that we prefer death (for ourselves and everyone else) to tyranny. What right have we to choose death for everyone else? Is not that an act of supreme tyranny and injustice? . . .

We are rational and responsible beings. *No form of defeatism is permitted to us, neither appeasement nor bullying*. We have no right to solve our problems by blowing ourselves up. Even if it were possible to destroy Russia and survive ourselves, this would not be permitted. It would be a crime greater than any of Hitler's acts of genocide and such crimes never go unpunished. We have no right to abandon the Christian moral values on which our society was built and adopt the moral opportunism and irresponsibility of atheistic materialism. If we live and act like atheists we shall turn our world into a living hell, and that is precisely what we are doing—for the Russians are not the only men in the world who are Godless! We who still try to be Christians must be warned. Even for the best of ends it is not permitted to do evil. Total war is nothing but mass murder.

We have got to find a human and reasonable way of solving our problems. And above all we must refuse to believe in any form of propaganda which tell[s] us that nuclear war is necessary and right. We must say *no* to such propaganda and demand that our government continue to seek a sane and prudent way to disarmament. If we give up hope of the only rational solution our blood and the blood of all mankind will be upon our own heads.

Martin Luther King, Jr.
1929–1968

We have thus far been considering war largely in the abstract, but this selection and those that follow it will concentrate on the impact on the Christian conscience of a specific conflict: Vietnam. Aside from absolute pacifism, which treats this as any other war, all the issues raised thus far have come together in this, the largest war of the nuclear era.

Beginning in 1950 with its agreement to help finance France's bid to reconquer her former colony of Indochina, the United States has almost imperceptibly become deeply engaged on the Asiatic mainland. In terms of lives and treasure, Vietnam is, next to World War II, the most costly foreign war in American history. By no means the smallest cost has been the infliction upon the American people of their most painful trial of conscience since the Civil War. Self-doubt and shame, verging in some on self-hatred, have combined to create an unprecedented antiwar movement; indeed, it would hardly be an exaggeration to call it an antiwar crusade, with all that the word implies.

Neutrality has proven impossible, and sooner or later conscience or circumstance or both have drawn all elements of the religious and intellectual communities into the controversy. For conscientious men the dilemma is real, involving the squaring of time-honored Western concepts of justice with guerrilla warfare, in which the fundamental nature of conflict differs drastically from so-called "conventional" warfare.

Although he was always concerned about world peace, not until a gathering in the Riverside Church in New York City on April 4, 1967 (exactly a year before his death), did Martin Luther King speak out decisively against the Vietnam war. The history of "Vietnam and the Struggle for Human Rights" is as revealing as its contents. A man whose time and energies needed to be devoted almost entirely to the cause of black freedom, Dr. King felt he must husband his resources carefully. Moreover, he hesitated to commit himself for tactical reasons, a hesitation he later regretted as an unworthy concession to expediency.

Dr. King eventually came to believe that war is not an isolated phenomenon, but indivisible from the total pattern of a people's life. The point of his speech is that one does not "confuse the issues" by linking the war in Vietnam to the cause of social justice in America; but that this linkage must be made because both issues spring from the assumptions and style of American life. The immediate reaction to the speech was strong, criticism coming both from within the civil rights movement and from the press, whose editorials and cartoons depicted King as an ivory-tower moralist pontificating on something he knew nothing about. Undeterred, he followed this speech with others equally hard-hitting, until his assassination.

Vietnam and the Struggle for Human Rights

I come to this platform tonight to make a passionate

From Speeches by The Rev. Dr. Martin Luther King, Jr., About the War in Vietnam (*New York: Clergy and Laymen Concerned About Vietnam, 1968). Reprinted with special permission.*

plea to my beloved nation. This speech is not addressed to Hanoi or to the National Liberation Front. It is not addressed to China or to Russia.

Nor is it an attempt to overlook the ambiguity of the total situation and the need for a collective solution to the tragedy of Vietnam. Neither is it an attempt to make North Vietnam or the National Liberation Front paragons of virtue, nor to overlook the role they can play in a successful resolution of the problem. While they both may have justifiable reason to be suspicious of the good faith of the United States, life and history give eloquent testimony to the fact that conflicts are never resolved without trustful give and take on both sides.

Tonight, however, I wish not to speak with Hanoi and the NLF, but rather to my fellow Americans who, with me, bear the greatest responsibility in ending a conflict that has exacted a heavy price on both continents. . . .

As I ponder the madness of Vietnam and search within myself for ways to understand and respond in compassion, my mind goes constantly to the people of that peninsula. I speak now not of the soldiers on each side, not of the junta in Saigon, but simply of the people who have been living under the curse of war for almost three continuous decades now. I think of them too because it is clear to me that there will be no meaningful solution there until some attempt is made to know them and hear their broken cries.

They must see Americans as strange liberators. The Vietnamese people proclaimed their own independence in 1945 after a combined French and Japanese occupation, and before the communist revolution in China. They were led by Ho Chi Minh. Even though they quoted the American Declaration of Independence in their own document of freedom, we refused to recognize them. Instead we decided to support France in its re-conquest of her former colony. . . .

The only change [in American policy] came as we increased our troop commitments in support of governments which were singularly corrupt, inept and without popular support. All the while the people read our leaflets and received regular promises of peace and democracy—and land reform. Now they languish under our bombs and consider us—not their fellow Vietnamese—the real enemy. They move sadly and apathetically as we herd them off the land of their fathers into concentration camps where minimal social needs are rarely met. They know they must move or be destroyed by our bombs. So they go—primarily women and children and the aged. . . .

What do the peasants think as we ally ourselves with the landlords and as we refuse to put any action into our many words concerning land reform? What do they think as we test out our latest weapons on them, just as the Germans tested out new medicine and new tortures in the concentration camps of Europe? Where are the roots of the independent Vietnam we claim to be building? Is it among these voiceless ones?

We have destroyed their two most cherished institutions: the family and the village. We have destroyed their land and their crops. We have cooperated in the crushing of the nation's only non-communist revolutionary political force— the Unified Buddhist Church. We have supported the enemies of the peasants of Saigon. We have corrupted their women and children and killed their men. What liberators! . . .

Perhaps the more difficult but no less necessary task is to speak for those who have been designated as our enemies. What of the National Liberation Front—that strangely anonymous group we call VC or Communists? What must they think of us in America when they realize that we permitted the repression and cruelty of Diem which helped to bring them into being as a resistance group in the South? What do they think of our condoning the violence which led to their own taking up of arms? How can they believe in our integrity when we speak of "aggression from the North" as if there were nothing more essential to the war? How can they trust us when now we charge them with violence after the murderous reign of Diem, and charge them with violence while we pour every new weapon of death into their land? Surely we must understand their feelings even if we do not condone their actions. Surely we must see that the men we supported pressed them to their violence. Surely we must see that our own computerized plans of destruction simply dwarf their greatest acts. . . .

At this point I should make it clear that while I have tried in these last few minutes to give a voice to the voiceless on Vietnam and to understand the arguments of those who are called enemy, I am as deeply concerned about our own troops there as anything else. For it occurs to me that what we are submitting them to in Vietnam is not simply the brutalizing process that goes on in any war where armies face each other and seek to destroy. We are adding cynicism to the process of death, for they must know after a short period there that none of these things we claim to be fighting for are really involved. Before long they must know that their government has sent them into a struggle among Vietnamese, and the more sophisticated surely realize that we are on the side of the wealthy and the secure while we create a hell for the poor.

Somehow this madness must cease. We must stop now. I speak as a child of God and brother to the suffering poor of Vietnam. I speak for those whose land is being laid waste, whose homes are being destroyed, whose culture is being subverted. I speak for the poor of America who are paying the double price of smashed hopes at home and

death and corruption in Vietnam. I speak as a citizen of
the world, for the world as it stands aghast at the path we
have taken. I speak as an American to the leaders of my
own nation. The great initiative in this war is ours. The
initiative to stop it must be ours. . . .

. . . [Yet] the war in Vietnam is but a symptom of a far
deeper malady within the American spirit, and if we ignore
this sobering reality we will find ourselves organizing clergy
and laymen-concerned committees for the next generation.
They will be concerned about Guatemala and Peru. They
will be concerned about Thailand and Cambodia. They will
be concerned about Mozambique and South Africa. We will
be marching for these and a dozen other names and attending rallies without end unless there is a significant and profound change in American life and policy. Such thoughts
take us beyond Vietnam, but not beyond our calling as sons
of the living God.

In 1957 a sensitive American official overseas said that it
seemed to him that our nation was on the wrong side of the
world revolution. During the past ten years we have seen
emerge a pattern of suppression which has now justified
the presence of U.S. military "advisors" in Venezuela. This
need to maintain social stability for our investments accounts for the counter-revolutionary actions of American
forces in Guatemala. It tells why American helicopters are
being used against guerrillas in Colombia and why American napalm and Green Beret forces have already been
active against rebels in Peru. It is with such activity in mind
that the words of the late John F. Kennedy come back to
haunt us. Five years ago he said, "Those who make peaceful revolution impossible will make violent revolution
inevitable."

Increasingly, by choice or by accident, this is the role our
nation has taken—the role of those who make peaceful

revolution impossible by refusing to give up the privileges and the pleasures that come from the immense profits of overseas investment.

I am convinced that if we are to get on the right side of the world revolution, we as a nation must undergo a radical revolution of values. We must rapidly begin the shift from a "thing-oriented" society to a "person-oriented" society. When machines and computers, profit motives and property rights are considered more important than people, the giant triplets of racism, materialism, and militarism are incapable of being conquered. . . .

These are revolutionary times. All over the globe men are revolting against old systems of exploitation and oppression and out of the wombs of a frail world new systems of justice and equality are being born. The shirtless and barefoot people of the land are rising up as never before. "The people who sat in darkness have seen a great light." We in the West must support these revolutions. It is a sad fact that because of comfort, complacency, a morbid fear of Communism, and our proneness to adjust to injustice, the Western nations that initiated so much of the revolutionary spirit of the modern world have now become the arch anti-revolutionaries. This has driven many to feel that only Marxism has the revolutionary spirit. Therefore, Communism is a judgment against our failure to make democracy real and follow through on the revolutions that we initiated. Our only hope today lies in our ability to recapture the revolutionary spirit and go out into a sometimes hostile world declaring eternal hostility to poverty, racism, and militarism. With this powerful commitment we shall boldly challenge the status quo and unjust mores, and thereby speed the day when "every valley shall be exalted, and every mountain and hill shall be made low, and the crooked shall be made straight and the rough places plain."

Paul Ramsey
1913–

Among the foremost Christian ethicists of the post-World War II period, Paul Ramsey is professor of religion at Princeton University and author of several books, among them *Nine Modern Moralists, Christian Ethics and the Sit-In,* and *Who Speaks for the Church?* As an exponent of the just war, Ramsey today finds himself in the minority of articulate Christian opinion vis-à-vis international relations, nuclear deterrence, and Vietnam.

Throughout his writings, but particularly in his most recent work, *The Just War* (1968), a collection of articles on the ethics of international politics and war, Ramsey has sought, by "quite consciously drawing upon a wider theory of statecraft and of political justice to propose within the Christian realism of Reinhold Niebuhr, an added note within his 'responsibilistic' ethics" (p. 260). Whereas Niebuhr was concerned primarily with legitimatizing war by an appeal to a doctrine of greater/lesser evil, he said little about the actual employment of force. Ramsey seeks to fill this gap. Discrimination and proportionality are the threads running through all his writings on war. It will not do merely to calculate consequences and choose the lesser evil, because the ends, however exalted, never justify any means. The objective of combat, he affirms, must always be counter-force, never counter-people.

The rule of discrimination leads Ramsey to his second objective. As Niebuhr reproached the pacifists of the thirties for lack of realism and for overlooking the evil in human nature, so Ramsey sees himself recovering, in the sixties, the just war from the hands of the liberal "messianists," Catholic and Protestant, who hold that negotiation is always possible and always preferable to fighting, and that "an ethic of reconciliation based on the Gospel of Peace" (see A. J. Muste) is now a viable option.

The following excerpt brings to bear on the Vietnam issue Ramsey's views on discrimination and the misconceptions of religious liberalism in politics. Insofar as he casts his net over a smaller area, it is in striking contrast to Dr. King's earlier (1967) speech in the Riverside Church. For Ramsey, the question of the United States' national depravity is irrelevant to the issue at hand, as are the propagandistic claims of both sides in the war. He seeks rather to determine whether either side or both sides in the conflict are waging a war immoral in its basic design.

Is Vietnam a Just War?

It is Christian realism or any other realistic theory of statecraft that has been most lacking in our discussions of Vietnam. One has to go elsewhere than to a Christian view of politics even to understand the animus, the exacerbation, the petulance infecting our public debate and protests over this war. The explanation is to be found in the utopian notion that it is bound to be the case that the government must be doing something wrong if there has to be, or if there has to continue to be, a political use of violence. The explanation is to be found in the conviction that it is always possible to negotiate so that negotiation will never fail, and yet attain a just peace, or one that will barely hold together. Then, of course, if our political leaders don't know this it must be because they haven't listened to the right people. . . . The expansion of the petulance of the protests lies in the optimistic denial that there can be such a thing as an arbitrament of arms, a denial that conflicts can arise among men and nations that are so unbridgeable that they defy *ratio* and drive nations to the *ultima ratio* of war. . . .

A Christian who has taken the non-pacifist road must thereafter be concerned with the *morality of war,* and not mix this up with the morality *contra bellum* [against war] on which his pacifist brother relies.

He will, first, know something about the intention, direction and thrust of an act of war if this is ever justifiable. The object of combat is the incapacitation of the combatant from doing what he is doing because he is this particular combatant in this particular war; it is not the killing of a man because he is this particular man. The latter and only the latter would be murder. From the proper direction of just action in war upon the combatant and not upon the man flows the prohibition of the killing of soldiers who have been captured or who by surrender have taken themselves out of the war and incapacitated themselves from continuing it. The robbers are not to be killed when effective robbery is no longer in them, since it was the robber and not the man who had to be stopped.

From this also follows the cardinal principle governing just conduct in war, namely, the moral immunity of non-combatants from deliberate, direct attack. In this *principle of discrimination* there are two ingredients. One is the prohibition of "deliberate, direct attack." This is the immutable, unchanging ingredient in the definition of justice in war. You have only to get to know the meaning of this in contrast to "aiming indiscriminately." The second ingredient is the meaning of "non-combatancy." This is relativistic and varying in application. "Non-combatancy" is a function of how the nations or the forces are organized for war, and of military technology.

I myself have no hesitation in saying that the counter-insurgency in South Vietnam in its chief or central design falls within the principle of discrimination. It is directed upon combatants as these have organized themselves for war, i.e., among the people like fish in water. No Christian and no moralist should assert that it violates the moral immunity of non-combatants from direct, deliberate attack to direct the violence of war upon vast Vietcong strongholds whose destruction unavoidably involves the collateral deaths of a great many civilians.

Yet this is asserted today by intellectuals and churchmen who have forgotten, if they ever knew, the meaning of a legitimate military target. With such leadership it is no wonder that people march in the streets with banners proclaiming that they prefer education or a domestic Peace Corps to "murder." They simply do not know the qualitative difference between "murder" and "killing in war." While this is to be expected of a complete pacifist, it is neither expected nor excusable in anyone who does not, like the universal pacifist, propose to withdraw from the political life of this nation insofar as politics in the nation-state system must also be organized for the political use of armed force. . . .

For the rest, decisions in regard to the political use of violence are governed by political prudence. This is to say, whether a particular war should be fought, or whether it should be fought at a higher level of violence for hopefully a shorter time or be de-escalated and fought for a longer time, and many other questions one must ask in justifying a particular political option rather than another, depend on one's count of the costs and the benefits, upon weighing greater and lesser evils in the consequences. In technical language, this is called the *principle of proportion,* which requires that the good achievable or the evil prevented be greater than the values destroyed or the destruction involved in any resort to arms.

A deliberately imprudent act that from inflexibility or bravado or for the sake of "why not victory?" undertakes to do more than we can do without greater harm would certainly be wrong. But so also would an uncharitable exercise of political prudence that in order to get on with our own Great Society would be content to do less than we might do for the just ordering of the world and for the good of other people in coincidence with our own, if these goods can at all be secured by anything we do or do not do. The principle of proportion, or prudence, can be violated only by acts of commission. These are the main limits which the Christian who engages in politics knows to govern the political use of violent means. Then no one should fling around the word "immoral" with any other meaning when he is debating these questions, or when he criticizes the Administration's course of action.

On the matter of weighing the greater and the lesser evil, one can only mean to say that the present policy is prudentially wrong—which may be disastrous enough!—not that it is inherently "immoral." . . .

One must pause to grasp the nature of insurgency's use of violence (whether this is aggression from outside or revolution inside a country, or both). We need to dissect the basic design of insurgency warfare no less than that of counter-insurgency. Only then can we tell how to distribute judgments about the inherent evil of their respective resorts to military force.

One does not justify adultery by saying it is *selective*. Not even with the additional finding that with one's various mistresses one mainly enjoys the finer things of life and has achieved an orderly domestic economy. Neither does one justify deliberate terror in the conduct of war or revolution by saying that it is selective. Not even with the additional finding that the insurgents win the allegiance of the people by many other appeals or also by a program of national liberation. The fact that insurgency resorts to terror, when it does, only minimally or only upon selected people does not qualify it as a discriminating use of force. That is simply not the meaning of the principle of discrimination in the use of means of violence. It is in fact, morally, the meaning of total war. Decision as to the inherent evil of an act of war or revolution cannot be settled by the body count. There is not a prudent number of villagers, school teachers, or petty local officials and their families that it would be right to disembowel in the village square to dissuade others from allegiance to the existing social processes and institutions, all to the good end of destroying the social fabric of the traditional society and taking over and reforming the country.

Guerrilla war by its main design strikes the civil population (albeit selectively and as rarely as need be) in order to subvert, while striking as few legitimate military targets as possible. This terrible terror, while "selective," is not therefore limited or a rarity. In 1960–61 alone, the Vietcong murdered 6,130 and abducted 6,213 persons, or a total of over 12,000. Proportionally, this is as if the U.S. were under subversive assault in which 72,000 prominent persons, crucial in the life of the nation and its community services, were murdered or abducted annually! This is an inherently immoral plan of war or of revolution, and one that cannot be rendered morally tolerable by reference to the social reforms by which insurgency mainly proposes to succeed. . . .

The question facing the world for decades to come is whether it is possible to oppose these revolutionary wars successfully without joining them in *direct* attacks upon the very people a government may be trying to protect while social progress is secured with liberty. Is counter-insurgency, like insurgency, bound to be warfare over people as a means of getting at the other's forces?

Of course, if the guerrilla lives among the people like a fish in water, he must be opposed mainly by withdrawing the water to see what then happens to the fish. This is to say, insurgency can be finally defeated only by social, economic, and political reformation. But what of the military force that still must be used? If the guerrilla chooses to fight between, behind, and over peasants, women, and children, is it *he* or the counterguerrilla who has enlarged the legitimate target and enlarged it so as to bring unavoidable death and destruction upon a large number of innocent people?

It is the shape of insurgency warfare that defines the contours of the legitimate combat destruction and the unavoidably associated civil damage it may then (so far as the principle of discrimination is concerned) be just to inflict in order to oppose evil, subject only to the limitation that this be the proportionately lesser evil. To draw any other conclusion would be like, at the nuclear level, granting an enemy immunity from attack because he had the shrewdness to locate his missile bases in the heart of his cities. It is rather *he* who has deliberately enlarged the extent of foreknowable but collateral civil destruction in the attempt to gain a privileged sanctuary through a military posture that brought more of his own population into range.

The design of insurgency does this to the people of a society it assaults. The onus of the wickedness of placing multitudes of peasants within range cannot be shifted from insurgency to counter-insurgency, any more than it could be called an indiscriminate act of war on the part of some enemy if in the future Omaha, Neb., or Colorado Springs, Colo., are tragically destroyed in the course of destroying the [Strategic Air Command] bases and command posts *we* located there.

The principle of discrimination governing the proper conduct of war has no other meaning than this. Some call this a "medieval" notion. One should then be able to recognize a medieval fortress when he sees or hears of one buried underground in South Vietnam—command headquarters, munitions factories, stores of rice and intricate tunnels connecting many villages, with openings into countless peasant huts, or under the water in lakes, streams, rice paddies, by which the guerrillas may fight and run away and live to fight another day through these same egresses. Plainly, there are here extensive areas subject to the laws of siege; i.e., "catapults" from as far away as Guam may then not be indiscriminate acts of war. These are unpleasant facts. I did not make them so; originally, Mao Tsetung did. No Christian or moralist has a right to demand that statesmen or commanders fail to take account of these facts in their policies and plans. This is to suggest, all too briefly, that the main design of the counter-insurgency mounted in Vietnam need not be and likely is *not* an inherently evil or morally intolerable use of armed force—not in any meaning that the distinction between discriminate and indiscriminate conduct in war ever had or should have.

This is not to deny that peripheral to the "central war" against the insurgents there may be taking place many intrinsically wrong actions in this confused and bloody war. (I only say that this is not proved by reference to "the bombing of villages," etc., that may in fact lie within a vast Vietcong stronghold.) There are those who say that if any of the acts of war violate the canons of justice in war, or if justice is violated by frequent actions that, however, do not or need not fall within the main thrust or design of the war, it is still on the whole unjust and no Christian should support or participate in it. This position is far more to be honored than the indiscriminate use of the principle of discrimination that is current today. Still, to uphold it seems to me to uphold a legalist-pacifist version of the just-war doctrine, as if the purpose of this teaching was to bring peace by discrediting, one by one, all wars. Instead, the just-war doctrine is intended to indicate to political decision-makers how, within tolerable moral limits, they are to defend and preserve politically embodied justice in this world. . . .

Determining the greater and lesser evil in accord with the *principle of proportion* and the application of the *principle of discrimination* in the face of some new organization of military forces calls for an exercise of political prudence on the part of magistrates and citizens alike. In the particulars of this, no Christian can fault the conscience of another. This is especially the case in judgments whether acts of war directed upon *where the guerrillas are* still may not be doing *disproportionate* damage. In this there may certainly be legitimate disagreement. It may be the case that the conflict in South Vietnam has long since been destructive of more values than there is hope of gaining. If this seems to be the case as far as the Vietnamese alone are concerned, one must not forget that there are more values and securities and freedoms to be reckoned in any judgment concerning the proportionately lesser evil. Tragically, or in God's inscrutable providence, neither villagers nor nations are impervious to one another in our fated and fateful togetherness. Again in the particular decision concerning the greater or lesser evil in the whole of Southeast Asia, no Christian can fault the conscience of another. Then in this no Christian can fault the possible correctness of the conscientious estimations made by his government when he states with all urgency his disagreement with it. And no assembly of churchmen should pronounce—as did the 1966 Geneva Conference on Church and Society—that recent U.S. actions in Vietnam "cannot be justified."

Opposition to the Draft

Official United States government policy in Vietnam has so enraged large segments of the public that a certain amount of overt opposition has become inevitable. This opposition has tended to focus on the Selective Service system, the most visible and in many ways the most vulnerable agency involved in carrying on the war. In New York City, for example, the Armed Forces Induction Center was seriously damaged by an explosion. Less violent, but in the long run perhaps more effective, have been the symbolic acts of protest. At first, draft-eligible individuals burned their registration cards in public or returned them to Washington. Later, however, raids on the files kept in the offices of local Selective Service boards took place throughout the country.

The numerology of protest has climbed steadily, from the Baltimore Four, the New York Eight, and the Catonsville Nine to the Chicago Fifteen. A religious element has been in the forefront of several of these actions: two Roman Catholic priests, Daniel Berrigan, S.J., and his brother Philip, S.J., were the moving spirits at Catonsville. To a degree all these protesters have rephrased the fundamental question of responsibility toward others: If my brother, whether he understands what is being asked of him or not, is called upon by the government to do something *I* know to be wrong, may I, in love and good conscience, and if rational argument seems to have failed, take nonviolent though overt actions against the structures of that government? Does certain property have the right to exist?

The largest raid thus far took place on September 24, 1968, when fourteen men, including six Roman Catholic priests and a Protestant minister, invaded the offices of the draft board in Milwaukee, removed more than ten thousand files, and burned them in a nearby square dedicated to America's war dead. As in Dr. King's speech, their statement, which follows, faults America not only for an unjust war, but for harboring a social system and world-view that make such atrocities inevitable; it also bears, in certain respects, strong affinities to Tolstoy's "Letter to a Non-Commissioned Officer."

The Statement of the Milwaukee 14

Generation after generation religious values have summoned men to undertake the works of mercy and peace. In times of crisis false values have further required men to cry out in protest against institutions and systems destructive of man and his immense potential.

We declare today that we are one with that history of mercy and protest. In destroying with napalm part of our nation's bureaucratic machinery of conscription we declare that the service of life no longer provides any options other than positive, concrete action against what can only be called the American way of death: a way of death which gives property a greater value than life, a way of death sustained not by invitation and hope but by coercion and fear.

We confess we were not easily awakened to the need for such action as we carry out today. In order for communities of resistance to come into being, millions had to die at America's hands, while in the process millions of America's sons were torn from family, friends, health, sanity and often life itself. Victim and executioner have been trapped in the same dragnet of death.

Roots of the Vietnamese Struggle

We have had to trace the roots of the Vietnamese strug-

Reprinted with the special permission of the Milwaukee 14 Defense Committee, Chicago.

gle and suffering and admit that all too many of those roots converge in the soil of American values and priorities.

And we have had to adjust to the discovery that in that same soil have been engendered many of the other tragedies already underway. At home and abroad, opponents of America's economic, political and military commitments share with the innocent death by overt violence and the gunless violence of the status quo: death by starvation and malnutrition, death from despair, death from overwork and exhaustion and disease. America, in the meantime, celebrates its "way of life": the canonization of competition and self-interest, a high standard of living which rests on the backs of the poor. The values of brotherhood, joy, liberation and love become less and less comprehensible to our society. The world's wealthiest, most heavily armed people, inheritors of a nation born in genocide against the Indians and built in great measure upon the toil of slaves, suffocate beneath myths of freedom and popular political control. Leaders of the religious establishment—preoccupied with mortgage payments, film-ratings, pills—automatically conscript the Creator of life into the ranks of America's high command, leaving others to apply the prophetic message they ritually recite. Vietnamese burn, Biafrans starve, tanks dominate the streets of Prague; at home Americans buy diet colas and flesh (that is, caucasian) colored bandaids, see dissenters clubbed in the streets, counsel the poor to patience, cry out for law and order. . . .

A Movement of Resistance to Slavery

We who burn these records of our society's war machine are participants in a movement of resistance to slavery, a struggle that remains as unresolved in America as in most of the world. Man remains an object to be rewarded insofar as he is obedient and useful, to be punished when he dares declare his liberation.

Our action concentrates on the Selective Service System because its relation to murder is immediate. Men are drafted—or "volunteer" for fear of being drafted—as killers for the state. Their victims litter the planet. In Vietnam alone, where nearly 30,000[1] Americans have died, no one can count the Vietnamese dead, crippled, the mentally maimed.

Today we destroy Selective Service System files because men need to be reminded that property is not sacred. Property belongs to the human scene only if man does. If anything tangible is sacred, it is the gift of life and flesh, flesh which is daily burned, made homeless, butchered—without tears or clamor from most Americans—in Vietnam, Thailand, Cambodia, Laos, Peru, Guatemala, Bolivia, Colombia, Nigeria, South Africa, Harlem, Delano, Watts, and wherever the poor live and die, forgotten people, the anonymous majority. So property is repeatedly made the enemy of life; gas ovens in Germany, concentration camps in Russia, occupation tanks in Czechoslovakia, pieces of paper in draft offices, slum holdings, factories of death machines, germs and nerve gas. Indeed our nation has seen, with such isolated exceptions as the Boston Tea Party, devotion to property take ever greater precedence over devotion to life. So we today, in the face of such a history, proclaim that property has sanction only insofar as it serves man's need and the common good.

America's Marriage to Coercion

We strike at the Selective Service System because the draft, and the vocational channelling connected with it, are the clearest examples at hand of America's marriage to coercive political methods, exercised within as without its borders. In destroying these links in the military chain of command, we forge anew the good sense of the Second Vatican Council: "Man's dignity demands that he act according to a free conscience that is personally motivated from within, not under mere external pressure or blind internal impulse" (*Constitution on the Church in the Modern World*).

We use napalm because it has come to symbolize the American way of death: a merciless substance insensitive to life and the sound of the human heart, blind to human pain, ignorant of guilt or innocence. Indeed napalm is the inevitable fruit of our national un-conscience, the sign of our numbness to life. . . .

We have no illusions regarding the consequences of our action. To make visible another community of resistance and to better explain our action, we have chosen to act publicly and to accept the consequences. But we pay the price, if not gladly, at least with a profound hope. . . .

Our action is not an end in itself. We invite those who are ready to lay aside fear and economic addictions in order to join in the struggle to confront injustice in words and deeds, to build a community worthy of men made in the image and likeness of God . . . a society in which it is easier for men to be human.

1. Two years later, September 1970, the total was more than 46,000 dead.—Ed.

New Aspects of Conscientious Objection

The unpopularity of U.S. intervention in Vietnam has manifested itself in diverse ways. As never before in the nation's history, attention has focused on the problem of the individual's conscience versus the will of society, or at least the will of the government claiming to speak for society. The law, of course, recognizes within narrowly defined limits the right to hold a conscientious objection to military service. According to the "Supreme Being" clause of the Selective Service Act, one may be exempted from service if he is "by religious training and belief conscientiously opposed to participation in war in any form." Designed primarily to accommodate members of the historic peace churches, the clause makes no provision for objections on other grounds. Furthermore, conscientious objectors are required to perform alternative service, under the supervision of a governmental agency, in an area promoting "the national health, safety or interest."

Apart from the fact that the Selective Service system is unfair and discriminatory, drawing disproportionately from the black and the poor, while allowing the financially able to escape through educational deferments, the options are indeed distasteful for the young man convinced of the immorality of only a given conflict. As a rule, in the Vietnam war he has had little support from the large organized religious bodies, whether Christian or Jewish. To be sure, Pope Pius XII's statement in his Christmas message of 1956, the year of the Hungarian revolution, undoubtedly has an ecumenical appeal in the present situation: "a Catholic citizen cannot invoke his own conscience in order to refuse to serve and fulfill those duties the law imposes." Consequently, hundreds of draftable men have migrated to Canada, while many men already in the armed forces have deserted and sought sanctuary in Scandinavia.

Another course, described variously as "unjust war" or "selective conscientious objection," has recently come in for detailed discussion. In a sense this view is an extension of Vitoria and the "natural law" doctrine that all men have in them a divinely implanted sense of right and wrong; and its exponents hold that the individual's conscience alone should be the deciding criterion. The Supreme Court has seen some merit in this argument, and has accordingly modified the "Supreme Being" clause. In the case of the *U.S.* vs. *Seeger* [380 U.S. 163 (1965)] the majority ruled as follows:

> We believe that . . . the test of belief "in relation to a Supreme Being" is whether a given belief that is sincere and mean-

ingful occupies a place in the life of its possessor parallel to that filled by the orthodox belief in God of one who clearly qualifies for the exemption. Where such beliefs have parallel positions in the lives of their respective holders we cannot say that one is "in relation to a Supreme Being" and the other not.

Finally, in June 1970, in the case of E. A. Welsh, the Supreme Court departed entirely from the concept of parallelism, exempting "all those whose consciences, spurred by deeply held moral, ethical, or religious beliefs, would give them no rest or peace if they allowed themselves to become a part of an instrument of war. . . ." It will be noted, however, that in both the Seeger and the Welsh cases the objection was construed as applying to all wars; the selective principle has thus far met with no success.

Of the selections included in this section, "The Church as a Sanctuary of Conscience" (a speech delivered at the First Unitarian Church, Boston, October 16, 1967, by the Rev. William Sloane Coffin, Jr., Chaplain of Yale University) and "Conscience and Conscription" (a statement by Clergy and Laymen Concerned about Vietnam, a broadly based interdenominational group) both state the case for selective conscientious objection and call for a much more activistic stance on the part of the churches.

The third selection, "Selective Conscientious Objection," by Father John Courtney Murray, S.J., was a commencement address given on June 4, 1967, at Western Maryland College. Here Father Murray, known for his elucidations of the thought of Pius XII, is more cautious, examining the issue against the background of the just war and present political realities.

The Church as a Sanctuary of Conscience

Most words are dispensable. They can perish as though

From the Rev. William Sloane Coffin, Jr., "The Church as a Sanctuary of Conscience," leaflet published by Clergy and Laymen Concerned about Vietnam (New York, 1967). Reprinted with special permission.

they had never been written or spoken. Some few, however, must forever remain alive if human beings are to
remain human. "I love my city, but I shall not stop preaching that which I believe is true: you may kill me, but I
shall follow God rather than you," and: "We must obey
God rather than men."

Why are these words of Socrates and St. Peter so indispensable? Because in the first place they tell us that the
most profound experience of the self is the experience of
the conscience, and not as frequently suggested today the
experience of private sensations and interior visions. And
secondly, they tell us that because there is a higher and
hopefully future order of things, men at times will feel constrained to disobey the law out of a sense of obedience to a
higher allegiance. To hundreds of history's most revered
heroes, not to serve the state has appeared the best way to
love one's neighbor. To Socrates, St. Peter, Milton, Bunyan,
Gandhi, Nehru, it was clear that sometimes bad subjects
make good neighbors.

Let us remember these men were not out to destroy the
legal order. By accepting the legal punishment they actually
upheld it. Nor were they disrespectful of the law. They
broke it as a last, not as a first resort. But they respected
the law only, they did not worship it, and were determined
to bend their every effort to the end that the law reflect
and not reject their best understanding of justice and
mercy. . . .

If only Americans could remember their own heritage
they could at least applaud the spirit, even if they do not
share the views, of those who here today are refusing to
surrender their consciences to the state.

The issue *is* one of conscience. Let us be blunt. To us the
war in Vietnam is a crime. And if we are correct, if the war
is a crime, then is it criminal to refuse to have anything to

do with it? Is it we who are demoralizing our boys in Vietnam, or the Administration which is asking them to do immoral things? . . .

To us then the war is an issue of conscience. So too is the draft. For not only does the National Selective Service Act inexcusably defer the rich and better educated; it also insists that a man's conscientious objection be based on "religious belief and training."

Could anything be more ethically absurd? Have humanists no conscience? Why, many men become atheists because they think Christians are so inhuman that the only way to be a good humanist is to be an atheist. . . . But it is absurd once again that a man must be a believer in order to be conscientious.

Then despite numerous appeals by numerous religious leaders and groups, Congress last spring chose to recognize only the rights of conscience of the absolute pacifist. This too, as every good pacifist knows, is absurd. For the rights of a man whose conscience forbids him to participate in a particular war are as deserving of respect as the rights of a man whose conscience forbids him to participate in any war at all. This is an ancient Jewish and Christian tradition. Yet the tradition we honor the government steadfastly continues to dishonor.

So the war and the draft are both issues of conscience.

When an issue is one of conscience then surely it is one we may not wish to seek but it is one we cannot properly avoid—particularly the synagogues and churches. So what are we to do?

"Thou spreadest a table before me in the presence of mine enemies."

As men have always felt certain times to be more sacred than others, i.e., the Sabbath, so also they have felt certain places to be more sacred, i.e., the home, the temple, the church. And closely associated with these more sacred places has been the belief that there a man should find some sort of sanctuary from the forces of a hostile world. "Thou spreadest a table before me in the presence of mine enemies." These familiar words from the 23rd Psalm refer to an ancient 'desert law which provided that if a man hunted by his enemies sought refuge with another man who offered him hospitality, then the enemies of the man had to remain outside the rim of the campfire light for two nights and the day intervening. . . .

Then during the Middle Ages all churches on the continent were considered sanctuaries, and in some instances in England the land within a mile of the church was included. And according to the Justinian Code sanctuary was extended to all law breakers, Christian, Jewish, and non-believer alike, with the exception only of those guilty of high treason or sacrilege. Now if in the Middle Ages churches could offer sanctuary to the most common of criminals, could they not today do the same for the most conscientious among us? And if in the Middle Ages they could offer forty days to a man who had committed both a sin and a crime, could they not today offer an indefinite period to one who had committed no sin?

The churches must not shirk their responsibility in deciding whether or not a man's objection is conscientious. But should a church declare itself a "sanctuary of conscience" this should be considered less a means to shield a man, more a means to expose the church, an effort to make a church really to be a church.

For if the state should decide that the arm of the law was long enough to reach inside a church there would be little church members could do to prevent an arrest. But the members could point out what they had already dramatically demonstrated, that the sanctity of the conscience was being violated. And further, as the law regarding "aiding and abetting" is clear—up to five years in jail and a fine of ten thousand dollars—church members could then say: "If you arrest this man for violating a law which violates his conscience then you must arrest us too, for in the sight of that law we are now as guilty as he."

What else can the churches do? Are we to raise conscientious men and then not stand by them in their hour of conscience? And if there is a price to pay, should we hold back? . . .

Gentlemen, it is fitting that your action should take place within two weeks of the 450th celebration of the Reformation. For what we need today is a new reformation, a reformation of conscience. What you do today gives substance to the question: "What in our technical age shall it profit a man that he be able to fly through the air like a bird and swim through the sea like a fish, if he be not able to walk the earth like a man?"

Conscience and Conscription

Congressional indifference to appeals for justice has convinced us that it is no longer enough to speak in defense of the rights of conscience. The time has come to act in defense of these rights. It is no longer enough to protest the injustice of the present military conscription system. The time has come to pledge active support to all who in conscience and through non-violent means decide to resist its injustice. . . .

The Selective Service Act asserts that anyone "who knowingly counsels, aids or abets another to refuse or evade registration or service in the armed forces . . . shall be liable

A statement by Clergy and Laymen Concerned about Vietnam, October 25, 1967. Reprinted with special permission.

to imprisonment for not more than five years or a fine of ten thousand dollars or both."

We hereby publicly counsel all who in conscience cannot today serve in the armed forces to refuse such service by non-violent means. We pledge ourselves to aid and abet them in any way we can. This means that if they are now arrested for failing to comply with a law that violates their consciences we too must be arrested, for in the sight of that law we are now as guilty as they.

When true to their tradition, churches and synagogues have always been sanctuaries for conscience. We therefore call upon our fellow clergy and laymen to sign this statement, to set up draft counselling centers, to do everything possible in their communities for these conscientious objectors, and to be prepared to pay whatever price may be exacted to defend the rights of conscience our government refuses to honor. As clergy and laymen we could live neither with ourselves nor with God if today we did not keep faith with those who refuse to surrender their consciences to the state.

Selective Conscientious Objection

My subject is the issue of selective conscientious objection to particular wars, or, as it is sometimes called, discretionary armed service.

The theoretical implications of this issue are complex and subtle. The issue raises the whole question of war as a political act and the means whereby it should be confined within the moral universe. The issue also raises the

From *John Courtney Murray, S.J.,* Selective Conscientious Objection *(Huntington, Indiana. Our Sunday Visitor, 1968). Reprinted with the special permission of Western Maryland College, Westminster, Maryland.*

question of the status of the private conscience in the face of public law and national policy. In fact, the whole relation of the person to society is involved in this issue.

Moreover, the practical implications of the issue are far reaching. Selective conscientious objection, as Gordon Zahn has pointed out, is an "explosive principle."

If once admitted with regard to the issue of war, the consequences of the principle might run to great lengths in the civil community. . . .

The American attiude towards war has tended to oscillate between absolute pacifism in peacetime and extremes of ferocity in wartime. Prevalent in American society has been an abstract ethic, conceived either in religious or in secularized terms, which condemns all war as immoral. . . . On the other hand, when a concrete historical situation creates the necessity for war, no ethic governs its conduct. There are no moral criteria operative to control the uses of force. . . . One may pursue hostilities to the military objective of unconditional surrender, and the nation may escalate the use of force to the paroxysm of violence of which Hiroshima and Nagasaki are forever the symbols, even though they were prepared for by the fire bomb raids on Tokyo and by the saturation bombing of German cities. And all this use of violence can somehow be justified by slogans that were as simplistic as the principles of absolute pacifism.

These extreme alternatives are no longer tolerable. Our Nation must make its way to some discriminating doctrine —moral, political, and military—on the uses of force. . . .

To state the problem quite coldly, the war in South Vietnam is subject to opposition on political and moral grounds, and also on the grounds of national interest. This opposition has been voiced, and voiced in passionate terms. It has evoked a response in the name of patriotism, that is also passionate. Consequently, in this context, it is difficult to raise the moral issue of selective conscientious objection. There are even some to whom it seems dangerous to let the issue be raised at all.

The issue of selective conscientious objection must be distinguished from the issue of the justice of the South Vietnam war. If this distinction is not made and enforced in argument, the result will be confusion and the clash of passions. The necessary public argument will degenerate into a useless and harmful quarrel.

The distinction can be made. I make it myself. I advocate selective conscientious objection in the name of the traditional moral doctrine on war and also in the name of traditional American political doctrine on the rights of conscience. I am also prepared to make the case for the American military presence and action in South Vietnam.

The advocacy of selective conscientious objection in the midst of the South Vietnamese war is provocative, and the political response to it has been an overreaction. If you want the evidence you need only read the record of the hearings in the Congress, both Senate and House, on the revision of the Selective Service Act, when the issue of conscientious objection was brought up. The claim that the selective objector should be recognized was met with the response that all conscientious objection should be abolished.

I should like to continue in this practical vein. Strictly on grounds of moral argument, the right conscientiously to object to participation in a particular war is incontestable. The practical question before all of us is to get the right itself legally recognized, declared in statutory law....

Perhaps the one central practical question might be put in this way. Do the conditions exist which make it possible for the responsible exercise of the right of selective conscientious objection? The existence of these conditions is the prerequisite for granting legal status to the right itself.

There are two major conditions. The first is an exact understanding of the just war doctrine, and the second is respect for what Socrates called "the conscience of the laws." Let me explain.

Not long ago a young man in an anti-Vietnam protest on television declared that he would be willing to fight in Vietnam if he knew that the war there was just, but since he did not know he was obliged to protest its immorality. This young man clearly did not understand the just war doctrine and he did not understand what Socrates meant by the "conscience of the laws."

Similarly, in a statement issued by a Seminarians' Conference on the Draft held recently in Cambridge there appears this statement: "The spirit of these principles [of the just war doctrine] demands that every war be opposed until or unless it can be morally justified in relation to these principles." Socrates would not have agreed with this statement nor do I. The dear seminarians have got it backwards.

The root of the error here may be simply described as a failure to understand that provision of the just war doctrine which requires that a war should be "declared." This is not simply a nice piece of legalism, the prescription of a sheer technicality. Beyond the provision lies a whole philosophy of the State as a moral and political agent. The provision implies the recognition of the authority of the political community by established political processes to make decisions about the course of its action in history, to muster behind these decisions the united efforts of the community, and to publicize these decisions before the world.

If there is to be a political community, capable of being a moral agent in the international community, there must be some way of publicly identifying the nation's decision. These decisions must be declared to be the decisions of the community. Therefore, if the decision is for war, the war must be declared. This declaration is a moral and political act. It states a decision conscientiously arrived at in the interests of the international common good. It submits the decision to the judgment of mankind.

Moreover, when the decision-making process of the community has been employed and the decision has been reached, at least a preliminary measure of internal authority must be conceded by the citizens to this decision, even by those citizens who dissent from it. This, at least in part, is what Socrates meant by respect for the "conscience of the laws." This is why in the just war theory it has always been maintained that the presumption stands for the decision of the community as officially declared. He who dissents from the decision must accept the burden of proof. . . .

In a word the burden of proof is on him, not on the government or the administration or the nation as a whole. He does not and may not resign his conscience into the keeping of the State, but he must recognize that the State has its conscience which informs its laws and decisions.

When his personal conscience clashes with the conscience of the laws, his personal decision is his alone. It is valid for him, and he must follow it. But in doing so he still stands within the community and is subject to its judgment as already declared.

Only if conceived in these terms can the inevitable tension between the person and the community be properly a tension of the moral order. Otherwise, it will degenerate into a mere power struggle between arbitrary authority and an aggregate of individuals, each of whom claims to be the final arbiter of right and wrong. . . .

There is a further requisite for legal recognition of selective conscientious objection. It is the prior recognition of the difference between moral objection to a particular war and political opposition to a particular war. This seems to be the sticking point for the political community. It brings into question the whole ethos of our society in the manner of the uses of force.

Historically, we have been disposed to regard the intuitive verdict of the absolute pacifist that all wars are wrong as having the force of a moral imperative. The same moral force is not conceded to the judgment of the conscientious man, religious or not, who makes a reflective and discriminating judgment on the war in front of him. The general disposition is to say that objection to particular wars is and can only be political and, therefore, cannot entitle anyone to the status of conscientious objector.

Here again there is a misunderstanding of the just war doctrine. In fact there seems to be a misunderstanding of the very nature of moral reasoning.

The just war doctrine starts from the moral principle that the order of justice and law cannot be left without adequate means for its own defense, including the use of force. The doctrine further holds that the use of force is subject to certain conditions and its justice depends on certain circumstances. The investigation of the fulfillment of these conditions leads the conscientious man to a consideration of certain political and military factors in a given situation. There is the issue of aggression, the issue of the measure of force to be employed in resisting it, the issue of probable success, the issue of the balance of good and evil that will be the outcome. The fact that his judgment must take account of military and political factors does not make the judgment purely political. It is a judgment reached within a moral universe, and the final reason for it is of the moral order.

There is some subtlety to this argument. But that is not, I think, the reason why the political community refuses to assimiliate or accept it. The reasons are of the practical order.

The immediate reason is the enormous difficulty of administering a statute which would provide for selective conscientious objection. The deeper reason is the perennial problem of the erroneous conscience. It may be easily illustrated.

Suppose a young man comes forward and says: "I refuse to serve in this war on grounds of 'e Nuremberg principle." Conversation discloses that he has not the foggiest idea what the Nuremberg principle really is. Or suppose he understands the principle and says: "I refuse to serve because in this war the United States is committing war crimes." The fact may be, as it is in South Vietnam, that this allegation is false. Or suppose he says: "I refuse to serve because the United States is the aggressor in this war." The reason again may be demonstrably false. What then is the tribunal to do?

Here perhaps we come to the heart of the difficulty and I have only two things to say. First, unless the right to selective objection is granted to possibly erroneous consciences it will not be granted at all. The State will have to abide by the principle of the Seeger case, which does not require that the objection be the truth but that it be truly held. One must follow the logic of an argument wherever it leads.

On the other hand, the political community cannot be blamed for harboring the fear that if the right to selective objection is acknowledged in these sweeping terms, it might possibly lead to anarchy, to the breakdown of society, and to the paralysis of public policy.

Second, the reality of this fear imposes a further burden on the consciences of those who would appeal to freedom of conscience. Selective objection is not a trivial matter. As Professor Ralph Potter has said: "The nation is ultimately

a moral community. To challenge its well established policies as illegal, immoral and unjust, is to pose a threat, the
seriousness of which seems at times to escape the critics
themselves, whether by the callowness of youth or the cal-
lousness of usage." It will be recognized that society will
defend itself against this threat, if it be carelessly wielded.

The solution can only be the cultivation of political discretion throughout the populace, not least in the student
and academic community. A manifold work of moral and
political intelligence is called for. No political society can
be founded on the principle that absolute rights are to be
accorded to the individual conscience, and to all individual
consciences, even when they are in error. This is rank in-
dividualism and to hold it would reveal a misunderstanding
of the very nature of the political community. On the other
hand, the political community is bound to respect conscience. But the fulfillment of this obligation supposes that
the consciences of the citizens are themselves formed and
informed.

Therefore, the final question may be, whether there is
abroad in the land a sufficient measure of moral and political discretion, in such wise that the Congress could, under
safeguard of the national security, acknowledge the right of
discretionary armed service.

Suggested Additional Readings

The literature on war and on war and religion is vast and growing, so that even a moderately representative bibliography would make a hefty volume in itself. I have found the titles listed below, along with those in the notes accompanying the introductory essay, most valuable. Especially relevant pieces have been annotated.

PERIODICAL LITERATURE

Bulletin of the Atomic Scientists. Useful for information about weapons technology and about current thinking in the scientific community.

Fellowship. The monthly journal of the Fellowship of Reconciliation, it publishes material pertaining to war and Christianity, as well as notices of recent literature.

Worldview. The publication of the Council on Religion and International Affairs, it contains articles of the highest quality by authorities in the fields of war, international relations, and ethics.

GENERAL BOOKS ON WAR, THE STATE, AND RELIGION

ABRAMS, RAY H. *Preachers Present Arms.* New York: Round Table, 1933. A mass of quotations without much explanation about how the American churches waged the First World War as a crusade. Originally published in part as a series of articles for the pacifist and isolationist *Christian Century,* the book's aim was to reinforce these tendencies.

BARTH, KARL. *Community, State and Church.* Garden City, N.Y.: Doubleday, 1960. Contains several of his lesser works on these subjects.

BENNETT, JOHN C. *Foreign Policy in Christian Perspective.* New York: Scribner, 1966.

BUTTERFIELD, HERBERT. *International Conflict in the Twentieth Century: A Christian View*. London: Routledge, 1960. Incisive comments by a leading English historian.

CLARKSON, JESSIE D., ed. *War as a Social Institution*. New York: Columbia University Press, 1941.

CULLMANN, OSCAR. *The State in the New Testament*. London: 1957.

DAKIN, MARTIN. *Peace and Brotherhood in the Old Testament*. London: Bannisdale, 1956.

ELBE, JOACHIM VON. "The Evolution of the Concept of the Just War in International Law," *American Journal of International Law* (October 1939).

FITZROY, MARK, ed. *War, Conscience and the Rule of Christ Compiled from the Encyclicals of Leo XIII, Benedict XV, Pius XI and Pius XII*. London: Pax Society, 1940.

FRANK, JEROME D. *Sanity and Survival: Psychological Aspects of War and Peace*. New York: Random House, 1967. A valuable study.

JONES, RUFUS M., ed. *The Church, the Gospel and War*. New York: Harper, 1948. Edited by a leading Quaker historian.

KAHN, HERMAN. *On Thermonuclear War*. Princeton: Princeton University Press, 1961. A standard work on the philosophy and strategy of war in the modern world; Kahn's views have drawn much fire from moralists.

KHADDURI, M. *The Law of War and Peace in Islam*. London: Luzac, 1940.

McREAVY, L. L. *War and Peace in Catholic Doctrine*. Oxford: Catholic Social Guild, 1963.

MOLLERING, R. L. *Modern War and the American Churches*. New York: American, 1957. Not a very complimentary account of the role of the churches in the World Wars.

ROMMEN, HEINRICH A. *The State in Catholic Thought.* St. Louis: Herder, 1945.

ROPP, THEODORE. *War in the Modern World.* New York: Collier, 1962. A history of philosophy and methods since the Renaissance.

RYAN, JOHN K. *Modern War and Basic Ethics.* Milwaukee: Bruce, 1940. A study of how modern methods of warfare relate to the traditional teaching on the just war; from the standpoint of the late thirties.

SMITH, J. M. P. "Religion and War in Israel," *American Journal of Theology* (1915).

STRATMANN, FRANZISKUS. *The Church and War: A Catholic Study.* London: Kenedy, 1928.

TOOKE, JOAN B. *The Just War in Aquinas and Grotius.* London: SPCK, 1965. A careful examination of both writers in terms of revelation and the natural law.

TUCKER, ROBERT W. *The Just War: A Study of Contemporary Doctrine.* Baltimore, Johns Hopkins, 1960. An important work by a political scientist.

VAGTS, ALFRED. *A History of Militarism.* New York: Free Press, 1959.

WRIGHT, QUINCY. *A Study of War.* Chicago: University of Chicago Press, 1942. A massive work on every aspect of the subject by a renowned authority.

PACIFISM AND PEACE MOVEMENTS

BROCK, PETER. *Pacifism in the United States from the Colonial Era to the First World War.* Princeton: Princeton University Press, 1968. An exhaustive study, incorporating material on many lesser known individuals and movements.

CURTI, MERLE E. *Peace and War: The American Struggle.* New York: Norton, 1936. Deals specifically with antiwar movements.

FINN, JAMES. *Protest: Pacifism & Politics.* New York: Random House, 1968. A series of interviews with, among others, Paul Ramsey, A. J. Muste, Daniel Berrigan, S.J., and John C. Bennett.

GANDHI, M. K. *Non-Violent Resistance (Satyagraha).* New York: Schocken, 1961. A useful collection of short pieces from his journalism. ERIK H. ERIKSON'S *Gandhi's Truth: The Origins of Militant Nonviolence* (New York: Norton, 1969) is a study of Gandhi and nonviolence by a noted psychiatrist-teacher-author.

HUXLEY, ALDOUS. *An Encyclopedia of Pacifism.* New York: Harper, 1937. Far from encyclopedic, and overloaded with issues peculiar to the thirties, it nevertheless contains some material of abiding interest.

MARTIN, DAVID. *Pacifism: An Historical and Sociological Study.* London: Routledge, 1965.

MAYER, PETER, ed. *The Pacifist Conscience.* Chicago: Regnery, 1967. Contains a well-rounded survey of the subject, as well as an extensive bibliography.

MUSTE, A. J. *Nonviolence in an Aggressive World.* New York: Harper, 1940.

————. *The Essays of A. J. Muste,* ed. Nat Hentoff. New York: Bobbs-Merrill, 1966.

NUTTALL, GEOFFREY. *Christian Pacifism.* Oxford: Blackwell, 1958.

RAVEN, C. R. *The Theological Basis of Christian Pacifism.* New York: Fellowship, 1951.

REGAMEY, P. *Non-Violence and the Christian Conscience.* New York: Herder, 1966. A sympathetic study by a French Dominican.

SIBLEY, MULFORD Q., ed. *The Quiet Battle.* Boston: Beacon, 1963. A useful anthology with commentary.

UNIVERSITY GROUP ON DEFENCE POLICY. *The Role of the Peace Movements in the 1930's.* London: U.G.D.P., 1959.

YODER, JOHN H. *Reinhold Niebuhr and Christian Pacifism.* Pamphlet, The Church Peace Mission, 1955.

————. *The Pacifism of Karl Barth.* Pamphlet, The Church Pamphlet, Peace Mission, 1968.

SECTARIAN CHRISTIANITY AND THE SOCIAL GOSPEL MOVEMENT

BOWMAN, R. D. *The Church of the Brethren and War, 1708–1941.* Elgin, Ill.: Brethren, 1944.

CARTER, PAUL A. *The Decline and Revival of the Social Gospel: 1920–1940.* Ithaca: Cornell University Press, 1956.

ELLWOOD, CHARLES A. *The Reconstruction of Religion.* New York: Macmillan, 1922.

HERSCHBERGER, GUY F. *The Mennonite Church in the Second World War.* Scottdale, Pa.,: Herald, 1951.

————. *War, Peace and Non-Resistance.* Scottdale, Pa.: Herald, 1944. Useful survey of war and sectarian Christianity, with an emphasis on the Mennonites.

'T HOOFT, W. A. VISSER. *The Background of the Social Gospel in America.* Haarlem, Netherlands, 1928.

HOPKINS, CHARLES H. *The Rise of the Social Gospel in American Protestantism, 1865–1915.* New Haven: Yale University Press, 1941.

KNOX, RONALD. *Enthusiasm: A Chapter in the History of Religion with Special Reference to the Seventeenth Century Churches.* New York: Oxford University Press, 1961. A life's-work dealing fairly, if critically, with the history and theology of sectarian Christianity.

MATTHEWS, SHAILER. *The Social Teachings of Jesus.* New York: Macmillan, 1917.

NIEBUHR, H. RICHARD. *The Social Sources of Denominationalism.* New York: Holt, 1929. A classic in the sociology of religion, dealing especially with Methodism and Baptism in the early American experience.

PAGE, KIRBY, AND EDDY, SHERWOOD. *The Abolition of War*. New York: Doran, 1923.

PAGE, KIRBY. *National Defense*. New York: Farrar, 1931.

————. *Jesus or Christianity*. New York: Doran, 1929. A scathing attack, amply documented, on organized Christianity and its attitude toward social questions.

RAUSCHENBUSCH, WALTER. *A Theology for the Social Gospel*. New York: Macmillan, 1917.

RUTENBER, CULBERT G. *The Dagger and the Cross*. Nyack, N. Y.: Fellowship, 1958.

CONSCIENTIOUS OBJECTION AND THE DRAFT

FINN, JAMES, ed. *Conflict of Loyalties: The Case of Selective Conscientious Objection*. New York: Pegasus, 1968.

GRAHAM, JOHN W. *Conscription and Conscience*. London: Allen & Unwin, 1922. A chronicle of the bigotry and stupidity the English conscientious objectors during the First World War had to endure.

SIBLEY, MULFORD, AND JACOB, PHILIP E. *Conscription of Conscience*. Ithaca: Cornell University Press, 1952. Study of American COs in the period 1940–1947.

TAX, SOL, ed. *The Draft: A Handbook of Facts and Alternatives*. Chicago: University of Chicago Press, 1967.

WARFARE SINCE 1945

ANSCOMBE, G. E. M., ed. *Nuclear Weapons: A Catholic Response*. New York: Sheed & Ward, 1962.

BENNETT, JOHN C., ed. *Nuclear Weapons and the Christian Conscience*. New York: Scribner, 1962.

CLANCY, WILLIAM, ed. *The Moral Dilemma of Nuclear Weapons: Essays from Worldview*. New York: Council on Religion and International Affairs, 1961.

FINN, JAMES, ed. *Peace, the Churches, and the Bomb*. New York: Council on Religion and International Affairs, 1965.

FLEMING, D. F. "Is Containment Moral?", *Annals of the American Academy of Political and Social Science*, vol. 362 (October 1965).

FORD, JOHN C. "The Morality of Obliteration Bombing," *Theological Studies*, vol. 5 (September 1944). Perhaps the best brief statement of the problem by a Catholic theologian in terms of the just war. Written as a response to the great raids on Germany early in 1944.

KING-HALL, STEPHEN. *Defense in the Nuclear Age*. Nyack, N. Y.: Fellowship, 1959. A former Commander in the Royal Navy and no pacifist states the case for nonviolent defense—indeed, he can see no sane alternative—in the face of weapons of total destruction.

LONG, EDWARD LE ROY. *The Christian Response to the Atomic Crisis*. Philadelphia: Westminster, 1950.

MUMFORD, LEWIS. "The Morals of Extermination," *The Atlantic Monthly* (October 1959).

MURRAY, JOHN COURTNEY, S.J. *Morality and Modern War*. New York: Council on Religion and International Affairs, 1959. His idea that nuclear war must be made a possibility within the context of the just war stirred a great deal of controversy when first put forth.

NAGLE, WILLIAM J., ed. *Morality and Modern Warfare*. Baltimore: Helicon, 1960.

RAMSEY, PAUL. *The Limits of Nuclear War: Thinking about the Do-able and the Un-doable*. New York: Council on Religion and International Affairs, 1963.

STEIN, WALTER, ed. *Nuclear Weapons and the Christian Conscience*. London: Merlin, 1961.

THOMPSON, CHARLES S., ed. *Morals and Missiles: Catholic Essays on the Problem of War Today*. London: J. Clarke, 1959.

342   SUGGESTED ADDITIONAL READINGS

TUCKER, ROBERT W. *The Just War and Vatican II: A Critique.* New York: Council on Religion and International Affairs, 1966.

WEBER, THEODORE R. *Modern War and the Pursuit of Peace.* New York: Council on Religion and International Affairs, 1968.

VIETNAM

FALL, BERNARD B. *Vietnam Witness: 1953–1966.* New York: Praeger, 1966. One of the few American experts in this field, Fall was killed during a visit to the war zone.

————. *The Two Vietnams.* New York: Praeger, 1967.

GOODWIN, RICHARD N. *Triumph or Tragedy: Reflections on Vietnam.* New York: Random House, 1966.

HANH, THICH NHAT. *Vietnam: Lotus in a Sea of Fire.* New York: Hill & Wang, 1967. A plea to end the war by a Buddhist leader.

SCHLESINGER, ARTHUR M., JR. *The Bitter Heritage: Vietnam and American Democracy.* Boston: Houghton Mifflin, 1968. A well-written historical analysis by one of the outstanding liberal historians of our time.

ZAHN, GORDON. *War, Conscience, and Dissent.* New York: Hawthorn, 1967.